"Ivan Savic and Zachary Shirkey have written a masterful book. By combining rigorous, game theoretic reasoning with nuanced case studies they have created a new and superior understanding of different facets of uncertainty. And then, in clear prose they tease out fundamental policy implications for global politics and US foreign policy. Every international relations student should read this book."

— Bruce Bueno de Mesquita, Julius Silver Professor of Politics, NYU and co-author of *The Dictator's Handbook* and *Spoils of War*.

Uncertainty, Threat, and International Security

The rise of China is changing the strategic landscape globally and regionally. How states respond to potential threats posed by this new power arrangement will be crucial to international relations for the coming decades. This book builds on existing realist and rationalist concepts of balancing, bandwagoning, commitment problems, and asymmetric information to craft explanations about how states respond when faced with potential threats. Specifically, the book explores the role different types of uncertainty play in potential balancing situations. Particular attention is given to the nature of the rising state's actions, the balance of forces, and the value of delay. These concepts are analyzed and illustrated through a series of case studies on Europe in the 1930s as well as present-day Southeast Asia, looking at great powers such as Britain and France, and also a wide range of smaller powers including Poland, Yugoslavia, Vietnam, and the Philippines.

Ivan Savic teaches Political Science at Memorial University of Newfoundland, Grenfell Campus. He received his M.Phil. in Political Science (with a minor in Economics) from Columbia University and a B.Com. from the University of Toronto, specializing in commerce and finance, and international relations. He has also taught at the University of Toronto, Brown University, Columbia University, and Hunter College, CUNY. His primary research interest is in international finance, specifically financial governance, the relationship between political and financial policy, and the politics of international crisis response. He is also interested in the interplay of economic and security issues such as the nature of economic interdependence under globalization and its impact on conflict.

Zachary C. Shirkey is an Associate Professor in the Department of Political Science at Hunter College, CUNY. He received his PhD from Columbia. His research on military intervention, war duration, and alignment choices has been published in the *Journal of Peace Research*, the *International Studies Review*, and the *Journal of Theoretical Politics*. His two previous books, *Is This a Private Fight or Can Anybody Join?* and *Joining the Fray*, examine the causes and timing of military intervention in interstate and civil wars respectively.

Rethinking Asia and International Relations
Series Editor – Emilian Kavalski
Australian Catholic University (Sydney)

This series seeks to provide thoughtful consideration of both the growing prominence of Asian actors on the global stage and the changes in the study and practice of world affairs that they provoke. It intends to offer a comprehensive parallel assessment of the full spectrum of Asian states, organizations, and regions and their impact on the dynamics of global politics.

The series seeks to encourage conversation on:

- what rules, norms, and strategic cultures are likely to dominate international life in the 'Asian Century';
- how global problems will be reframed and addressed by a 'rising Asia';
- which institutions, actors, and states are likely to provide leadership during such 'shifts to the East';
- whether there is something distinctly 'Asian' about the emerging patterns of global politics.

Such comprehensive engagement not only aims to offer a critical assessment of the actual and prospective roles of Asian actors, but also seeks to rethink the concepts, practices, and frameworks of analysis of world politics.

This series invites proposals for interdisciplinary research monographs undertaking comparative studies of Asian actors and their impact on the current patterns and likely future trajectories of international relations. Furthermore, it offers a platform for pioneering explorations of the ongoing transformations in global politics as a result of Asia's increasing centrality to the patterns and practices of world affairs.

Titles

India–US Relations in the Age of Uncertainty
An Uneasy Courtship
B. M. Jain

One Korea
Visions of Korean Unification
Edited by Tae-Hwan Kwak and Seung-Ho Joo

Asia in International Relations
Unlearning Imperial Power Relations
Edited by Pinar Bilgin and L. H. M. Ling

Uncertainty, Threat, and International Security
Implications for Southeast Asia
Zachary C. Shirkey and Ivan Savic

Theorizing Indian Foreign Policy
Edited by Misha Hansel, Raphaelle Khan and Mélissa Levaillant

Russia's Geoeconomic Strategy for a Greater Eurasia
Glenn Diesen

Uncertainty, Threat, and International Security
Implications for Southeast Asia

Ivan Savic and Zachary C. Shirkey

First published 2017
by Routledge
2 Park Square, Milton Park, Abingdon, Oxon OX14 4RN

and by Routledge
52 Vanderbilt Avenue, New York, NY 10017

Routledge is an imprint of the Taylor & Francis Group, an informa business

© 2017 Ivan Savic and Zachary C. Shirkey

The right of Ivan Savic and Zachary C. Shirkey to be identified as authors of this work has been asserted by them in accordance with sections 77 and 78 of the Copyright, Designs and Patents Act 1988.

The Open Access version of this book, available at www.taylorfrancis.com, has been made available under a Creative Commons Attribution-Non Commercial-No Derivatives 4.0 license.

British Library Cataloguing in Publication Data
A catalogue record for this book is available from the British Library

Library of Congress Catalogingi-in-Publication Data
Names: Savic, Ivan, author. | Shirkey, Zachary C., author.
Title: Uncertainty, threat, & international security : implications for Southeast Asia / Ivan Savic and Zachary C. Shirkey.
Other titles: Uncertainty, threat, and international security.
Description: New York : Routledge, 2017. |
Series: Rethinking Asia and international relations | Includes bibliographical references and index.
Identifiers: LCCN 2016049727| ISBN 9781472483201 (hardback) | ISBN 9781315610658 (e-book)
Subjects: LCSH: Security, International--Southeast Asia. | Southeast Asia--Foreign relations--21st century. | Southeast Asia--Foreign relations--China. | China--Foreign relations--Southeast Asia. | Comparative government.
Classification: LCC JZ6009.S644 S38 2017 | DDC 355/.033059--dc23
LC record available at https://lccn.loc.gov/2016049727

ISBN: 978-1-472-48320-1 (hbk)
ISBN: 978-0-367-26490-1 (pbk)
DOI: 10.4324/9781315610658

To Ed Shirkey and in memory of Fred Neidhardt who both showed me that an academic life was possible.

Zachary C. Shirkey

To my loving parents Ana and Selimir and my wonderful brother Vladimir.

Ivan Savic

Contents

List of figures and tables x
Acknowledgments xi
List of abbreviations xii

Introduction: threats and the challenges of uncertainty 1

1 Balancing as a commitment problem 16

2 Balancing and buck-passing I: a dynamic model with uncertainty 39

3 Balancing and buck-passing II: Western Europe in the 1930s 48

4 To bandwagon or hide I: a theoretical examination of the alternatives to balancing 67

5 To bandwagon or hide II: East Central Europe before World War II 75

6 Balancing and bandwagoning by other means: how the outbreak of war affects states' responses to threats 99

7 The rise of China: will states balance, bandwagon, or hedge in the South China Sea today? 115

Conclusion 145

References 150
Index 164

Figures and tables

Figures

1.1	Basic structure of the game	23
1.2	Potential balancer's action rule with certainty	27
1.3	Case of unique equilibrium: status quo (SQ)	28
1.4	Case of two possible equilibria: status quo (SQ) or balanced equilibrium (BE)	29
1.5	Case of three possible equilibria: status quo (SQ), unchallenged revision of the status quo (UC), or balanced equilibrium (BE)	30
1.6	Potential balancer's action rule with uncertainty	32

Tables

0.1	Core hypotheses: uncertainty and balancing	10
0.2	Ancillary hypotheses I: nature of the challenge	10
0.3	Ancillary hypotheses II: bandwagoning and uncertainty	11
6.1	States which joined wars after being attacked	102
6.2	Types of joining, their likelihood, and underlying motives	103
6.3	Types of joining and the likelihood of winning	106
6.4	Joining by type, belligerent, and war	107
6.5	List of COW interstate wars v.4.0	108

Acknowledgments

We would like to thank Timothy Crawford, Erik Gartzke, Craig B. Greathouse, Stuart Gottlieb, Christopher Layne, Paul MacDonald, M. J. Peterson, Christopher M. Sprecher, Alex Weisiger, and Scott Wolford for their helpful suggestions and advice at various stages of this project. Any mistakes are our own.

Abbreviations

ARF	ASEAN Regional Forum
ASEAN	Association of Southeast Asian Nations
COW	Correlates of War
INF	Intermediate-Range Nuclear Forces Treaty
NATO	North Atlantic Treaty Organization
PLA	People's Liberation Army
RAF	Royal Air Force
UNCLOS	United Nations Convention on the Law of the Sea

Introduction
Threats and the challenges of uncertainty

How do states respond to threats issued by rivals or that result from regional or systemic power shifts? What options are available to states? What difficulties do states face in crafting successful strategies to confront potential challengers? These questions have shaped states' foreign policies since states were formed. With the rise of China and its increasing assertiveness in the South China Sea, Russia's renewed attempts to increase its influence in its near abroad, and the altered balance of power[1] in the Middle East – a result of the Arab Spring, shifting demographics, and a weakened Iraq – these questions are as important as ever. How states respond to these new conditions will shape global and regional landscapes for years to come. Thus, while these questions are important for security specialists in particular, they have resonance well beyond the field.

Equally important is that the answers to these questions are not immediately obvious. Will states coordinate to array their strength against rising powers, work with the rising powers to ensure their own safety and obtain rewards, or simply try to avoid any resultant diplomatic entanglements altogether? Historically, states have pursued strategies at least as varied as these (Schroeder 1994). States ultimately decide what strategy to pursue based on their calculations of threat, risk, reward, the probable responses of other powers, and their ability to influence the distribution of power. In doing so, states face a great deal of uncertainty about their opponents' intentions, relative capabilities, the best time to act, and other potential balancers' behaviors. How states deal with all of these types of uncertainty and what strategies they would choose given their beliefs are all vital questions for understanding global politics today.

Yet, academic work on how states respond to potential threats has stalled in recent years. Existing realist and liberal explanations have been insufficiently integrated with newer rationalist insights on the roles that commitment problems and uncertainty play in influencing states' responses to potential threats. Also much, although not all, existing work focuses on great power behavior to the exclusion of smaller states.[2] Therefore, this book builds on existing realist, liberal, and rationalist concepts of balancing, bandwagoning, hiding, commitment problems, and asymmetric information to craft explanations about how states respond to potential threats. We generate several formal models which provide new insights into key types of uncertainty states face when making decisions about

DOI: 10.4324/9781315610658-1

how to respond to potential threats and to shifts in relative power. We then use the well-known 1930s cases of the failed attempts at balancing by British and French and the equally disastrous mix of hiding and bandwagoning by smaller states in East Central Europe in response to the growing German threat to illustrate the concepts of the models. Finally, the lessons learned about how states respond to potential threats resulting from shifting local power distributions are applied to the contemporary case of the South China Sea.

From our formal models we derive three new propositions which are vital to understanding responses to threats and power shifts. First, all balancing results from commitment problems. In the absence of such problems, states would be able to strike bargains to avoid the costs of balancing and being balanced against. This finding is entirely new, though it is consistent with much of the rationalist literature on commitment problems.[3] Second, uncertainty about the rising state's capabilities is more problematic for potential balancers than uncertainty about the rising state's intentions. Third, states are more likely to delay balancing to the future than to pass the buck to another state. These last two findings run contrary to what might be expected from some of the existing realist literature (Christensen and Snyder 1990; Mearsheimer 2001; Pape 2005; Powell 1999), which argues that buck-passing is central in understanding failed balancing especially in 1930s Europe. Each of these findings will be discussed in turn below, beginning with why commitment problems are a necessary cause of balancing – a finding which is formally derived in Chapter 1.

Before proceeding further, however, it would be profitable to discuss what is meant by balancing, bandwagoning, and hiding since the terms are used in different ways throughout the literature. While there is a fuller discussion about the terms' definitions in Chapter 1, a preliminary presentation of our definitions is necessary. Balancing is the marshaling of military resources, either internally or externally, against a threat which has yet to be actualized (Brooks and Wohlforth 2011). Thus, our definition of balancing is what many scholars call hard balancing and excludes the concepts of soft and asymmetric balancing.[4] Bandwagoning on the other hand is a state aligning itself militarily with a challenger to the status quo, either to protect itself from that challenger (Walt 1985; 1987), to gain spoils as a result of aiding the challenger's success (Jones 1994; Schweller 1994), or some combination thereof. Finally, hiding entails not responding to a threat even though it has been recognized. This may be out of a hope that the threat will not become actualized, that the best way to avoid being attacked is to not antagonize the threatening state, or that both balancing and bandwagoning are too costly or risky. In other words, hiding is a conscious, calculated policy of inaction in response to a recognized threat which has yet to be actualized. While other responses are certainly possible, these three have received the most attention in the international relations literature and thus are the behaviors we aim to explain.

Commitment problems and balancing

As indicated earlier, the book's first major claim is that commitment problems are a necessary cause of *all* balancing. Commitment problems are an important rationalist explanation of conflict in the international system (Copeland 2000; Powell 2006; 2012; Reiter 2009; Weisiger 2013). Commitment problems, along with private information and indivisibility, are one of the few rational causes of costly international conflict (Fearon 1995; Bueno de Mesquita, Morrow, and Zorick 1997).[5] This is because if each side knew how the costly conflict was going to end and could credibly commit to honor agreements, they would simply agree to that outcome *ex ante* without paying the costs. Yet uncertainty and expected future power shifts often make this impossible.

Balancing is a form of costly, and often tacit, interstate bargaining requiring significant increases in armament expenditures or settling with and making concessions to former rivals in order to create alliances. The state or states engaged in balancing hope that by mobilizing resources and forming alliances against the perceived threat, the threatening state or coalition of states would be deterred from attacking and ultimately desist from attempting to overturn the status quo. Failing this, the balancer aims to aggregate sufficient power to defeat the revisionist state in either a defensive or preventive war.

Given that balancing is costly and that it is not a response to a direct attack (thus not immediately necessary for a state's survival) states must consider whether the benefits of balancing are worth the costs. A state would balance only if it believed that it would be cheaper or more effective to address a potential threat now rather than at some future point when it may or may not materialize (He 2012; Powell 1999). In other words, balancing entails assuming definite short-term costs to avoid greater expected, but uncertain, long-term costs.

Also, it must be the case that no cheaper, satisfactory alternative to balancing, such as passing the buck to another potential balancer or accommodation through appeasement, exists. No state wants to be the target of balancing as this threatens its security and autonomy in the international system. Thus, reaching a compromise to avoid balancing may be possible and is certainly desirable. So why do potential balancers and revisionist states sometimes fail to come to an agreement, tacit or otherwise? The answer as suggested above is commitment problems. It is often difficult for revisionist states to credibly commit to limit themselves to the immediate and localized changes to the status quo they are proposing. This is because potential aggressors often seek agreement with potential balancers so that they can isolate and defeat their opponents piecemeal or gain time to further strengthen themselves, striking only when they are confident of success. It is this inability of revisionist states to bind themselves and commit to never using the relative power gained to harm potential balancers which results in balancing behavior.

Thus, potential balancers are faced with the problem that both aggressive and benign challengers of the status quo (from the potential balancers' points of view) have incentives to declare that they do not harbor future hostile intentions toward the potential balancers and thereby avoid being balanced against. It can, therefore, be difficult for balancers to determine which revisionists they need to concern themselves with. Not only is the challenger's "type" hard to determine but also it is subject to change. A government challenging the status quo may sincerely not intend to take advantage of their enhanced power at present but it could change its mind at a later date or be replaced by a new, more aggressive, government.

For example, it would be quite difficult for Iran to credibly commit to refrain from building a nuclear bomb once it had the capacity to do so even if Iran had no intention of become a nuclear power. The enhanced status and greater freedom from US military threats that possessing a nuclear bomb would give Iran to expand its influence throughout the Middle East creates an additional commitment problem.[6] Thus, Israel, Saudi Arabia, several other Persian Gulf states, and many western powers including the United States have pressed Iran to dismantle much of its uranium enrichment capability. Yet, the Iranians were reluctant to do so. Whether this was because the Iranians wanted a bomb or wanted the enrichment program for other reasons is unknown outside of top Iranian leadership circles.[7] The confrontation proved costly, with sanctions hurting the Iranian economy and the United States having to strike deals with many states in order to keep the sanctions in place. The 2015 agreement struck between Iran and the P5+1 states[8] in Geneva, for an easing of the sanctions in return for Iranian concessions on enrichment and the initial compliance on both sides for carrying it out, show that Iran and the United States would like to escape from the confrontation if possible. However, the great difficulties experienced during negotiations and the continued and widespread opposition to the agreement show just how hard that is, given the nature of the commitment problem. Whether the agreement will continue to hold in the long term remains to be seen.[9]

This conclusion that balancing is always the result of commitment problems is new. Neither work on commitment problems nor balancing has previously advanced it. This is important as it identifies when balancing is a possibility and when it is certain to not occur. Also, given the difficulty in eliminating commitment problems it suggests that if balancing occurs it is likely to endure for some time and it will be quite difficult to solve the underlying problems which brought it about.[10] Thus, this is the most important of the book's claims and it serves as the theoretical basis for further explorations about how uncertainty and asymmetric information affect the likelihood of balancing in response to commitment problems.

For instance, states in Southeast Asia would be unlikely to balance against China if the Chinese could credibly commit to not use their growing power to harm Southeast Asian states in the future. In particular, if there was some way for China to renounce its territorial ambitions in the South China Sea in a decisive and irrevocable way, it would be hard to see why any state in Southeast Asia would forego the benefits of closer economic ties with China and instead balance against growing Chinese power. Yet, it is hard to see how China could do that as it could always renege on any agreement not to push its territorial claims once it was in a better position to do so and of course China is at present already aggressively pushing those claims. Likewise, fears amongst Arab Gulf monarchies about growing Iranian power would be much reduced if Iran could irrevocably commit itself to not revise the status quo in the region. Thus, it is not power itself that causes balancing, but rather the fear that a rising state would use its growing power to harm another state's interests in the future.

Uncertainty about capabilities and intentions

As mentioned above, the book's two remaining major claims involve the role of uncertainty in potential balancing situations. The first of these is uncertainty about the rising state's intentions and capabilities. Generally, public rhetoric about and academic studies on balancing have focused on uncertainty surrounding the rising challenger's intentions (Glaser 1997; Taliaferro 2001; Walt 1985). In other words, does the challenger intend to use the change in the status quo to harm the potential balancers or is the challenger benign (i.e., simply interested in the revision for its own sake and not the advantage it provides over the potential balancers). Realists often argue that intentions are particularly devilish as they reside within the minds of leaders, meaning they cannot be directly observed and they are highly changeable, either due to leadership changes or an alteration in preferred strategy by a given leadership group. In addition, capabilities are arguably easier to observe and assess. While some in fact dispute the realist claim regarding the difficulty of observing intentions (Hopf 2010; Wendt 1999), it is widely advanced in the literature.[11] Thus, one would expect that a central problem potential balancers face in deciding if a potential challenger is in fact a threat is determining what the challenger intends to do rather than what the challenger is capable of doing.

We, however, find that uncertainty over relative capabilities is more problematic for determining whether a state should balance than is uncertainty over intentions. This finding, which runs counter to common intuition and much of the academic literature, is originally derived through formal modeling in Chapter 2 and is borne out in our case on 1930s Europe in Chapter 3 – a case often cited as driven by French and especially British uncertainty over Hitler's true intentions. This suggests that while policy makers should consider both what states are capable of doing and what they intend to do, it is more important to resolve uncertainty surrounding the former question than the latter in potential balancing situations. This in turn has implications for what sorts of intelligence gathering techniques and programs should receive funding when targeting rising states. Incidentally, this is consistent with classic advice from defensive realists that states should focus on capabilities rather than intentions though the reasons for this are completely different (see Waltz 1979). We, unlike many realists, are not arguing that intentions are unknowable or even harder to discern than capabilities – we are agnostic on the point – but rather that it is easier to devise strategies given uncertainty about intentions rather than uncertainty about capabilities. In other words, if a state knows its potential opponent's strength, it can determine the appropriate scale of any needed military response if its potential opponent is indeed hostile. If it is unsure of its opponents' strength, however, determining the appropriate scale of any military buildup is highly problematic even if the opponent's hostility is assured.[12]

This is also illustrated by the Russian proverb – "Trust, but verify!" – which Reagan adopted as his watchword during the negotiation of the Intermediate-Range Nuclear Forces Treaty (INF) in the mid-1980s. Reagan came into office as a hawk who criticized the US–Soviet Détente of the 1970s. Although his views of the Soviet Union softened during his presidency, he never trusted the intentions of either the Soviet Union or international communism. The INF treaty was not signed and ratified because the Regan administration was finally convinced of the benign intentions of Gorbachev and his sincere commitment to reduce the Soviet intermediate ballistic missile arsenal. It was signed and ratified because it included carefully negotiated provision that would allow both parties to monitor the progress made by the other. The provisions helped to reduce their uncertainty over the commitment problem created by the agreement. This shows that because the changes in capabilities could be monitored, the uncertainty surrounding Soviet intentions could be overcome through a cleverly constructed agreement.

Furthermore, if realists are correct that it is easier to determine capabilities than intentions, our finding is good news for states facing potential challengers as they should be able to resolve one of the key uncertainties facing them in deciding whether to balance. If realists are wrong in this regard, the problem becomes thornier. Thus, this finding has important policy implications in addition to theoretical implications.

Uncertainty about timing or the value of delay

The final major contribution of this book is that it explores the impact of uncertainty surrounding the value of delay in balancing. It is tempting to think about the decision to balance – or indeed to bandwagon or hide – as a onetime decision, but this is not the case. States must make this decision repeatedly. In the regular course of relations between states it can recur over a period of months or years, especially in cases of established rivalries such as the Cold War. Therefore, even a state that is inclined to balance faces a tricky choice. It is not "should I balance?", but rather "should I start balancing now or wait for a more opportune moment?" States may wish to save resources now to make a maximum effort later if they do not anticipate the threat materializing until some point in time down the road. Additionally, if there is uncertainty about the need to balance, delay could be tempting given the hope that time will reveal whether the challenger really is a threat and the scale of that threat.[13] Finally, if leaders discount the future somewhat it may be tempting to put off costs provided the risk of doing so is not too severe. Complicating this further, it is often unclear whether it will be cheaper and easier to meet a threat now or at some point in the future due to uncertainties about the speed of rearmament, economic growth, shifting alliances, and evolving technologies. Hence deciding when and if to balance is very difficult and fraught with uncertainty.

Given the complicated nature of the question of the value of delay, subjecting it to formal modeling makes sense. Much as with uncertainty about capabilities and intentions, this too has a clear payoff. The model in Chapter 2 shows that the temptation to pass off threats to the future is more compelling than the temptation to pass the buck to another state. This is important as much discussion of coalition balancing behavior focuses on concerns about free-riding rather than passing the burden off to a future date (Christensen and Snyder 1990; Mearsheimer 2001;

Pape 2005; Powell 1999). Our historical case supports the model's insights. We find that Britain and France in the 1930s were more apt to pass off balancing to the future rather than to each other. The French in particular realized the threat the Germans posed, yet both France and Britain hoped that their rearmaments programs would allow them to confront Germany more successfully in 1940 than they could in 1936 or 1938. Thus, time considerations are important when thinking about if and when states balance.

Other factors affecting balancing

While the above three hypotheses form the core of the book's argument they do not capture everything affecting states' propensity to balance. We, therefore, develop two ancillary hypotheses about the likelihood of balancing. First, the offensive value of the challenger's move influences the likelihood of balancing. Second, the degree to which the challenger's move is motivated by a desire to revise the distribution of power as opposed to the intrinsic value of the move itself affects both the propensity to balance and potential balancers' ability to find accommodation with the challenger. Each of these is discussed below in turn.

The first of these, the offense value of the move of the rising state's actions, has been explored in the security dilemma and offense/defense balance literatures (Biddle 2001; Jervis 1978; Reiter 1999), but has direct bearing on the propensity to balance (Powell 1999). To understand what is meant by the offensive value, consider that actions taken to strengthen a state militarily may be more or less threatening in nature. New fortifications and a new tank division may both enhance a state's security, but the latter move is far more offensive in nature and hence more threatening to its neighbors than the former. This is also distinct from intentions. A state which is not intending to take advantage of its move to threaten a neighbor may not have a move available which is mainly defensive. Thus, while states may take the move as a signal of intentions, it is not the same thing. Yet, the greater the offensive value of the move, the more need there is to balance. It is important to understand that we do not conceptualize this aspect of the problem as an either/or issue. In other words, it is not that some moves are inherently defensive and others are inherently offensive. Rather, threats fall on a continuum between two ideal types: purely defensive vs. purely offensive changes to the balance of power. As with capabilities and intentions, uncertainty can surround this variable.

Second, we argue counter-intuitively that less revisionist challengers are more willing to risk being balanced against than are more revisionist challengers. This is because less revisionist states are likely making the threatening move mostly for the move's intrinsic value and not because they are trying to alter the relative balance of power. Thus, a state's threats to balance against the challenger and wipe out any relative power gains which would accrue to the challenger are not compelling. On the other hand for a challenger that was mainly interested in the relative gains, such threats to balance might remove most or all of the incentive to make the threatening move in the first place. Returning to the earlier example of the Iranian nuclear program, this argument means that if Iran wanted the program either for reasons of domestic politics or its own security – in other words the intrinsic value of the program – rather than for altering the strategic balance of the Middle East, it would have been hard to dissuade Iran from pursuing the program through threats of counterbalancing to offset the increased Iranian capabilities.[14] Actions such as economic sanctions which cause direct pain to Iran to offset the intrinsic value of the nuclear program, however, were more likely to be effective as the costs sanctions inflict would directly reduce Iran's utility assuming it values economic gains, whereas balancing would only reduce Iran's ability to further alter the status quo, something Iran would not value if it were true that it pursued a nuclear program for the program's intrinsic rather than relative value. Of course states, including Iran, can value both the intrinsic and relative gains values of a move and Iran's willingness to strike a deal regarding its enrichment program does not indicate whether Tehran was more interested in intrinsic or relative gains.

On the other hand, Russia's seizure of the Crimea may also be due to the intrinsic value of the territory rather that the strategic advantage it gives. First, regaining this "lost territory" satisfies domestic Russian irredentism and thus boosts Vladimir Putin's domestic popularity. Second, this redemption of lost territory also likely has a strong emotional value for Putin and his view of himself and his role in Russian history. Alternatively, the argument could be made that this is just about securing Russia's naval base in Sevastopol. However, there are a number of reasons to doubt this. Under the 2010 Kharkiv Pact, Russia's lease of Sevastopol was extended from 2017 to 2042 in exchange for a multi-year gas contract. This accord was only unilaterally terminated by Russia on 31 March 2014, two weeks after Russia's annexation of Crimea and the accord was not in any clear trouble before Russia's actions. Furthermore, annexing an entire province to keep one base is unnecessarily provocative and risky. After all, the US has dealt with similar issues surrounding Guantanamo by simply ignoring Cuba's demands to leave while paying rents to the Cuban government for the base. On the other hand, it seems likely that in supporting separatists in the Donbass region of Ukraine, Russia is concerned about relative gains (or avoiding relative losses) in relation to the West. This may explain why Putin has modulated Russian behavior in the Donbass in response to Western reactions far more than he has in Crimea. Thus, understanding a state's motives behind an action which is perceived as threatening is important in crafting the most effective strategy for dissuading that state from continuing its provocative strategy. This hypothesis, as well as the argument about the offensive nature of the challenger's move, is fully developed in Chapters 1 and 2 and applied to the case French and British balancing against Nazi Germany in the 1930s in Chapter 3.

Factors affecting the propensity to bandwagon

The book also explores what drives states to bandwagon with potential challengers. Bandwagoning is often seen as the opposite side of the coin from balancing and thus to understand balancing behavior it is necessary to have a firm grasp on bandwagoning as well. States may bandwagon with a rising power to protect themselves from that power (Walt 1985; 1987), to obtain spoils in return for assisting that power's rise (Schweller 1994), or to obtain both protection and spoils. The book derives three ancillary hypotheses about factors which makes states more or less likely to bandwagon.

First, states which are geographically isolated from other potential balancers and alliance partners are more likely to bandwagon than those that are geographically proximate to their potential allies and other balancers. This is taken from Walt (1985; 1987) who makes the same argument when developing his Balance of Threat theory which argues that states often bandwagon to protect themselves from threats. Geographically isolated states are more apt to bandwagon because balancing is less likely to be effective as they would have difficulty pooling their efforts with those of another state and also because if they get into a war with the rising challenger, they would likely be unable to receive outside military help (Rothstein 1968; Walt 1987; Waltz 1979). Such isolation is more problematic for relatively weak states than it is for great powers, but it should matter to some extent for all states.

Second, the book argues that shared membership in multilateral international organizations with other potential balancers can reduce the appeal of bandwagoning. In arguing this, we are building off a significant amount of neo-liberal institutional theory.[15] We argue that intergovernmental organizations matter because such institutions can act as fora for communicating and coordinating with other states which face the same security challenges. Thus, institutions help reduce the diplomatic isolation that can prompt security seeking states to see bandwagoning as the best strategy to protect themselves. States can find reassurance that they will not be alone in opposing the rising challenger nor the only one missing out on potential spoils of bandwagoning. Also, such organizations can help mediate and resolve existing tensions between potential balancers, allowing them to more easily cooperate with one another. Finally, institutions can act as a credible check on the aspirations of the rising state by reducing the odds that the state would be able to provide significant spoils to states which bandwagon with it, meaning that even revisionist states seeking spoils should be less likely to bandwagon due to the presence of powerful multilateral organizations. Given that such revisionist states make up much of the pool of states which bandwagon (Schweller 1994), this effect of institutions is empirically important. Taken together, these independent effects of institutions add up to a considerable factor in determining whether states bandwagon.

Third, states which are economically dependent on the rising state and which lack credible substitutes for their economic relationships with the rising state – including trade, investment, and aid – are more likely to bandwagon with the rising challenger than are states which have a variety of important international economic connections, are economically interdependent rather than unidirectionally dependent upon the challenger, or have plausible substitutes for their economic ties with the challenger should those ties be severed (Hirschman 1980). In effect, states which have multilateral economic ties and which are interdependent with a variety of states rather than dependent on the rising challenger are less constrained and have more foreign policy options available to them. Thus, they are freer to balance.

We develop these ancillary hypotheses in Chapter 4 and apply them to bandwagoning in East Central Europe in the 1930s. We also apply these concepts,

10 *Introduction*

along with the previously developed hypotheses on balancing, to the contemporary case of states in Southeast Asia in Chapter 7 to determine if those states are likely to balance, bandwagon, hide, or do something else entirely. A summary of the work's hypotheses discussed in the preceding sections can be found in Tables 0.1 to 0.3.

Table 0.1 Core hypotheses: uncertainty and balancing

Hypothesis	Empirical evaluation
1. Commitment problems and balancing	
Chapter 1 All balancing results from commitment problems. In the absence of such problems, states would be able to strike bargains to avoid the costs of balancing and being balanced against.	**Chapters 3, 5, and 7** Germany posed a commitment problem for Britain, France, and Poland in the 1930s and China poses a commitment problem for Vietnam and the Philippines today.
2. Uncertainty of capabilities vs. intentions	
Chapter 2 Uncertainty about the rising state's capabilities is more problematic for potential balancers than uncertainty about the rising state's intentions.	**Chapter 3** In the 1930s Britain and France were largely convinced of Hitler's revisionist goals but they were uncertain about how much he had been able to build up his capabilities.
3. Uncertainty of timing (value of delay)	
Chapter 2 States are more likely to delay balancing to the future than to pass the buck to another state.	**Chapter 3** In the 1930s Britain and France were more apt to pass off balancing to the future (in order to rearm) rather than to each other.

Table 0.2 Ancillary hypotheses I: nature of the challenge

Hypothesis	Empirical evaluation
4. Degree of offensive advantage	
Chapters 1 and 2 The offensive value of the challenger's move influences the likelihood of balancing.	**Chapters 3 and 7** France and Britain discounted the offensive value of the German occupation of the Rhineland and Sudetenland in the 1930s. Chinese installations in the South China Sea do little to alter the military equation today.
5. Relational vs. intrinsic value	
Chapters 1 and 2 The degree to which the challenger's move is motivated by a desire to revise the distribution of power as opposed to the intrinsic value of the move itself affects both the propensity to balance and potential balancers' ability to find accommodation with the challenger.	**Chapters 3 and 7** Germany valued the Rhineland and Sudetenland for both relational and intrinsic reasons. China has strong intrinsic and more limited relational reasons for valuing establishing sovereign control over the South China Sea.

Table 0.3 Ancillary hypotheses II: bandwagoning and uncertainty

Hypothesis	Empirical evaluation
6. Geostrategic position	
Chapter 4 States which are geographically isolated from other potential balancers and alliance partners are more likely to bandwagon than those that are geographically proximate to their potential allies and other balancers (Walt 1985; 1987).	**Chapters 5 and 7** In the 1930s, the states of East Central Europe were geographically cut off from their great power allies, while the sea gives the maritime states of Southeast Asia access to American aid today.
7. International organizations	
Chapter 4 Membership in multilateral international organizations with other potential balancers can reduce the appeal of bandwagoning.	**Chapters 5 and 7** In the 1930s, regional organizations were collapsing in East Central Europe and the League of Nations was ineffective. Today, ASEAN offers a regional forum for addressing issues in the South China Sea and there are also relevant global organizations to which states can turn, such as the Permanent Court of Arbitration and the United Nations.
8. Economic dependence	
Chapter 4 States which are economically dependent on the rising state and which lack credible substitutes for their economic relationships with the rising state are more likely to bandwagon with the rising challenger (Hirshman 1980).	**Chapters 5 and 7** In the 1930s, many of the states of East Central Europe were unidirectionally dependent on Germany as trading partner. Today, while Southeast Asian states have important economic ties to China, the pattern is one of multilateral interdependence.

Outline of the book

The rest of the book is laid out as follows. Chapter 1 constructs a formal model in order to demonstrate that balancing is not only a response to power shifts as argued within much of the realist literature, but that in order for balancing to occur the power shift in turn must create a commitment problem. Thus, commitment problems are a prerequisite to all balancing. We argue that whether or not a commitment problem exists depends on the nature of the challenge[16] being made by the revisionist state as well as the relative power of the states. The chapter also explores what types of revisionist states are willing to risk being balanced against. Specifically, we argue that states which are less revisionist are more willing to risk being balanced against.

Chapter 2 relaxes some of the assumptions of the model in Chapter 1 by developing a multiplayer, dynamic model which explores the impact of uncertainty about the challenger's type, the pre-crisis balance of power, the nature of the challenge to the status quo, and the value of delay on the prospects for balancing. In contrast to the model in Chapter 1, the model in Chapter 2 allows for buck-passing and for players to defer balancing to the future. We conclude that uncertainty about capabilities is more problematic for effective balancing than uncertainty about intentions. In addition, uncertainty about the pre-crisis balance of power is more difficult to resolve than uncertainty about the strategic impact of the challenge on the balance of power, though the latter is still more important than uncertainty over intentions. Also, delay is shown to be more seductive than buck-passing.

Chapter 3 explores the model's findings through a case study of German and Allied behavior prior to World War II, from the German militarization of the Rhineland in 1936 through the Sudetenland crisis of 1938. We find that Britain and France focused primarily on the relative balances of forces and to a lesser extent on the nature of the German challenge. However, the latter still figured more prominently in their calculation than German intentions. Ultimately, uncertainty about the reliability of third parties and the conviction that delay was valuable swayed Britain and France toward appeasement.

Chapter 4 takes the concepts developed in the models in Chapters 1 and 2 and applies them to the behaviors of smaller states which may be more inclined to bandwagon or hide than more powerful states would be. In particular, the chapter examines how states trade off potential spoils versus security. All of this is again done considering uncertainty over the nature of the challenge, the balance of power, and the actions of other states. Chapter 5 examines the foreign policies of Poland, Yugoslavia, Romania, and Hungary – cases which have been given insufficient attention in the international relations literature – in light of the concepts developed in Chapter 4.

We selected the pre-World War II era in Chapters 3 and 5 to develop our argument for two reasons. First, it is an important case on its own merits as World War II and the alignment decisions leading up to it affected the international system for decades. Second, the case, at least as it pertains to Britain and France, is well known, allowing us to illustrate and test our ideas using the behaviors of states which will be familiar to most readers. Given that the actions of Britain and France have been used by other international relations scholars to make different arguments about balancing, it also provides a fairly difficult hurdle for our explanations. Thus, the case is important, accessible, and provides a difficult challenge for our hypotheses.

Chapter 6 looks at balancing and bandwagoning behavior after war breaks out. It draws connections between the motives for militarily intervening in a war (balancing or bandwagoning) and the likely timing of such interventions. It also argues that the spoils bandwagoners are seeking (territory versus other forms of spoils) should affect the timing of intervention. Additionally, the likelihood of a state ending up on the winning side of a war should be influenced by both its motives and the timing of its entry. The various arguments are examined by looking at all military interveners in the Correlates of War Interstate War dataset version 4.0 (1816–2007). In general, once the role of alliances is accounted for, bandwagoners should join later than balancers and later bandwagoners should be more likely to win than earlier bandwagoners. Also, states joining for non-territorial spoils should be less careful about picking the winning side. The rate of balancing versus bandwagoning is also considered as is the success rate of these strategies.

Chapter 7 examines whether states near or bordering the South China Sea – specifically Brunei, Indonesia, Malaysia, the Philippines, Singapore, and Vietnam – are likely to bandwagon with, balance against, or respond in another fashion to a rising China. To answer this question, the chapter contrasts these states' geographic, institutional, and economic positions with those of the European states in the 1930s discussed in Chapters 2 and 3. The chapter also examines the behavior of these Southeast Asian states in light of the models in the preceding chapters. This chapter concludes that while China is less of a threat than Germany was in both territorial and ideological terms, there are significant differences in each of the areas listed above between the present and the 1930s, indicating that neither balancing nor bandwagoning are likely to occur in Southeast Asia today, unlike in 1930s Europe when many states bandwagoned with Germany. We have chosen the South China Sea case for its relevance to contemporary international relations and especially US foreign policy today. Growing Chinese power and assertiveness have prompted intense debates about two related but distinct questions. What sort of foreign policies should states adopt and what policies are states likely to adopt? We hope that by applying our theories to this case we will shed light on these questions and make a useful contribution to contemporary foreign policy debates.

Finally, the Conclusion summarizes and brings together the findings from the previous chapters. It also makes policy recommendations based on these findings. In particular, it offers suggestions about alliance management, intelligence gathering, and how challengers can avoid being balanced against.

How states respond to potential threats is an important theoretical and policy question. Building on existing realist, liberal, and rationalist work, this book advances several new claims about what types of uncertainty are most problematic for the creation of effective strategies and which situations are most likely to produce balancing, bandwagoning, hiding, or some other behavior. In order to do this, we will begin in Chapter 1 by reviewing previous explanations of balancing and demonstrating that all balancing occurs as a response to a commitment problem.

Notes

1 Throughout the book we use the terms balance of power, balance of forces, and balance of capabilities interchangeably.
2 Elman (1995) and Whitaker (2010) both make this exact point and are rare examples of works that focus on balancing behavior among smaller powers. For examples of works which focus solely on great powers in relation to balancing, see He (2012), Levy and Thompson (2005; 2010), Lieber and Alexander (2005), Mearsheimer (2001), Pape (2005), and Paul (2005).

14 *Introduction*

3 For instance see Fearon (1995) and Powell (2006).
4 Paul (2005, 47) defines soft balancing as states forming "limited diplomatic coalitions or ententes, especially at the United Nations, with the implicit threat of upgrading their alliances if the [potential challenger] goes beyond its stated goals." Asymmetric balancing refers to balancing against non-state actors or balancing by non-state actors against states (Paul 2004, 3).
5 Rationalists argue that since war is costly, states would prefer *ex post* to have arrived at the post-war settlement without having had to pay the costs. Thus, war is a highly inefficient dispute resolution mechanism and why states would rationally engage in it is an important question. Rationalists have concluded that given unitary actors wars are caused by uncertainty resulting from private information, commitment problems, or indivisibility. The first of these, uncertainty due to private information, makes it impossible for the two sides to agree upon the probable outcome of the war. Second, commitment problems make it impossible for states to commit to not revise a settlement after they become more powerful, meaning that their opponents may prefer to fight them now rather than settle only to have to fight later when the odds are longer. Finally, indivisibility makes striking a bargain impossible as the stake itself is not divisible and thus must either be conceded in its entirety or fought for. Incentives arising out of domestic politics can also rationally lead to war (Bueno de Mesquita et al. 2004; Chiozza and Goemans 2004; Croco 2011; Stanley 2009).
6 Iran can commit to refrain from using nuclear weapons in an offensive manner as existing nuclear retaliatory threats are credible and overwhelming. In other words, unless one believes that the Iranian government is suicidal or that for some reason Iranian nuclear strikes would not bring about swift and massive retaliation, then it should be quite possible to deter Iran from using its nuclear weapons offensively, just as every other nuclear power has been deterred since the United States lost its nuclear monopoly in 1949. However, the protection from invasion by the United States that the possession of a nuclear arsenal would afford Iran should allow it to behave more aggressively using conventional forces within the Middle East as Iran would be protected from the worst potential repercussions of such adventurism. This is the stability–instability paradox. See Liddell Hart (1960), Rauchhaus (2009), and Snyder (1965).
7 Both motives are likely at work here since Iran is not a monolith. Like any other government it is composed of various factions with different strategic outlooks and goals.
8 The P5+1 consist of the five permanent members of the United Nations Security Council (China, France, Russia, the United Kingdom and the United States) plus Germany.
9 One promising sign is the victory of more moderate candidates in the February 2016 elections for both the Iranian Parliament and the Assembly of Experts. The latter is an assembly of *mujtahid* (religious experts) who chose and supervise the Supreme Leader of Iran.
10 Rationalists argue that commitment problems can only be eliminated through major power shifts, regime change, outside guarantors, or substantial destruction of the good at stake (Powell 2006; Reiter 2009; Weisiger 2013).
11 For instance see Glaser (1997) and Taliaferro (2001).
12 This is one reason why intelligence gathering was so crucial during the Cold War even though East and West were fairly sure of the other side's hostile intent once the Cold War was well underway. Of course, if benign intent is certain, the problem disappears.
13 This would also allow the state to avoid Jervis' (1978) security spiral: the unnecessary triggering of a costly arms race due to uncertainty.
14 Such actions could include building closer military alliances between the United States and Israel or Arab monarchies in the Persian Gulf region. This general logic is

similar but not identical to Davis (2001) who examines when threats work better than appeasement and vice versa. He argues threats work against aggressive states and appeasement works with security seeking states.

15 For instance see Keohane (1986), Keohane and Martin (1995), Kupchan and Kupchan (1995), Lake (2001), Oneal (1990), Ostrom (1990), Oye (1986), Rafferty (2003), and Weber (1997).
16 Throughout the book we use the terms nature of the challenge, nature of the move, and nature of the opportunity interchangeably.

1 Balancing as a commitment problem

As discussed in the introduction, a major trend in the study of international relations in the last decade has been an increasing focus on the roles that strategic interaction and information play in influencing state behavior in the international system.[1] This trend has been quite fruitful, yet concepts from older schools of thought remain important to our understanding of international relations. In this chapter, we take an older concept, that of balancing, and place it within a new framework of commitment problems and informational asymmetries. Specifically, in this chapter using a formal model we will argue that commitment problems are a necessary, but not sufficient, cause of all balancing. While this general conclusion is perhaps unsurprising, the model goes further. It shows that whether uncertainties about intentions lead to balancing or not depends upon two factors: first, the relative power differences between the challenger of the status quo and the potential balancer; and second, the long-run advantage that a specific challenge to the status quo creates for a revisionist state (such as beneficial tactical positions for future military offensives). It further argues that while informational asymmetries are important they are not a necessary part of balancing because under some circumstance balancing would happen even with perfect information about intentions.

In arguing this, we are attempting to improve on Walt's (1985) conception of balancing against threats as well as taking up Schweller's (1997) call for scholars to state the conditions under which their propositions hold. To this end, we distinguish between commitment and information problems and analyze how these two aspects of balancing influence each other. Additionally, the model departs from the standard literature by breaking the revisionist state's benefits from challenging the status quo into two components: the action's intrinsic value and any relative gains vis-à-vis potential balancers.

The first section of the chapter will examine the concept and definition of balancing. The second will examine the role that commitment and informational problems play in balancing behavior. The third outlines the basic structure of the game-theoretic model used to analyze the role that commitment problems play in balancing behavior. The chapter then examines the implications of this model under complete information, while the fifth section introduces informational asymmetries. The sixth section discusses the implications of our model for balancing behavior. The final section concludes and summarizes the chapter's findings.

What is balancing?

Though balancing has long been an accepted concept in the study of international relations and is a core principle of the realist framework, its definition is somewhat nebulous. In large part, this is because of its association with the term "balance of power" and with balance of power theory. The concept of the "balance of power" is used in a sufficiently wide variety of ways that its meaning has become unclear (Gulick 1955). Haas (1953) claims there are eight distinct meanings in the literature for the term "balance of power" and Wright (1965) finds nine. Even Morgenthau (1973) admits he uses the term in four distinct ways. Claude (1962) finds that balance of power is used to describe the current distribution of power, to identify a particular type of policy, and as a symbol of *realpolitik*. However, even within these broad categories it is often used in distinct and even contradictory ways. Thus, it might seem that balancing as a concept is hopelessly muddled and should be discarded. This, however, is not the case. Rather, it is the concept of the balance of power and not balancing that has many meanings, is ill defined, and empirically suspect (Kaufman, Little, and Wohlforth 2007; Nexon 2009; Vasquez and Elman 2002). Additionally, the vast majority of international relations scholars see balancing as a distinct type of state behavior. This is true even of scholars that do not support balance of power theory or the realist framework.[2] Thus, it should be possible to form a clear definition of balancing.

A key role in defining balancing is played by the concept of threat perception. Walt (1985, 12) argues that balancing is a response to a threat and that states balance "to avoid domination by stronger powers." In particular, aggressive behavior will prompt balancing. Wolfers (1962, 125) sees balancing as the response of a status quo power to a threat.[3] Similarly, Schweller (1994) and Schroeder (1994) see balancing as a response to a threat, though Schroeder argues that balancing is only one of a number of possible responses, along with bandwagoning, hiding, and transcending (Schroeder 1994, 111 and 116–17).[4] Lieber and Alexander state that balancing is "motivated by some perception of threat" and is not a "general desire for influence or the pursuit of power" (Art et al. 2006, 192).[5] Both Schweller and Walt agree that not all threatened states will balance,[6] but none of the balancing scholarship argues that states that are not threatened will balance.

Equally important is that balancing is a response to a threat that has yet to be actualized, rather than a response to an actual attack (Levy 2002, 135; Schweller 1994, 83). Responding with force to an invasion or some other military attack is defense, not balancing. Belgium and the Netherlands entered World War II not to balance against Nazi Germany, but because they had been invaded. To conflate their reasons for acting against Germany with those of France and Britain would be misleading and would obscure the rich variety of state behavior that exists in the security realm. Finally, balancing need not be directed at a hegemon, but may be directed at a regional or minor power (Art et al. 2006, 184). For example, in the nineteenth century Argentina balanced against Brazil and Bolivia balanced against Chile. Thus, for the purposes of this analysis, balancing will be defined as the arraying of power by a state or states against a perceived future threat. Balancing may be either internal – building up one's own military forces – or external – forming alliances to counter the perceived threat (Waltz 1979). Successful balancing will manage to array sufficient power against the threat to either defeat or deter it. Of course, not all balancing will be successful.

Some might argue that this definition is flawed as it ignores balancing as described by defensive realists such Waltz and Layne. Waltz (1979; 2000) and Layne (1993; 2006) argue that states balance against power, not threat.[7] However, this claim is not actually in opposition to the idea that states balance against threats. Waltz argues that states balance against states capable of being a threat because they can never be sure when or if that potential threat will become real (Morgenthau 1973; Vasquez 1997, 904). In determining whether another state poses a threat, leaders look at two aspects of that state, its capabilities and intentions. Waltz is essentially arguing that intentions cannot be discerned, therefore, capabilities are inherently threats and should be balanced against. In essence, this makes all balancing the result of the inherent commitment problems found in any power imbalance. Many classical realists, however, concede that intentions can be discerned to some extent and that estimates about intentions do factor into threat perception (Claude 1962, 64–5). Some neo-realists, such as Walt (1985), also argue that intentions matter to threat perception and that states balance against threat, not power. Certainly, constructivists and neo-liberals believe that intentions matter and can be discerned to some degree.[8] Walt, however, connects the view that power is an implicit threat with the view that intentions matter in threat perception. He states that, "To ally with the dominant power means placing one's trust in its continued benevolence" (Walt 1985, 5). Thus, power is a threat, but only if the state's continued benevolence is unlikely. If the dominant power (or any other power), however, could credibly commit to remaining benevolent there would be no need to balance against it.[9] Thus, this definition of balancing is consistent with the literature at large and the apparent disagreement between our definition and certain strains of realism is simply the result of some realists seeing all capabilities as threats. The disagreement also highlights that commitment problems play a central role in balancing.

Additionally, Waltz (1979) suggests balancing is automatic, thereby implying that balancing is not a conscious choice made by individual states. Waltz, however, is careful to point out that his theory is one of international politics, not foreign policy. He argues that the system as a whole will tend to balance; thus it seems that balances form automatically, even though individual states may choose not to balance.[10] Many others concur that balancing is not automatic, certainly not for states and perhaps not for the system as a whole either (Levy and Thompson 2005; Lieber and Alexander 2005; Paul 2005). Whether or not Waltz is correct that balancing is the predominant behavior, and there are reasons to think he is not (Cusack and Stoll 1991; Rosecrance and Lo 1996; Schroeder 1994; Schweller 1994; 1997; Vasquez 1997),[11] is unimportant for our argument. What is important is that even Waltz recognizes that individual states must choose whether or not they should balance. Viewing balancing as a conscious decision by a state is in line with an older school of realism. Wolfers (1962) concludes that though balancing may appear to be automatic, it is in fact the result of conscious decisions by individual states (Wolfers 1962, 122–4). Morgenthau (1973) certainly does not see balancing as automatic and frequently encouraged status quo states to balance.[12] Similarly, Rosecrance and Lo (1996) argue that for systemic balancing to occur, collective action problems must be overcome and the "buck-passing" described in Christensen and Snyder (1990) must be avoided. This implies that the decision to balance is up to individual states. Thus, there is no conflict between the way realists traditionally use the concept of balancing and defining balancing within the framework of strategic interaction and individual state choice.

A final, possible criticism of the definition of balancing advanced herein is that balancing requires states to join the weaker side and that this should be explicit within any definition of balancing (Schroeder 1994; Schweller 1994; Waltz 1979). This implies that joining the stronger side is bandwagoning. However, many of the examples of balancing given by political scientists do not fit within this restriction. The United States was more powerful than the Soviet Union, yet the formation of NATO is generally described as an act of balancing on the part of the United States and the Western European states.[13] Additionally, any coalition that wishes to deter a threat does not wish to simply achieve parity with that threat, but rather wants to achieve supremacy over it. As Claude (1962, 59) notes, "Balance of power theorists tend to put more stock in defeating aggressors by preponderant power than in deterring them by equivalent power." Finally, it is not always clear what the true distribution of power is. Thus, states may join what they believe to be the weaker side, but what is in fact the more powerful. Would such an act be balancing under the restrictions suggested by Schweller and Schroeder? The answer is not clear. It is far clearer and more consistent with the literature to define balancing as the arraying of force against a perceived threat rather than attempting to define it in terms of whether a state is joining the stronger or weaker side. Thus, while the relative power of the challenger and potential balancer will be important, it need not be true that the challenger is more powerful than the potential balancer. With these definitional issues addressed we can now turn to examining the causes of balancing.

Balancing and commitment problems

In this section and in the rest of this chapter we will refer to *revisionist states* (or *challengers to the status quo*) and *balancers* (or *status quo states*) not in absolute terms but only in the context of a particular case of balancing. Thus, a state may be revisionist on some issues and a status quo state on other issues. In fact, it is hard to imagine any state which would not wish to change some aspect of the current international system and maintain the status quo in others (Mearsheimer 2001). We will also refer to *potential aggressors* as those revisionist states which cannot credibly commit to not using the change in the status quo to their advantage at some point in the future.[14] Finally, we refer to *potential balancers* as those states that can respond to the challenger but which have not yet done so.[15]

It is our contention that commitment problems are a necessary cause of all balancing. Commitment problems are in fact an important rational explanation of conflict in the international system.[16] Fearon (1995) demonstrates that commitment problems, along with private information and problems of indivisibility, are one of the few empirically significant rational causes of war.[17] Bueno de Mesquita, Morrow, and Zorick (1997) extend Fearon's logic and show that these same conditions must exist for crises to occur. This is because crises, like war, are a form of costly bargaining and if each side knew how the crisis was going to end, they would simply agree to that outcome ex ante without paying the costs of a crisis.[18] Thus, states will only engage in costly conflict if their dispute is irresolvable for the reasons stated in Fearon (1995).

Balancing is clearly a form of interstate bargaining, albeit often tacit. The state or states engaged in balancing hope that by mobilizing resources and forming alliances against the perceived threat, the threatening state or coalition of states will be deterred from attacking and ultimately desist from attempting to overturn the status quo. Failing this, the balancer aims to aggregate sufficient power to defeat the revisionist state in either a defensive or preventive war.

Like wars and crises, balancing is costly. It is generally seen as being more costly in the short term than other behaviors such as bandwagoning, though often it is less costly in the long term, hence the tension about whether to balance (Rosecrance and Lo 1996; Schroeder 1994; Schweller 1997). Balancing often requires significant increases in armament expenditures or settling with former rivals in order to create alliances. Such settlements are costly since they require sacrificing claims and potential advantages in order to bring about the alliance.[19] Additionally, all balancing runs the risk of war with the state or coalition being balanced against.

Given that balancing is costly and that it is not a response to a direct attack (thus not immediately necessary for a state's survival) states must consider whether the benefits of balancing are worth the costs. Such costs include not only the risk of war, the military expenditures necessary to oppose the threatening state, and the sacrifices necessary to bring about alliances, but also the forgone spoils that might have been available had the state bandwagoned with the revisionist state instead of having balanced against it. Why would a state undertake such a costly action and forgo potential benefits? A state would only balance if it believed that it would be cheaper or more effective to address a potential threat now rather than at some future point when it may or may not materialize. In other words, balancing entails assuming definite short-term costs to avoid greater expected, but uncertain, long-term costs.

Also, it must be the case that no cheaper alternative to balancing, such as buck-passing or accommodation, exists. This is crucial. No state wants to be the target of balancing as this threatens its security and autonomy in the international system. Further, if the state is truly revisionist, hostile balancing limits its long-term ability to change the status quo. Thus states which face potential balancers have incentives to come to some sort of accommodation in order to prevent balancing. This is true regardless of whether or not the revisionist state plans on attacking the potential balancer's interests in the future. Thus, states perceived as potential aggressors should be willing to come to terms with potential balancers, even if this is merely to ensure that when they are ready to strike they can do so with minimal cost. Also, given the high cost of balancing, potential balancers should find an agreement with potential aggressors' appealing, provided of course they can somehow ensure the potential aggressor will not exploit the agreement to challenge their interests in the future.

So why do potential balancers and revisionist states sometimes fail to come to an agreement, tacit or otherwise? The answer, as alluded to above, is commitment problems. It is often difficult for revisionist states to credibly commit to limit themselves to the immediate and localized changes to the status quo they are proposing. This is because potential aggressors often seek agreement with potential balancers so that they can isolate and defeat their opponents in a piecemeal fashion. Alternatively they may seek to use the time gained to strengthen themselves relative to the potential balancers, striking only when they are confident of success. It is this inability of a revisionist state to bind itself in the future, and thus commit itself never to use its relative power gain against the potential balancer, which results in balancing behavior. Asymmetric information is chiefly responsible for these commitment problems. If the future intentions of the revisionist state were known to potential balancers, the decision to balance or not would be quite simple. Potential balancers could focus solely on the subset of revisionist states which had malevolent intentions for the future (i.e., potential aggressors). By analyzing the nature of the moves and power of the challenger, potential balancers could determine if balancing was necessary or not. However, both aggressive and benign challengers of the status quo (from the potential balancers' point of view) have incentives to declare that they do not harbor future hostile intentions toward the potential balancers (and thus avoid being balanced against). It can be difficult for balancers to determine which revisionists they need to concern themselves with based on intentions. While balancers may be able to discern the intentions of some aggressors based on their behavior and capabilities, often the balancer will remain uncertain about the challenger's type. The decision to balance or not also depends on the nature of the challenge to the status quo. There are some changes that simply do not constitute enough of a threat no matter what the intentions behind them are. Thus, there may also be uncertainty about the nature of the challenge to the status quo. The model below helps illustrate these points.

Basic structure of the model

Our basic contention – that for balancing to occur, the existence of a commitment problem is a necessary but not sufficient condition – is not particularly controversial. However, clearly identifying those commitment problems and showing how they lead to balancing is a useful contribution to our understanding of balancing. As Powell (2006, 180) notes in his discussion of the role of commitment problems in war, unless this is done commitment problems become nothing more than a "catch-all" label that provides little insight. This section sets up the simple game-theoretic model we use to do this.

The first step is to realize that the traditional explanation for balancing – changes in capabilities and threat perception – are both insufficient and vague. The decision to engage in balancing by one state is not simply a response to a change in the capabilities of another. If this were so, then annual economic growth or any type of government action that improves the stability or well-being of a state would be grounds for balancing behavior. This would make the scope of balancing ridiculously large. We also cannot simply reduce balancing to threat perception. If this were the case, then a state could one day simply "wake up" to find itself being balanced against without it having in any way tried to change the balance of power vis-à-vis the other state. Such "preemptive balancing" also stretches the scope of the problem too far. Rather, for balancing to occur, both a change in capabilities and a perception that this change threatens a potential balancer are necessary. This fits with the widely accepted view that threat perception is a function of both capabilities and intentions. In essence, the change in capabilities will produce a threat if the state that is changing the status quo cannot credibly commit that this shift in power is not a threat to the potential balancer.

The game consists of two states: a challenger and a respondent/potential balancer. The challenger is a revisionist state that wishes to change the state quo in a particular area. The respondent is a potential balancer who prefers the status quo. As noted above, it is important to keep in mind that these labels ("status quo power" and "revisionist power") are not used in the absolute sense that the respondent does not want to change anything about the international system. Rather, these labels refer to the specific context in which the states find themselves in relation to a given issue.[20] Thus on any given issue and at any given time, certain states will favor the status quo while others would like to see a revision of it.

The basic version of the game consists of two decisions. First, the challenger must decide whether to change the status quo by taking advantage of some opportunity (e.g., engaging in an arms buildup, seizing a strategic territory, etc.) or not. The challenger benefits from the move in two ways. First, the challenger would receive a benefit from the move itself. In other words there is some sort of intrinsic, absolute benefit to building more armaments, occupying a territory, etc. The second benefit from such a move is that it may enhance the challenger's position relative to the respondent.[21] The key provision here is that the challenger's decision does not directly threaten the integrity or existence of the respondent or his core interests. As noted above, responding to such an act would be a case of defending against an actual aggressor, not balancing against a potential one. If the challenger decides not to make a challenge, then the status quo remains in effect. Otherwise, the respondent must decide whether to react to the challenge by balancing or allowing the balance of power to be revised by the challenger. This model investigates not only when balancing occurs, but also under what conditions the initial challenge to the status quo will be made. Thus we have three possible outcomes: the status quo (SQ), unopposed challenge (UC), and balancing (BE). See Figure 1.1.

The challenger's payoff is:

SQ: 0
UC: $v + r - c_c$
BE: $v - c_c$

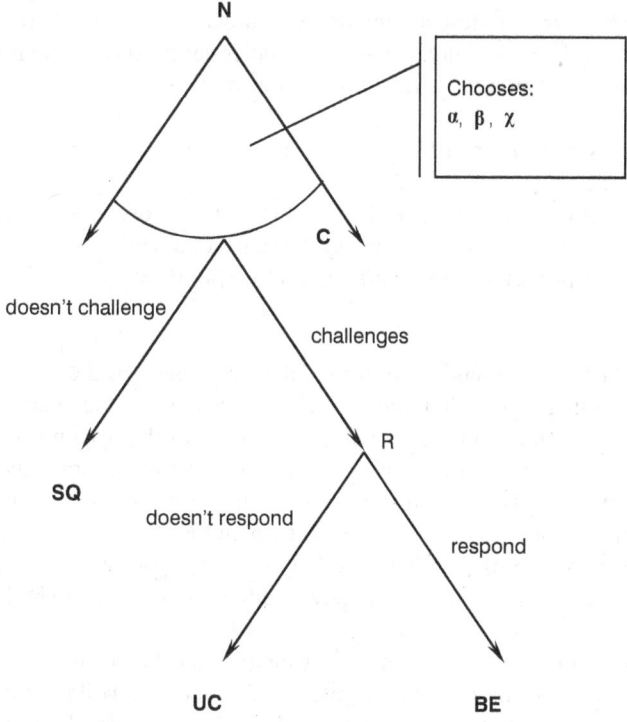

Figure 1.1 Basic structure of the game

where:
- v is the intrinsic value of the action the challenger undertook, $v \in \mathbb{R}^+$;
- r is the relative value of the challenge, that is the shift in the balance of power in favor of the challenger; and
- c_c is the cost of undertaking the action.

The respondent's payoff is:
SQ: 0
UC: $-r$
BE: $-c_r$

where:
- r is the same as for the challenger, reflecting that this is the measure of the relative power swing; and
- c_r is the cost to the respondent of balancing against the challenger's actions.

Game with perfect information

However, this is not the entire picture, as the relative advantage of making an unopposed revision to the status quo in a particular situation will vary according to three factors. Each of these are important in order to understand how a change to the status quo becomes threatening to the potential balancer; a simple change in capabilities is not enough. These three factors are:

1 **Intentions of the challenger**: i.e., the respondent's beliefs about the challenger;
2 **Relative difference in power**: i.e., the balance of power between the challenger and the respondent under the status quo; and
3 **Type of opportunity the challenger is responding to**: i.e., its offensive value.

The first factor, the intentions of the challenger, is perhaps the most important factor in assessing threat. It is not merely the change in the relative balance between the challenger and the respondent that worries the respondent, but what the challenger intends to do with this relative gain. Two important facts about the challenger's type must be recognized. First, it is not so much the challenger's type itself that matters but rather the respondent's belief about the challenger's type. Second, the relevance of the challenger's type is strongly tied to the other two factors: the opportunity type and the power differential between challenger and respondent.

This is illustrated by the often-cited example that the United States found Iraq, but not Britain, threatening despite the fact that the Britain not only has vastly greater capabilities than Iraq, but also has a nuclear arsenal. Thus, the mere possibility that Iraq may have had a WMD program was threatening enough to the United States to impose sanctions and eventually invade Iraq. Not only did the United States not find Britain's nuclear weapons program threatening, they actively helped and encouraged its development during the 1950s. Clearly, intentions matter in threat perception.

In order to operationalize this aspect of threat perception the concept of perceived challenger types is used. In this model there are two types of challengers: "aggressive" and "non-aggressive." Of course, these are simply ideal types each representing an extreme on a continuum $\alpha \in \mathbb{R}^+$, where $\alpha = 0$ is the least aggressive type and $\alpha \to +\infty$ is the most aggressive type. The implications of this for the value of r will be discussed below.[22]

The second factor affecting how a respondent will react to an attempt to change the status quo is the relative balance of power between the challenger and the respondent under the status quo. The impact of the change will directly depend on the magnitude of the change compared with the original balance of power. Imagine three cases. In the first, the respondent is assumed to be much stronger than the challenger. Here the challenger's gain will not warrant the costly balancing response by the respondent, provided it does not greatly diminish the respondent's autonomy on a given issue. For example, if Luxembourg decided to spend a very large portion of its GDP on increasing its armed forces it is hard to imagine that it could pose a threat to any of its neighbors, let alone to any great power.[23] In the second case, the challenger is assumed to be dominant. Any challenge it makes that is not directed at the territorial integrity of the respondent will not make much difference to the balance of power between them. Furthermore, as the power disparity increases, it becomes increasingly harder for the respondent to effectively balance against the challenger or even be motivated to try. Where challenging the status quo really matters is the third case: when the relative power of challenger and respondent are near parity. It is under this condition that even small changes to the balance between two states matters most. Thus, during the Cold War balancing appeared to be nearly automatic.

This factor is operationalized as the power differential $\beta \in \mathbb{R}$, where:

$\beta \to 0$ the relative power of challenger and respondent are near parity;
$\beta \to +\infty$ the relative power of the respondent is greater; and
$\beta \to -\infty$ the relative power of the challenger is greater.

The final factor is the strategic character of the opportunity presented to the challenger. This is important because certain changes to the status quo are simply more threatening than others. Of course, no action that changes the status quo is inherently defensive or offensive in nature. Even the most defensive capabilities can give an offensive advantage: securing your frontiers will make it easier for you to attack your neighbors without worrying about your core power base. And even the most offensive capabilities can be used in a purely defensive way: e.g., if a state has a second strike capability, then it can use nuclear weapons in a purely defensive way. However, the offensive capabilities of opportunities will vary from case to case.

In order to illustrate this it is useful to compare two instances: France building the Maginot Line (and the less famous Alpine and Corsican extension in the 1930s) and the satellite states the Soviet Union set up in Eastern Europe after World War II. Both had very similar motives. After the experience of World War One, France sought a ready-made defensive line to protect itself from future German aggression. Similarly, the Soviet Union was primarily motivated by a desire to create buffer states that would protect it in case of an attack like the ones it faced in World War One and World War II. However, despite similar intentions these actions were perceived very differently, in part because of the nature of each defensive solution.[24] Aside from the massive cost of the line, it soon became apparent that it would be very difficult for France to use the Maginot Line offensively. The mobile strategic reserve the line was supposed to produce proved illusionary since it was realized that manning the line would take up a large portion of France's military manpower.[25] On the other hand, the Soviets could easily use their satellites as staging areas for an attack on Western Europe once the Soviet Union recovered from its losses. Furthermore, the satellite states were not just buffers, but potentially provided the Soviets with manpower and resources to augment their power.[26] Thus, there are some capabilities that cause commitment problems regardless of the immediate intentions of the challenger, because even though the challenger does not want to use this advantage aggressively in the short run, it cannot credibly commit to never doing so in the long run.

26 Balancing as a commitment problem

This is operationalized in a similar way as the challenger type. Conceptually we can use the notion of two extreme types of opportunities: one "offensive" and one "defensive." The parameter $\gamma \in \mathbb{R}^+$ is such that if $\gamma = 0$ the opportunity is defensive in nature and if $\gamma \to +\infty$ the opportunity is offensive in nature. Thus, the relative value of the action is given by $r(\alpha, \beta, \gamma)$ such that r is an increasing function of α, the challenger's type, and γ, the opportunity's type – and a decreasing function of the absolute value of β (i.e., r decreases as $|\beta| \to +\infty$) – the relative balance of power between challenger and respondent in the status quo.

Thus, we have broken down the commitment problem that leads to balancing into three components. It is useful to think of the first two – the respondent's perception of the challenger's intention/type and the balance of power between challenger and respondent – as the context for the third component, the opportunity type. In turn, we can think of the opportunity type as the commitment problem proper. The context is important for two reasons. First, intentions and relative power differentials determine the significance of the commitment problem proper. Second, this context is generally fixed during balancing. That is, given the short time horizon, the respondent's perception and the balance of power are unlikely to shift dramatically. This means that the commitment problem proper – the strategic value of the opportunity the challenger is trying to capitalize on – is actually where the bargaining, explicit or tacit, will take place. Of course, the nature of the opportunity cannot be changed, but it can be rendered less threatening by the challenger (by taking a unilateral step to diminish its offensive value), by the respondent (by balancing), or by both (through a negotiated settlement). This approach differs from that of Fearon (1995) and Powell (2006), both of whom make the balance of power an integral part of commitment problems. Separating the two, however, provides useful conceptual and modeling leverage over the problem of balancing.

Outcomes with perfect information

If both players have perfect information about the strategic situation, then the outcomes depend on the payoffs. For the respondent, the decision is between balancing against the challenge or doing nothing and depends on the cost of balancing compared with the cost of ignoring the actions of the challenger. Obviously, if the cost of balancing is less than or equal to the relative value of the challenge, the respondent will balance, while if it is greater, the respondent will ignore the threat.[27] This leads to the critical value $r_r^* = c_r$. The respondent will balance against any threat that is equal or greater than r_r^* and will ignore all other threats. See Figure 1.2.

This means that the challenger's potential payoff of acting will be equal to $v + r$ if $r > r_r^*$, and v if $r \leq r_r^*$. The challenger's choice of action will depend on his net payoff, which means that there are three cost ranges that affect the outcome:

$c_c \geq v + r_r^*$: There is no level of r for which it is worthwhile to make a challenge so the only possible equilibrium is the status quo. See Figure 1.3.

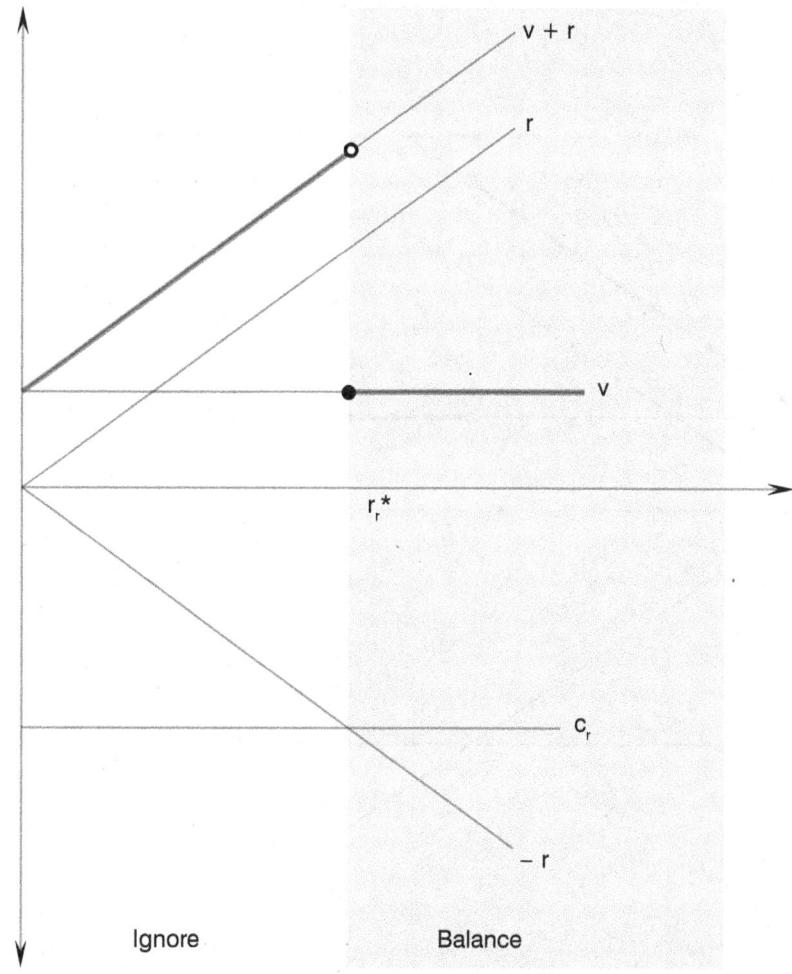

Figure 1.2 Potential balancer's action rule with certainty

$c_c \leq v$: It is always worthwhile to make a challenge and there are two possible equilibria. See Figure 1.4:

    $r < r_r^*$ unopposed challenge (UC)
    $r \geq r_r^*$ balancing equilibrium (BE)

$v \leq c_c \leq v + r_r^*$: The challenger will challenge only if $v + r \geq c_c$.

This leads to a second critical value $r_c^* = v + c_c$. If $r \geq r_c^*$, a challenge will be made, but if $r < r_c^*$, it will not. This leads to three possible equilibria (see Figure 1.5):

    $r < r_c^*$ status quo (SQ)
    $r_c^* \leq r < r_r^*$ unopposed challenge (UC)
    $r_r^* \leq r$ balancing equilibrium (BE)

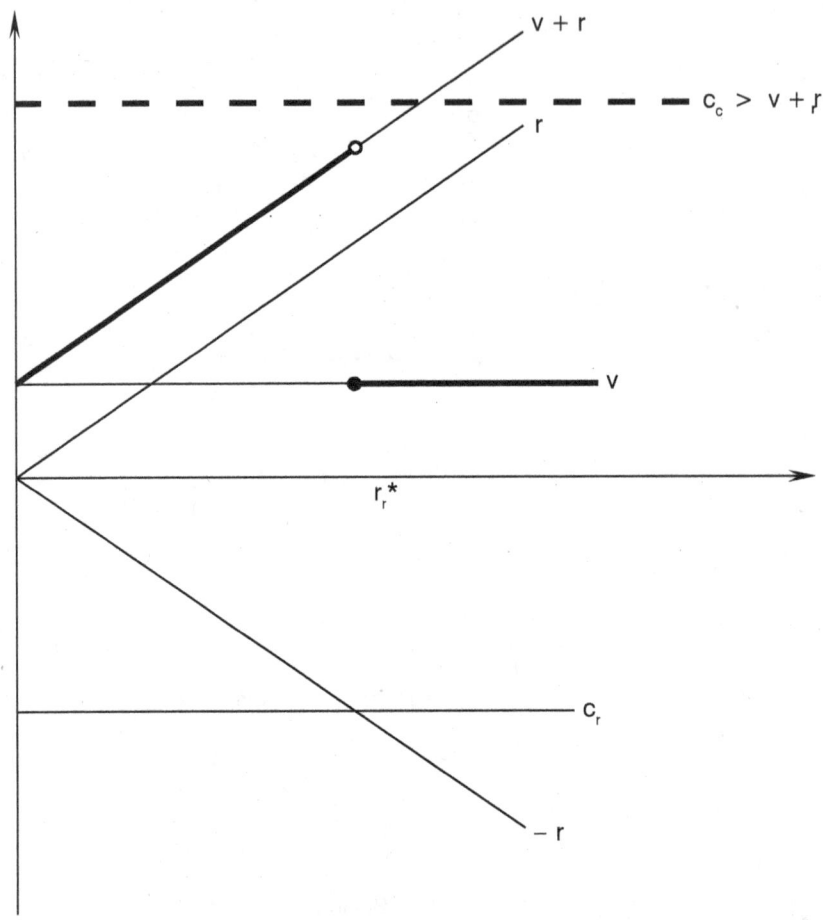

Figure 1.3 Case of unique equilibrium: status quo (SQ)

Game with uncertainty arising from asymmetric information

Uncertainty is introduced into the model through the challenger type parameter. As we discussed in section three, all three types of uncertainty are important. However, the uncertainty surrounding the type of challenger is the most common concern in theoretical discussions of balancing. The model does not consider uncertainty with respect to the type of opportunity or the balance of power between states as these are left to the next chapter.

However, before looking at the effect of uncertainty it is important to determine when uncertainty about intentions will have an effect. This depends on the values of β (the power difference between the two states) and γ (the offensive value of an opportunity). Remember that r is assumed to be a decreasing function of the absolute value of β, and an increasing function of γ. This means that as either

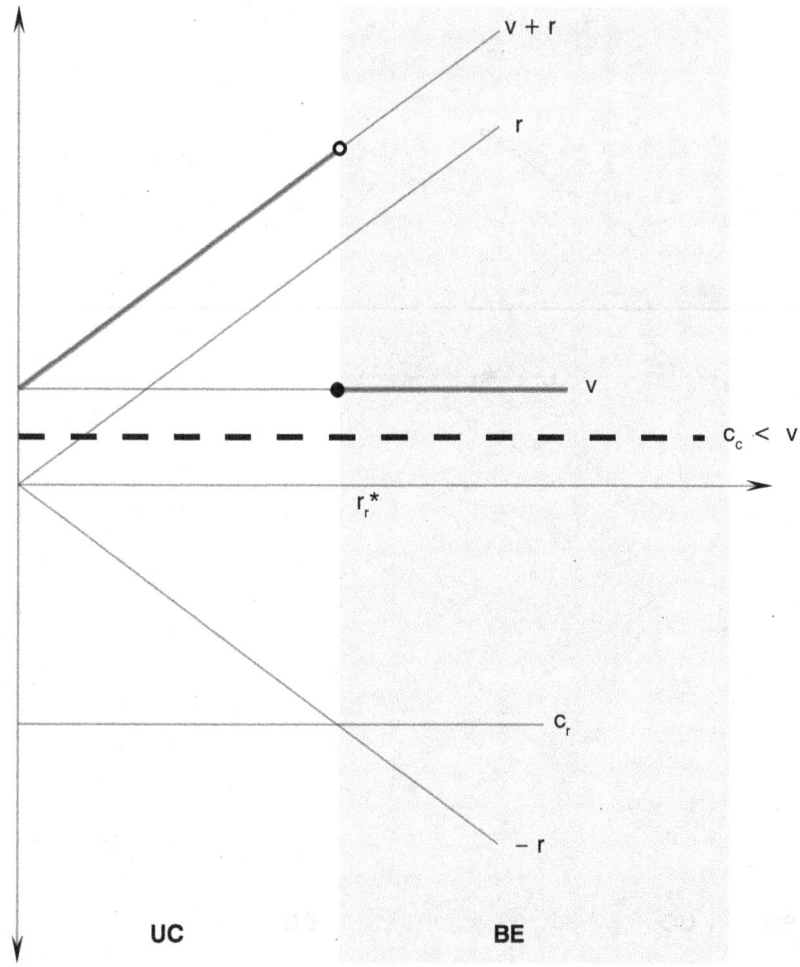

Figure 1.4 Case of two possible equilibria: status quo (SQ) or balanced equilibrium (BE)

$|\beta| \to +\infty$ or $|\gamma| \to +\infty$, the effect of challenger type becomes irrelevant. Thus, if the balance of power between states is so great that the power disturbance between them is relatively insignificant, then the intentions of the challenger will not matter. In this case, the more powerful state, whether it is the challenger or the respondent, will simply ignore the actions of the weaker state. Similarly, if the offensive potential of an opportunity is so great that it dramatically strengthens the challenger with respect to the respondent, then type will not matter. The respondent will always balance regardless of the short-term intentions of the challenger as even a less aggressive challenger would not be able to credibly commit not to use the advantage in the future.[28] Thus, for the challenger's type to

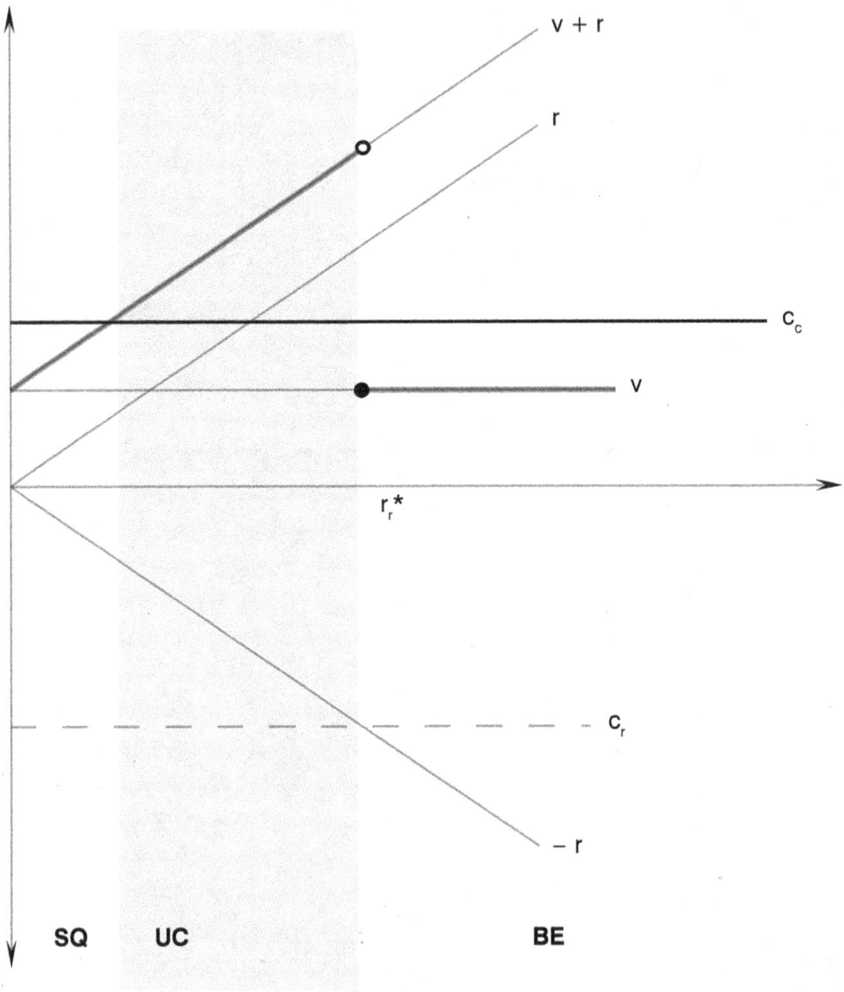

30 *Balancing as a commitment problem*

Figure 1.5 Case of three possible equilibria: status quo (SQ), unchallenged revision of the status quo (UC), or balanced equilibrium (BE)

matter the offensive value of the challenge cannot be too high nor can the relative power difference between the challenger and potential balancer be too great. For the rest of this discussion we will assume that β and γ are held at values that do not make challenger type α irrelevant.

We have so far assumed that α is a continuous parameter such that $\alpha \in \mathbb{R}^+$, however, for the respondent what matters is not the level of α itself but the relationship between the relative gain of the challenger, $r(\alpha)$, and the cost of balancing c_r. As was noted above this gives us the critical value for the potential balancer $r_r^* = c_r$, such that it will only respond to relative gains of the challenger that are greater than or equal to r_r^*. From this value, we can determine the critical value of the challenger type, α^* (for given levels of β and γ) which gives us r_r^*. Thus, challenger type only matters to the extent that $\alpha > \alpha^*$. Therefore, challenger type is categorized into two discreet categories: *aggressive* (where $\alpha > \alpha^*$) and *non-aggressive* (where $\alpha < \alpha^*$).[29]

It is further assumed that the respondent does not observe α but rather a signal sent by nature a. This signal is assumed to be related to the underlying challenger type but with an error or noise ε, such that $a = \alpha + \varepsilon$. It is further assumed that the respondent knows the value of the error term. The challenger of course knows his type, i.e., how aggressive his intentions are, but does not know the exact value of the signal, a, sent by nature. As we noted above for the respondent, the exact level of α is not as important as the relationship of $r(\alpha)$ to his cost of balancing c_r. What matters is whether $r(\alpha^*) = r_r^* = c_r$ and challenger type matters to the extent that his level of aggressiveness is above the threshold level, i.e., $\alpha > \alpha^*$. Since the respondent receives a signal, $a = \alpha + \varepsilon$, its value will be important to the extent that it is related to α^*. This means that the upper limit of "safe signals," i.e., those for which $r \leq r_r^* = c_r$, will be $a_{safe} < \alpha^* - \varepsilon$; and the lower limit of the "danger signal," i.e., those for which $r \geq r_r^* = c_r$, will be $a_{danger} > \alpha^* - \varepsilon$. This gives the action rule for the respondent. See Figure 1.6.

$a \in [0, \alpha^* - \varepsilon]$	or $r(\alpha) < r^*(\alpha^* - \varepsilon)$	never balance
$a \in [\alpha^* - \varepsilon, \alpha^* + \varepsilon]$		uncertain
$a \in (\alpha^* + \varepsilon, +\infty)$	or $r(a) > r^*(\alpha^* - \varepsilon)$	always balance.

Since the potential balancer always balances for $\alpha > \alpha^*$, under conditions of uncertainty the balancer will lower his threshold and always balance against a challenge if $r(a) > r^*(\alpha^* - \varepsilon)$. This will reduce the challenger's payoff from $v + r - c_c$ to $v - c_c$ in the range $a \in [\alpha^* - \varepsilon, \alpha^*)$. Thus, with uncertainty the challenger and the respondent will be made worse off in the range $a \in [\alpha^* - \varepsilon, \alpha^*)$, since the respondent will be bearing a cost c_r to meet a threat $r(\alpha)$ when $c_r > r(\alpha)$, where $a \in [\alpha^* - \varepsilon, \alpha^*)$.

Discussion

A number of interesting implications come out of our model. The first is that even with perfect information about the three relevant parameters that produce the commitment problems that lead to balancing – challenger type, the balance of power, and the opportunity type – balancing can still take place despite the fact that balancing is costly. This is driven by the fact that in our model the challenger is motivated by both the intrinsic value of the opportunity (i.e., absolute gains) and the relative advantage it confers (i.e., relative gains). Thus, under perfect information, balancing will occur if the challenger finds the intrinsic value of the opportunity high enough to act, despite the prospect of being balanced against, and the respondent finds the change in the balance of power threatening enough that it justifies the cost of responding.

32 Balancing as a commitment problem

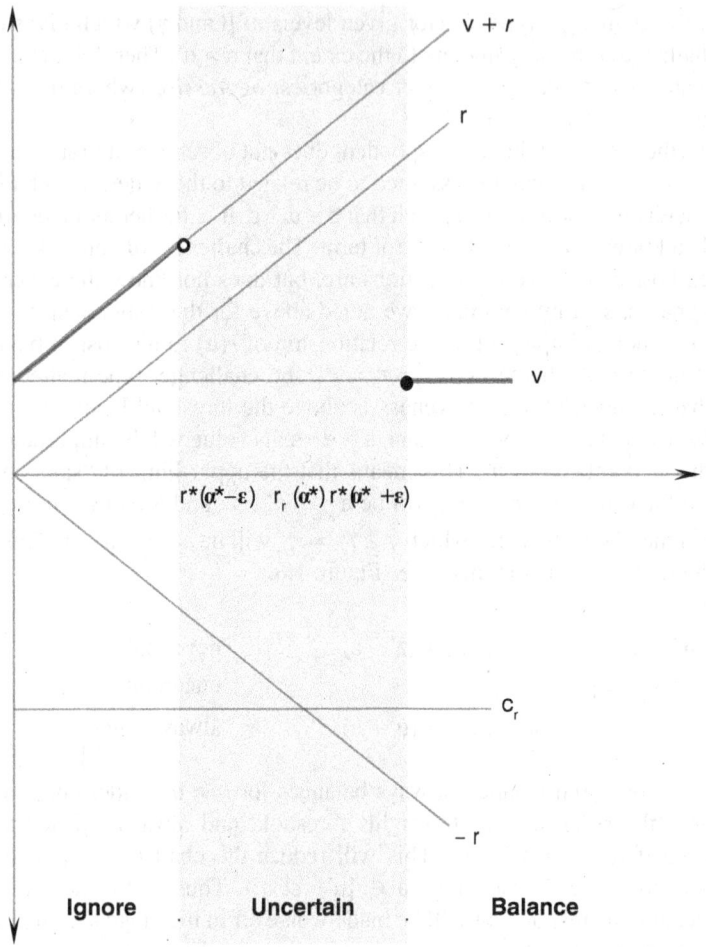

Figure 1.6 Potential balancer's action rule with uncertainty

It is also significant that this would not change even if we allow for negotiation between challenger and respondent. In this situation the challenger knows that the respondent will balance, so he knows he cannot hold on to any relative gains.[30] The only way to prevent balancing would be to voluntarily give up the relative gains of the opportunity. This is because no tacit understanding or treaty can remove this commitment problem unless it restores the balance of power prior to the challenger action. If we assume that such an action is costly, all else being equal, the challenger is better off letting the respondent bear the cost of restoring the balance of power.

It could be argued that such a refusal to negotiate by the challenger would negatively impact the respondent's perception of the threat posed by the challenger, thus exacerbating the commitment problem caused by perceptions of the challenger's type. However, this will only happen if the offensive value of the opportunity is very great. Even in this situation, the challenger may still be better off inviting the respondent to balance rather than trying to bear the cost of restoring the balance of power himself. If the challenger and balancer are already rivals, then the challenger has little incentive to make any such efforts especially as aggressive behavior will likely merely confirm the balancer's view of his rival, rather than change his perception.

This means private information is not necessary for balancing. Under certain circumstances the ultimate goal of the challenger will be to gain the intrinsic value of an action and not the relative advantage it confers. In this case, the disruption in the balance of power is an externality which the challenger cannot take advantage of, due to the respondent's reaction. Furthermore, if we assume that removing the externality is costly, then, just as in the case of dealing with pollution, the producer of the externality (i.e., the challenger) will not benefit from neutralizing it. Thus, the problem falls to the respondent, for whom this externality is of course negative and must be considered.

Another counterintuitive finding is that a credible balancing response is more likely to deter an aggressive (i.e., power-seeking) challenger than a non-aggressive one. Given that we assume a self-help system, we can redefine a state as aggressive if it places more value on the relative gains resulting from the opportunity (i.e., r) than on the intrinsic value of the opportunity (i.e., v). In the extremes, the most aggressive states will derive their entire benefit from the relative power gain of the opportunity (i.e., $r > 0$ and $v = 0$) and the least aggressive states will derive their entire benefit from the intrinsic value of the opportunity (i.e., $r = 0$ and $v > 0$). Thus, when facing a credible threat of balancing the expected payoff of the most aggressive state will be a net loss of $v - c_c = -c_c < 0$. This means that as long as the respondent balances (which in our model happens when $r > c_c$) an aggressive challenger will not initiate the challenge in the first place. On the other hand the least aggressive state will face an expected payoff of $v - c_c$. As long as $v - c_c < 0$ it will have an incentive to challenge the status quo no matter what the respondent does.

Thus, all else being equal, an aggressive challenger is more likely to be deterred by a credible threat of balancing than a non-aggressive challenger would be. For an aggressive challenger, strategic interaction plays an important part in their calculations because they place a great deal of importance on relative gains, which are dependent on the response of the potential balancer. Since non-aggressive challengers are less, if at all, concerned about relative gains, they are in effect able to act non-strategically. This result, of course, depends in part on the fact that in our model balancing is a one-shot game and does not incorporate the possibility of balancing escalating into all-out war. However, even with the possibility of escalation, the finding that non-aggressive challengers are more likely to act unilaterally can still hold. Because an aggressive challenger wants to gain a relative advantage over the potential balancer they are even less likely to act if their challenge is likely to not only produce balancing but also escalate into a conflict with the potential rival sooner than the aggressive challenger is ready.

On the other hand, because the non-aggressive challenger is more interested in the absolute gains of the challenge, it will be willing to face balancing and even escalation of the crisis up to the point where the cost of doing so outweighs the intrinsic value of the revision it wants to achieve. Thus, the possibility of escalation will make the non-aggressive challenger more mindful of the potential balancer's reaction, but it will still be more willing than an aggressive challenger to ignore the respondent.

This finding has a couple of interesting implications. First, while it is intuitive to assume that a challenger who does not back down when faced with a credible threat of balancing is aggressive, this is not necessarily the case. In our model, standing firm in the face of balancing is in fact a very costly signal that the challenger is not interested in changing the balance of power but only in gaining the intrinsic value of the opportunity. This is something an aggressive challenger, i.e., one focused on the relative gains the challenge would bring, would not do. Second, this means that aggressive challengers are more likely to opt for small revisions to the status quo that are too small to merit a response but are still worthwhile (i.e., when the relative gains in power are higher than the costs of challenging the status quo but smaller than the costs of balancing, $c_r \geq r \geq c_c$). As long as such actions are not perceived as threatening, they may accumulate into a long-term advantage.[31] On the other hand, non-aggressive challengers are more likely to make large, individual revisions to the status quo if their inherent value is greater than the cost of undertaking them. Finally, when dealing with an aggressive challenger, balancing should happen only if the challenger underestimates the balancer's resolve.

Given that balancing happens under perfect information, what impact does introducing uncertainty have in our model? As indicated in Figure 1.6, uncertainty produces a gray area where it is harder for the respondent to gauge the risks they are facing against the cost of responding to them. Assuming risk aversion, this will lead to a lowering of the threshold for the balancing response and increase the number of cases in which balancing will occur. Thus, introducing asymmetric information into our model does not dramatically change the nature of balancing; rather it lowers the threshold at which the respondent will balance.

Introducing uncertainty increases the stakes for an aggressive challenger. Since they are more likely to face a balancing response they are less likely to make a challenge in the first place. Of course, in keeping with our previous argument, non-aggressive challengers will not change their behavior and will still act non-strategically (i.e., without seriously considering the respondent's actions). Thus with the introduction of uncertainty, we are closer to the realist worldview where all challenges to the balance of power must be responded to (Morgenthau 1973; Waltz 1979; Wolfers 1962). But interestingly, the most common challengers to the balance of power will still be those states that are not really interested in grand revisions (i.e., revisions that would impact the system as a whole, rather than minor changes to some aspect of it).

Of course, the model does not capture all the complexity of balancing and there are a number of interesting extensions to the model that may prove fruitful.

Of these the most promising are: 1) exploring in more detail the implication of our three types of uncertainties and how they interact, 2) making an iterated rather than a one-shot game, and 3) increasing the number of players. All three refinements will be taken up in Chapter 2.

Conclusion

This chapter has shown that commitment problems play a central role in balancing. These commitment problems classically are conceptualized as arising out of uncertainty about the challenger's intentions (i.e., type) but other factors such as the relative balance of power and the opportunity available to the challenger play crucial roles in the creation of commitment problems. We find that due to incentives to misrepresent intentions, even challengers that do not plan to later harm potential balancers cannot easily resolve problems arising from asymmetric information. Under certain conditions such challengers are more likely to face balancing because they are less likely to back down in the face of credible threats. Most importantly, the model shows that uncertainties about the challenger's intentions are not sufficient in themselves to bring about balancing; the nature of the challenge and the relative power of the states involved must be considered. The model presented here, of course, does not address all facets of balancing behavior. Specifically, the model only has one potential balancer and does not allow states to delay balancing to the future, both of which are important considerations in real-world balancing. Chapter 2, therefore, builds a more complex model to further explore these facets of balancing. The implications of both that model and the model presented in this chapter are examined in a case on British and French behavior in response to the growing German threat in the 1930s in Chapter 3.

Notes

1 This chapter is reprinted with minor changes and the publisher's gracious permission from Savic and Shirkey (2009).
2 For example see Nye (2002) and Huth and Russett (1984).
3 It should be noted, however, that the archetypes of "status quo" and "revisionist" states are problematic. States often favor the status quo in one issue area, but are revisionist in another. Therefore, even a state that is primarily revisionist can engage in balancing. This is discussed in more detail in the next section.
4 Schweller (1994) argues that states may bandwagon for reasons other than as a response to a threat, most notably to fulfill revisionist aims and to acquire spoils. Also arguing balancing is a response to threat are Glaser (2011); He (2012); Levy and Thompson (2005); Pape (2005); Paul (2005); Schweller (2006; 2011); and Taliaferro (2001).
5 Gulick (1955) and Taliaferro (2001) also see threat perception as motivating balancing.
6 This may be due to a belief that balancing would be too costly, that it would be ineffective, or that superior strategies exist. It may also be due to internal divisions in the threatened state (Schweller 2006).
7 They are not alone in this contention. For instance see Hume (1898); Jones (1994); and Mattingly (1988).
8 In certain cases it may be easier to determine another state's intentions than capabilities. For example, leading up to the 2003 invasion of Iraq, the United States arguably had

36 *Balancing as a commitment problem*

less difficulty in determining Iraq's intentions toward the United States than Iraq's capabilities.

9   This point is discussed at length in the next section.
10 According to Waltz, they do so at their own peril.
11 Jones (1994) and to a lesser extent Levy and Thompson (2005), however, find support for Waltz.
12 See Claude (1962, 29–30 and 36–7) and Vasquez (1997, 903) for a discussion of Morgenthau's arguments on balancing.
13 Arguably, the relative proximity of the Soviet Union to Western Europe and the distance of the United States made the Soviet Union the stronger of the two from the perspective of Europe. However, given the US military presence in Europe, its economic strength, and the long recovery the Soviets faced, it is more reasonable to view the United States as the stronger state in 1949. See Kennedy (1989, 460–5).
14 Thus, the category "potential aggressor" includes both actual aggressors (those that want to use the change in the status quo as a means for further revisions) and non-aggressive revisionist states (those that do not). Therefore, the aggressiveness of the revisionist can be discussed in two ways. First, in terms of the status quo states' perception of the revisionist's intentions (this is the primary usage in the fourth and fifth sections below where we discuss the model). Second, in terms of the value that revisionist states place on the absolute gain from changing the status quo vs. the relative gain vis-à-vis the status quo state (this is the primary usage in the sixth section, where we discuss the implications of the model).
15 This will be discussed in more detail in the following section.
16 The term "rational" is used in the same way as it is commonly used in rational choice theory approaches and denotes explanations distinct from psychological and other non-rational explanations of conflict.
17 There are other ways to rationally get to war with unitary actors such as very high costs to peace, very high risk acceptance, or coordination problems but these have not been found to be empirically significant (Weisiger 2013).
18 Costs associated with crises include the possibility of lost prestige, the material costs associated with mobilization, and the possibility that the crisis may escalate into a war.
19 This is not to say that there will never be side benefits to balancing. The alliances formed and weapons built may have other uses and benefits. Weapons procurements, however, always have a clear monetary cost. Smith (1995) argues that alliance formation is always costly and it is states' willingness to pay these costs which makes their alliance commitments credible. Additionally, if the side benefits of balancing outweigh the costs then these actions would have been taken before the threat emerged. Of course, balancing could help a leader overcome domestic or international opposition to building up armaments or creating alliances, but in this case the leader is not really engaged in balancing but is using it as a pretext.
20 For example, in the case of the Cuban Revolution and the Missile Crisis that followed it, the Soviet Union was a revisionist power and the United States was a status quo power. This does not mean that on other issues, such as regime change in Hungary in 1956 or Czechoslovakia in 1968, the Soviet Union was not in favor of the status quo or the United States did not want to revise it.
21 Here we are not trying to rehash the old debate surrounding relative vs. absolute gains but rather build on the conclusion of that debate: that the relative importance of each type of gain depends on the strategic context.
22 Conceptually, one could also argue that respondents have types: a fearful respondent will increase his valuation of the relative gain achieved by the challenger (r) and a more trusting one would decrease the value of r. However, the "fearfulness" or "trustfulness" of the respondent should be based on the three above-mentioned factors: the challenger's type, the offensive value of the opportunity, and power

difference between the two players. Also, it is not the challenger's actual type but how he is perceived by the respondent that really matters. Therefore, in our model, the challenger's type incorporates the respondent's type because it depends on his perception. Under perfect information adding a respondent type would not make a difference. Under uncertainty, which will be examined in the next section, the level of fear will be reflected by the latter two factors and the signal that the respondent receives about the challenger's type.

23 Of course, this is assuming that the respondent has no intentions of attacking the challenger in the near future. Since we have defined the respondent as the status quo power in the context of the game this case is not possible in the framework of the game.

24 Obviously, the character of the French and Soviet regimes played a role in how their actions were perceived. However, it would be a mistake to paint one regime as inherently interested in the status quo and the other as inherently revisionist. For example, the original aims of Clemenceau at the 1919 Paris Conference included the French annexation of the Saar and the creation of independent Rhineland states under permanent allied occupation. France only gave these up in exchange for security guarantees from Britain and the United States and the promise of German reparations payments. See Graham (1996, 40).

While Stalin and the Bolsheviks were interested in expansion in the long run, in the late 1940s the Soviet Union was in no position to plan further conquests. It was much weaker than other states realized – a fact it actively tried to hide. The Soviets did see themselves as global players, but their initial priority was rebuilding their strength, not further expansion. See Kennedy (1989, 467–70). Stalin even refused Marshal Plan aid, which was theoretically available to him, because revealing the extent of recovery needs was a condition of receiving American aid. See Gaddis (1997, 41–3).

25 Despite the conventional wisdom that the Maginot Line was a financial white elephant and a strategic disaster there is still disagreement about the value of France's fortifications during World War II. The French did overcommit their field divisions to supporting the line. However, this may have less to do with the inherent weakness of the line and more to do with a failure of French strategic planning. See Kaufmann (1988, 74).

26 These benefits tended to be short run in nature. A reasonable argument can be made that over the long run, Soviet satellite states were actually a net drain on Moscow's resources.

27 It may at first seem a bit odd that the potential balancer will ignore a threat if the costs of balancing are too high, but this makes sense if you consider the fact that it would be a waste of resources to do so and this would be dangerous in a self-help system.

28 For example, historically it was a major tenet of British foreign policy that the Low Countries (especially the Southern Netherlands, i.e., modern Belgium) should not be controlled by any great power, no matter what its intentions, because it was a perfect staging ground for an attack on Britain. The one exception to this rule was Austria, which held the territory from 1713 to 1794. Britain did not oppose Austrian control because Austria's base of power lay in Central and South-Central Europe and Austria had virtually no navy. In fact, the British insisted Austria take over the territory in 1713, as Austrian control was seen as the way to prevent the more dangerous prospect of French control. In essence, like a minor power, the Austrians lacked the capability to exploit the possession of the Southern Netherlands in a fashion that was threatening to Britain. Thus, it was the Austrians' lack of naval capabilities and not their supposedly benign intentions that mattered. See McKay and Scott (1995, 63–6).

29 It may seem as if the challenger's perceived type is defined endogenously in this model, however, the underlying aggressiveness of the challenger is determined exogenously by nature. It is only the level of the challenger's aggressiveness as perceived by the potential balancer that is in part determined endogenously.

30 This is because in a self-help system a relevant change in the balance of power between two states will lead to a commitment problem. In other words, the challenger cannot credibility commit not to use the change in the balance of power to his advantage at some future date.
31 This is analogous to Schelling's (1966) concern about salami-slicing tactics.

2 Balancing and buck-passing I

A dynamic model with uncertainty

Whether to balance is often a difficult decision. While some scholars argue that great powers almost always balance (Parent and Rosato 2015), most agree that for individual states, balancing is not automatic (Morgenthau 1973; Waltz 1979; Rosecrance and Lo 1996; Wolfers 1962; Vasquez 1997).[1] So why do states sometimes choose to balance against threats while at other times they ignore or appease states making such threats? The previous chapter began to answer this question by looking at the role of commitment problems. Specifically, Chapter 1 argued that commitment problems can prompt balancing provided the costs of doing so are tolerable, but that uncertainty about states' intentions, the type of opportunity presented by the challenger's move, and the relative balance of power all complicate the picture and could potentially cause states to make poor decisions about whether or not to balance. However, the model in Chapter 1 has several important limitations. It left unaddressed which of these types of uncertainty is most problematic for states facing decisions about whether to balance.[2] Also, the model has only one potential balancer and lacks an extended time horizon. These are both unrealistic assumptions which prevented the possibilities of buck-passing and strategic delay from arising. This chapter develops a more realistic model which allows for tradeoffs between current versus future balancing and for buck-passing. The implications of this more realistic model are explored in Chapter 3 through a case study of the Rhineland and Sudetenland crises of 1936 and 1938.

When do states balance?

In determining whether another state poses a threat which should be balanced against, leaders look at two aspects of that state: its capabilities and intentions. Realists disagree about the extent to which intentions can be discerned. Mearsheimer in particular argues that others' intentions are opaque. He states "Intentions are ultimately unknowable, so states ... must make worse case assumptions ... In short, great powers balance against capabilities, not intentions" (Mearsheimer 2001, 45). Similarly, using 1930s Germany as an example, Schweller (2006) argues that it is very hard to infer intentions from behavior without the benefit of hindsight. This is especially troubling as he believes the key to successfully dealing with a rising dissatisfied state is understanding its intentions. Only then, he claims, is it clear whether the state will be satisfied by limited concessions. Not surprisingly then, while he acknowledges that uncertainty over capabilities is real and matters, Schweller spends most of his discourse on the challenges to determining threat by focusing on the difficulties of inferring intentions. Edelstein (2002) argues that this view is the norm among offensive realists.

Such a view, however, is not limited to offensive realists. Many defensive realists have focused their explanations for conflict on uncertainty about intentions (Claude 1962; Glaser 1992; 1997; Jervis 1978; Kydd 1997a; 1997b; Morgenthau 1973; Walt 1985; Waltz 1979). Rationalists have also examined the role of uncertainty about intentions, though not necessarily to the exclusion of uncertainty over capabilities. For example, Bueno de Mesquita, Morrow, and Zorick (1997) argue that uncertainties about both capabilities and intentions play important roles in crisis escalation and that uncertainty around either variable can never be entirely eliminated during crises. Likewise Gartzke (1999) focuses on the role of intentions in causing commitment problems which in turn make war unpredictable. Similarly, constructivists and neoliberals believe that intentions matter when it comes to alignment decisions. All of this leads Edelstein to conclude that the key to successful balancing is understanding other states' intentions. He states that, "Where states are confident that another state has either benign or malign intentions, formulating appropriate strategies is straightforward" but that uncertainty over intentions leads to mistakes (Edelstein 2002, 12). This view that uncertainty over the intentions of the revisionist state is the most problematic aspect of balancing decisions is common (Danilovic 2001; Mearsheimer 2001; 2010; Parent and Rosato 2015; Waltz 1979).

We disagree. In this chapter, we show that uncertainty over the specific nature of the change to the balance of power coupled with uncertainty about the relative balance of forces, including uncertainty over the behavior of potential third party allies, is more problematic than uncertainty over intentions. In doing so we agree with Powell (2012) who conceives of commitment problems as arising from expected shifts in the future balance of power. He stresses that they will exist even if there is absolute certainty about the challenger's intentions, though such certainty should prompt balancing. Thus, it is not uncertainty over the future power shift which leads to conflict, but rather the shared understanding that these shifts in power will occur.[3] This is consistent with our model in Chapter 1 which argued that uncertainty about the challenger's intentions is not sufficient to bring about balancing. It showed that the nature of the challenge, in particular the offensive value of the move and the relative power of the states involved, must be considered. It also showed that balancing can happen even with perfect information about the challenger's type, the balance of power, and the opportunity type provided two conditions are met: the challenger finds the intrinsic value of the opportunity high enough to act despite the prospect of being balanced against and the respondent finds the change in the balance of power threatening enough that it justifies the cost of responding.

We now expand on the findings of that model by creating a new model which allows for multiple time periods and multiple potential balancers. In doing so, we shed light on the relative importance of three types of uncertainty as they relate to balancing: the challenger's type, the relative balance of power, and the relative value (i.e., strategic implications) of the challenger's move. Also discussed, but not formally modeled, are two additional sources of uncertainty that arise from the dynamic multiplayer environment: uncertainty about whether the balancers' benefit from delaying their decision to balance and uncertainty about the commitment of allies. However, as discussed in more detail below, these sources of uncertainty can be understood as special cases of uncertainty about the relative balance of power.

A model of balancing with multiple time periods and players

There are N players: states that must decide whether to respond to a challenge by a revisionist state. The revisionist state is treated as a non-strategic player. This is potentially unsatisfying because it means the loss of some of the strategic possibilities, but it is necessary in order to make the dynamic multiplayer model manageable. It is also justifiable in light of the fact that we are primarily interested in balancing behavior and not in the decision to challenge the status quo. The potential balancers are not sure whether the challenge to the status quo warrants balancing due to uncertainty about one of three parameters: the intentions of the challenger, the existing balance of power, or the nature of the change to the balance of power. Nature decides the value of each parameter for the duration of the game in period $t = 0$.

It is further assumed that there is a fixed numbered of periods, T, in which the players can make an irrevocable decision to balance. Although the number of periods is somewhat arbitrary, most international crises have relatively short time horizons, making a limited number of moves a reasonable assumption. The assumption that the decision to balance can only be made once reflects the fact that for balancing to be meaningful it requires a costly mobilization of material, political, and diplomatic resources which cannot be easily undone. Otherwise, we are dealing with the threat of balancing and not balancing itself.

At the end of the crisis, i.e., at time $T + 1$, uncertainty is resolved and the potential balancers get the following payoff:

If they decided to balance: $\frac{n_T}{N}(x) + (x-c)\delta^{t-1} - \alpha(\beta+\gamma)$

If they decided not to balance: $\frac{n_T}{N}(x) - \alpha(\beta+\gamma)$

These payoffs can be broken down into three components:

$\frac{n_T}{N}(x)$ **Benefit from *common defense*:** the payoff from the creation of a balancing coalition. This is operationalized as the proportion of potential balancers that mobilize to balance against the challenger $\left(\frac{n_T}{N}\right)$ multiplied by the contribution of each balancer's response

$(x-c)\delta^{t-1}$ **Benefit from *national defense***: the payoff to an individual state that decides to balance, regardless of what other states do. The response, x, is modified by two parameters: the cost of balancing c (such that $0 < c < 1$) and the timing of the decision to balance δ^{t-1} (where $0 \leq \delta \leq 1$). This model assumes that the sooner governments are able to mobilize against the challenger the better.[4] These two parameters do not appear in the common defense payoff because states only bear the cost of their own balancing and because the value of the coalition is only realized once the final size of the coalition is known at time $T+1$.

$\alpha(\beta+\gamma)$ **Cost from the challenge**: the threat that the challenge to the status quo represents to the system (see below).

(x). For simplicity, this model assumes an equal distribution of power between the potential balancers. Thus, each state can contribute equally to a common defense. The value, n_r, is the number of states that have joined the balancing coalition. This will increase each time states decide to make the irrevocable decision to balance. States benefit from the common defense whether they join the coalition or not. This captures the free rider problem of collective balancing.

This means that there is a minimal necessary coalition that can meet the new threat: one that exactly balances against the new threat $\frac{n_T}{N}(x) = \alpha(\beta+\gamma)$. The minimal effective coalition is given by $n_T^* = \frac{\alpha(\beta+\gamma)}{x}N$. This will be important when discussing the implications of uncertainty. The strategic threat to the system breaks down into three parameters. The first is α, which represents the challenger's type; specifically how aggressively revisionist the challenger is. Of course, it can be argued that any state would revise the status quo given a favorable opportunity. Here aggressiveness means actively pursuing a revision of the status quo. The more aggressive the state, the more it values changing the status quo. This parameter can take a value in the range $0 \leq \alpha \leq 1$. As $\alpha \to 0$ the aggressiveness of the challenger diminishes (when $\alpha = 0$ the state is only concerned in the absolute not the relative gains). As $\alpha \to 1$ the aggressiveness of the challenger increases (when $\alpha = 1$ the state completely values the relative gains of its actions). The second parameter, β, represents the challenger's power relative to all other states in the system – whether that system is regional or global. Thus, $0 < \beta \leq 1$, and the combined power of all the potential balancers is equal to $1-\beta$. Therefore, as $\beta \to 0$ the less relevant is the challenger to the balance of power and the more likely the challenge will be ignored. On the other hand as $\beta \to 1$ the more powerful the challenger is and the less likely a coalition will be able to balance against it. Where balancing matters most is as $\beta \to 0.5$ since it is around this midpoint that challenges to the balance matter most. Finally, γ represents the value of the strategic opportunity that the challenger is taking advantage of, i.e., how much the challenge disrupts the balance of power. Therefore, the pre-crisis balance is determined by the parameter, β, and the value of the opportunity, γ, is the change in this balance. This means that $0 \leq \gamma \leq 1-\beta$; as $\gamma \to 0$ the challenge to the system becomes irrelevant and as $\gamma \to 1-\beta$ the opportunity transforms the challenger into a hegemon.

Before introducing uncertainty a few general points should be made. First, under full information the likelihood of balancing will depend on the parameters α, β and γ as outlined above. Second, while there is a potential for collective action problems among the balancers the extent to which this problem matters will depend entirely on two parameters: N, the number of states in the system, and $1-\beta$, the balance of power they represent. Thus, the smaller N is and the closer $1-\beta$ is to 0.5, the less likely are problems of buck-passing.

Variation I: Uncertainty over the challenger type (α)

We first assume the challenger's type is unknown. Before the first period, nature decides randomly and for the duration of the game the challenger's type by choosing the value of $\alpha \in \{\alpha_0, \alpha_1\}$, such that $\alpha_0 < \alpha_1$. Without loss of generality, the values are set as:

$\alpha_1 = 1$ **Power seeking** (revisionist) **state**: balancing is appropriate
$\alpha_0 = 0$ **Security seeking state**: balancing is a waste of resources.

The value of α is not perfectly observable, rather at the beginning of the first period each government is given a onetime private signal (i.e., *private information*) about the challenger's type which is not observed by the other states. Each country uses its signal along with some common knowledge about the challenger to form its *private belief*, μ_i, which is that government's probability assessment of the necessity of balancing. The initial distribution of private beliefs is defined by a cumulative distribution function $F_1^\theta(\mu)$.[5] Thus, in the first period the distribution of beliefs is supported by the bounds $(\underline{\mu}_1, \overline{\mu}_1)$. These bounds can be infinity but must be independent of θ. The distribution must satisfy the condition of compatibility with the Bayesian framework.[6] If it does, then they satisfy the assumption of first order stochastic dominance.

For the rest of the game, nature gives no new information and states update their beliefs by observing the actions of others. In each period, a government can make a onetime irreversible decision to respond. This decision is based on the government's updated beliefs for that period which consist of the beliefs at the beginning of the last period and an update based on observed balancing made by other governments in that period. Thus, in each period the government knows its initial beliefs (based on the signal it received and common knowledge) and the history, $h_t = (x_t, ..., x_{t+1})$, where x_k is the number of governments that decided to balance in period k.

The only decision that the government can make in each period is whether to balance. For simplicity, only symmetric equilibria and pure strategies will be considered. Given the initial distribution of beliefs, $F_1^\theta(\mu)$, and the history, h_t, a strategy in period t is defined by the decision set, $l_t(h_t)$, of beliefs of all states that balanced. Thus, a government balances in period t if and only if $\mu_t \in I_t(h_t)$, where μ_t is that government's belief at the beginning of that period.

At the end of a given period of the game, t, governments observe n_t: the total number of governments that have balanced. Updating of beliefs by individual governments transforms the distribution of belief from F_t^θ to F_{t+1}^θ. At the beginning of the next period the governments that have not balanced, $N - n_t$, use their private information and the equilibrium strategies of all agents for any future date and future history to choose a strategy that maximizes their expected payoff. A government decides to balance if and only if the potential payoff of this decision is greater than doing nothing. If a government is indifferent between balancing and not balancing the model assumes that it will do nothing. The model focuses only on symmetric sub-game perfect Bayesian equilibria.

Suppose now that governments have the option to share their private information through diplomacy. Specifically, suppose that during the first period after they have received their private signal about α, governments have the options of sharing their signal by sending a message, m_i. For simplicity it is assumed that governments reveal their private signal about the challenger's intentions α, $m_i(s_i) \in \{0, 1\}$. If we assume that diplomatic talks take place at time t then each government's log likelihood ratio will be updated as follows:

$$\lambda_{t+1} = \lambda_t + \zeta_t \text{ where } \zeta_t = Log\left(\frac{P(M_t|H_t,\theta_1)}{P(M_t|H_t,\theta_0)}\right),$$

M_t is the number of governments that say they received a signal to balance

$$M_t = \sum_{i=0}^{N} m_i$$

H_t is the set of truth-telling conditions and

$$P(M|H,\theta) = \frac{N!}{M_t!(N_t - M_t)!}\pi_\theta^{M_t}(1-\pi_\theta)^{N_t - M_t}, \quad \pi_\theta = P(m_i \in H|\theta).$$

Consequently, two key questions arise. First, will potential balancers tell the truth? Second, will they delay their decision to exchange information or their decision to balance once the information is revealed? The answers are that the likelihood of truth-telling will depend on the cost of balancing and the threat that the challenger poses and that states do not have an incentive to delay truth-telling because of the cost of postponing the decision.

Variation II: Uncertainty over the balance of power (β)

What if countries are certain about the value of α, but are uncertain about the balance of power? Assuming that the challenger is known to be aggressive, as otherwise there is no need to balance regardless of the uncertainty over the value of β, then $\alpha = 1$ and the payoffs for potential balancers become:

If they decided to balance: $\frac{n_T}{N}(x)+(x-c)\delta^{t-1}-(\beta+\gamma)$

If they decided not to balance: $\frac{n_T}{N}(x)-(\beta+\gamma)$

The problem becomes determining the size of the coalition necessary to effectively balance against the challenger. As noted above, the size of the minimal coalition that can defend against the challenger is given by $\frac{n_T}{N}(x)-(\beta+\gamma)=0$ that is $n_T = N\frac{(\beta+\gamma)}{x}$. Since in the first version of the model the values of both β and γ were known, the minimal necessary balancing coalition was a known value, which we will refer to as n_T. By introducing uncertainty in the balance of power or the nature of the challenge, the size of the minimal coalition becomes unknown.

We will first explore uncertainty about the balance of power β. As noted above, the pre-crisis balance of power is assumed to be continuous in the range $0 < \beta \leq 1$. Thus, each state will receive a signal $b = \beta \pm \varepsilon$. The outcome of this variation is similar to the first with one important difference. Namely, because states are uncertain about the balance of capabilities, they cannot easily determine the exact coalition needed to effectively balance against the challenger.

Variation III: Uncertainty over the opportunity type (γ)

Finally, there can be uncertainty about the impact of the challenge on the status quo (i.e., the value of γ). This situation is similar to the previous variant with one key difference: since the pre-crisis balance of power is unknown, so is the lower limit of the possible coalition that is necessary to balance. That is, given a pre-crisis balance of power, β, the absolute smallest balancing coalition will be $n_T = N\frac{\beta}{x}$. Thus the uncertainty comes down to the question of whether a larger than minimal coalition is necessary.

Discussion

Incorporating multiple players and multiple periods leads to some interesting results. Generally, the arguments presented in Chapter 1 hold true in this framework. The biggest contribution of the new model is that it allows for the exploration of different sources of uncertainty leading to the following conclusions. First, uncertainty about capabilities is more problematic than uncertainty about intentions.[7] When capabilities are known (i.e., both the pre-crisis balance and the potential change in that balance) states know the size of the coalition that will be able to deter or defend against the challenger. In this situation, states can form a balancing coalition and wait for intentions to be revealed. However, if intentions are known but there is uncertainty about capabilities, then the necessary size of the balancing coalition cannot be easily determined. This opens the door to well-known problems associated with balancing, especially buck-passing. States in this situation are more likely to miscalculate and gamble that they can shift the burden of balancing onto others. In addition, this also leads to the possibility that states will conclude that balancing is less likely to work and as a result they may choose to either hide or bandwagon with the challenger in the hopes of ensuring their security or of picking up spoils.

Second, uncertainty about the initial balance of power is more difficult to deal with than uncertainty about the opportunity the challenger has seized. However, the latter is still more of a challenge to balancing than uncertainty over intentions. Thus, when states are uncertain about the nature of the opportunity at least they know what the minimal balancing coalition would be. In addition, for certain pre-crisis balances, specifically those where the challenger is powerful enough that any disturbance of the status quo is dangerous to the potential balancer, then the nature of the challenge is largely irrelevant.

Finally, two further sources of uncertainty exist: the timing of balancing (δ) and the size of the coalition $\left(\frac{n_T}{N}\right)$. Before discussing them in detail, it is important to systematically categorize the different sources of uncertainty we have discussed. They fall into one of two broad categories: intentions and capabilities. Uncertainty about intentions includes both the challenger's intentions (referred to above as α) and the intentions of other potential balancers (which we have not discussed). Uncertainty about capabilities takes four forms, namely uncertainty about the current balance of power (β), the current challenge (γ), timing of balancing (δ), and the minimal size of the coalition $\left(\frac{n_T}{N}\right)$. To put it another way:

β: balance of power
δ: expected change in the balance over time
γ: change in the balance of power without balancing
$\frac{n_T}{N}$: minimal coalition necessary for balancing.

Turning first to timing, in the basic setup of the model it was assumed that the discount rate of the decision to balance was $0 < \delta \leq 1$. As $\delta \rightarrow 0$ the cost of delaying the decision to balance is low. But as $\delta \rightarrow 1$ the cost of delaying the decision to balance increases and potential balancers will be more likely to err on the side of caution. This in turn will affect how quickly the coalition is likely to form. However, it is possible that delaying balancing could be beneficial. For example, domestic politics could make it difficult to respond immediately. Alternatively, a state may be in the process of modernizing its military capacity. In these situations, delay could be beneficial since the later the state responds the more able it will be to neutralize the challenge. Of course, here the value of δ will depend on the positions of both the potential balancers and the challenger, thus creating uncertainty. If potential balancers are uncertain of the value of δ they will have problems coordinating their actions. In the case of coalition size, $\frac{n_T}{N}$, the uncertainty rests on questions about the final size of the coalition. In particular, the uncertainty would rest on the ability of states to observe the behavior of potential balancing partners. Thus, this comes down to the old issue of the reliability of external balancing and the problem of defection once a crisis comes to a head.

The insights from the model are supported by the case of British and French responses to the rise of Germany in the 1930s in the next chapter. Many members of both the French and British governments were largely alive to the nature of Hitler's regime. While there was some uncertainty over Hitler's intentions, this was not the fundamental obstacle to forming a balancing coalition. Rather, the key problem was uncertainty about whether a sufficiently large balancing coalition could be formed. This was due to both worries about buck-passing and uncertainty over the relative balance of power. This led France to doubt its ability to successfully balance and led to defeatism and essentially hiding behavior. Additionally, both France and Britain had doubts about whether changes to the status of the Rhineland and Sudetenland were sufficiently threatening to warrant fighting a major war before they were ready. In other words, uncertainty about the nature of the opportunity also played a role. Finally, both Britain and France believed that the balance of power would be more favorable in the future and hoped to delay war until a later date. Each of these factors will be examined in depth in Chapter 3.

Notes

1 In particular Parent and Rosato (2015) argue that bandwagoning and buck-passing are very poor options for great powers and thus rarely employed as strategies by great powers. Whether or not this is true in general, the 1930s fit poorly with such a view as the Soviets bandwagoned with the Germans and the British and French buck-passed – albeit to the future rather than to one another.
2 A potential problem with focusing on the role of uncertainty arising from private information in balancing is, as Fey and Ramsay (2007) argue, that mutual optimism arising from private information should never result in war. This is because a state's willingness to fight should cause the other state to reconsider its own willingness. Slantchev and Tarar (2011), however, show that this result depends entirely on the unrealistic assumption that a state can unilaterally impose peace on the dyad. Once this assumption is relaxed, mutual optimism arising from private information again becomes a cause of war.
3 Powell (2004) finds that offers during crises reveal information about states' cost tolerances, but not about their relative capabilities and concludes that uncertainty over capabilities is more likely to result in war than uncertainty over costs. This hints that uncertainty over capabilities may be worse than uncertainty over intentions. However, a state's tolerance for cost, though a component of its intentions, is not the sum of them.
4 The impact of relaxing this assumption is explored in the last subsection of the model.
5 For simplicity and without loss of generality it is assumed that the cumulative distribution function is differentiable.
6 For example, if private beliefs have density f^1 and f^0 in $\alpha_1 = 1$ and $\alpha_0 = 0$ then $f^1(\mu)/\mu = f^0(\mu)/(1-\mu)$.
7 This differs from the realist contention that determining intentions is more problematic than observing capabilities. We are not claiming which sort of uncertainty is more likely, only that uncertainty about capabilities, when it does arise, is more problematic than uncertainty about intentions.

3 Balancing and buck-passing II
Western Europe in the 1930s

The situation in Europe from the Rhineland crisis of 1936 to the Sudetenland crisis of 1938 closely resembles the conditions outlined in Chapter 2: multiple actors must make balancing decisions under conditions of uncertainty about intentions, capabilities, the reliability of allies, and the benefits of delay. Germany threatened to overturn the status quo and change the relative balance of power between it and the other great powers of Europe, notably Britain and France. One exception to this relatively good fit is that while the primary balancers, Britain and France, were roughly equal in power as assumed by the model, Britain's military was disproportionately focused on naval assets. This meant that in the short run France was the much more powerful potential balancer when it came to land forces. Also, given France's shared land border with Germany, it was likely to be subjected to the brunt of the German attack, though of course Britain would be immediately vulnerable to air attack.[1] This disparity in short-run land power and the likelihood of bearing costs played an important role in both crises as will be seen below.

The Rhineland crisis, 1936

The first crisis began on March 7, 1936 when Germany remilitarized the Rhineland. The Treaty of Versailles forbade Germany to maintain troops or build fortifications in the area. By moving troops into the Rhineland, Germany would be in a better position to both threaten France and defend against a French attack, thereby shifting the balancing of power. However, German remilitarization was also motivated by a desire to restore national pride, creating some uncertainty over long-run German intentions. Thus, while in retrospect Hitler's actions seem clear, during the crisis there was legitimate uncertainty about whether Hitler wanted to remilitarize the Rhineland as a first step in a program of broader revision to the European system or simply a means of reassertion of national sovereignty.[2] For their part, the French ultimately did not oppose the remilitarization. This was not a result of uncertainty regarding German intentions. Rather Paris acted the way it did because of its beliefs about the significance of the German move and their beliefs about the relative balance of forces in 1936.

First, the French did not believe the move itself did much to alter the relative balance with Germany. Paris had begun to devalue the Rhineland as a defensive buffer prior to the remilitarization and was not particularly surprised by Germany's actions (Adamthwaite 1977, 37; Alexander 1992, 76; Young 1996, 25). In fact, Hitler had already partially violated the demilitarization. Prior to the crisis, there were 200,000 men in *Sturmabteilung*, *Schutzstaffel*, and labor service battalions in the territory rebuilding roads and railways, plus another 22,000 regular infantry and one air regiment, all of which were dubiously classified as police (Schuker 1986, 308–9).[3] Additionally, modern military equipment, especially planes and tanks, had increased military mobility. This meant the Germans could move through the zone much more rapidly in the 1930s than in the 1920s. Simply keeping the zone demilitarized no longer bought France as much time as it did when the Treaty of Versailles was signed (Schuker 1986, 303; Young 1996, 25).

While keeping the Rhineland demilitarized was not without value to France – militarization would strengthen Germany's rail network and provide security for factories used in rearmament (Schuker 1986, 303–19) – in many ways the Rhineland was more important to the security of Poland and Czechoslovakia than to France (Young 1996, 25).[4] The zone's main value was in preventing Germany from fortifying the Rhine, thereby keeping Germany vulnerable to a French offensive if Germany moved east against either Poland or Czechoslovakia. Paris' alliances with these states rested on this offensive possibility (Kaufman 1992, 430).[5] In fact, this was the only thing that offset the defensive posture of the French army in Polish eyes (Sakwa 1973, 129–30).[6]

Furthermore, the weakness of France's offensive capabilities reduced the value of the Rhineland to Paris. French military planning in the 1930s assumed any European conflict involving France, including one over the Rhineland, would be a general war involving full mobilization and that France would remain on the defensive (Kaufman 1992, 422–3; Sakwa 1973, 137; Shirer 1984, 240–8). Broader diplomatic opinion agreed with this (Parker 1956, 305). For this reason, no force capable of undertaking a small-scale attack existed (Parker 1956, 363–4). In particular, the equipment possessed by the French army was ill-suited for an offensive. The French military lacked many modern weapons, especially rapidly mobile vehicles. French armor consisted of 200 poorly constructed light tanks which were designed to meet a colonial emergency and were incapable of undertaking an offensive in Europe (Sakwa 1973, 137; Schuker 1986, 304–16). France simply had not been building the necessary military equipment for aggressive action in part because of financial concerns (Steiner 2011, 139). The budget for weapons procurement had fallen by 17 percent from 1930 to 1934 due to the cost of the Maginot Line and the severity of the Great Depression reaching its nadir for the interwar period in 1935 (Steiner 2011, 138). The standing forces France did have available, even when supplemented by the *couverture* (a limited initial mobilization), were simply designed to hold the line in the east against the Germans for 17 days until a general mobilization could be completed (Parker 1956, 362–4). Therefore, a conflict with Berlin would likely require a full mobilization and British aid (Alexander 1992, 258–9; Schuker 1986, 304–16). Particularly worrisome was that any attempt to use the forces immediately available for an offensive would make any subsequent full-scale mobilization very difficult logistically (Parker 1956, 362–4). This meant that if the German army continued to fight after the initial offensive, France would be poorly positioned to carry on the war. Thus, any attempt by France to utilize the offensive potential of the demilitarized Rhineland would have harmed Fránce's defensive position.

Second, the French military was in no condition to fight even a defensive war. In 1935, France had no anti-tank weaponry, very little modern heavy and medium artillery, and most of France's 1,847 planes were still made of canvas. General Maurice Gamelin, head of the French General Staff, knew the French military equipment was badly outdated and that because of the decline of the French armaments industry, rectifying this deficiency would take years (Alexander 1992, 34–6, 62, and 128–30). The gradual rearmament that had only just begun left France in no position for war in 1936 (Alexander 1992, 76; Steiner 2011, 138; Young 1996, 28). Budget constraints were so tight that France had been unable to engage in full field maneuvers. Thus while France nominally had 651,000 soldiers, only 195,000 had been properly trained (Schuker 1986, 320–1). Depending on what forces on each side were counted as part of the standing military, and there were disagreements as to what were equivalent forces, France's peacetime army was only half the size of Germany's (Sakwa 1973, 133). Gamelin assumed that any military action against Germany would lead to a full-blown war – a war which he believed would result in initial deadlock and long-run defeat for France (Schuker 1986, 330). This attitude was broadly held by the French general staff and prompted it to oppose a military response to the remilitarization of the Rhineland. The military's attitude was a crucial factor in dissuading the French government from acting (Adamthwaite 1977, 37; Steiner 2011, 137).

At the cabinet meeting on March 7, right after German troops had entered the Rhineland, Gamelin presented the worse-case war scenario to the French cabinet. He overestimated the Germans' strength, refused to include Polish and Czechoslovak divisions in his analysis, and insisted that a full mobilization was necessary if any action was to be taken (Kaufman 1992, 429; Steiner 2011, 138).[7] He and the rest of the French military discouraged the politicians from acting. Albert Sarraut, the French Prime Minister, was also worried about whether Britain would aid France (Adamthwaite 1977, 37–9; Parker 1956, 362; Schuker 1986, 328–31). In the end, the cabinet did call out the *couverture*, but declined to issue orders for further mobilization. This amounted to a decision not to act. In the end, the French government threatened sanctions and passed the matter on to the League of Nations which in turn did nothing (Parker 1956, 358–60; Schuker 1986, 310). Indeed, even in denouncing the German move in parliament, Sarraut strongly indicated that the French would have accepted the remilitarization had it been done via negotiation and in accordance with international law (Great Britain 1990 v. 22, 145–8).[8] Thus, the French believed the value of the opportunity was low enough to not justify the costs of war and were sufficiently uncertain about the relative balance of forces to fear that France could not effectively balance the German threat. Both factors combined to convince the French to not oppose the German move.

Additionally, as suggested briefly above, the French decision rested in part on a belief that it would have had to confront Germany singlehandedly. Was this realistic? What of France's allies? In fact, Paris was correct to doubt that it would have had support in a fight over the Rhineland. The conflict between Italy and Britain over Ethiopia had forced France to choose between the two and the choice of Britain meant Italy would not oppose Germany. The United States was also unlikely to do anything. Washington still favored appeasement in 1936. Not only did the United States fail to condemn the remilitarization, but also Eleanor Roosevelt actually wrote an editorial supporting it (Marks 1985, 970–1). Likewise, the Belgians were strongly neutralist and had just denounced their 1920 military convention with France on March 6. Even had Brussels been inclined to act, it could not have done much. Belgian air defenses were a shambles and the army was in such poor shape that it was even unable to occupy some of its critical fortresses (Schuker 1986, 309–311; Thomas 1999, 136). Last, the Poles and the Czechoslovaks had no reason to fight if France was not going to launch an offensive. In such circumstances, they would bear the full burden of the war and likely be overrun. Because of this, Paris was uncertain whether Warsaw or Prague would act (Wandycz 1988b, 430). In the end, Belgium, Poland, and Czechoslovakia all declared fidelity to France during the crisis, but essentially waited for France to move (Sakwa 1973, 139).

That left Britain, but the British were unlikely to act even though as early as February 1936 they had anticipated the Rhineland would be Hitler's next move. British reluctance stemmed primarily from their position of perceived military weakness (Kaufman 1992, 431–33). Robert Vansittart, the Permanent Under-Secretary at the Foreign Office, warned that Britain was "in the matter of most armaments and all munitions, already weaker than Germany. ... [I]t is now inevitable that Germany will be ready for aggression long before we and the League can be ready for defense" (Ripsman and Levy 2008, 164). To this was added a report by the armed services committee which concluded that "the air position was deplorable" (Ripsman and Levy 2008, 165). Repeated intelligence from the British military attaché in Berlin emphasized the superiority of German equipment and rapid rearmament, especially in armored formations and aircraft (Great Britain 1990 v. 47, 220, 224, 292, 318, and 382–3). Thus, Vansittart warned that Britain would be unable to fulfill the request for aid in opposing the remilitarization that France would surely make. Prime Minister Stanley Baldwin was afraid any action against Germany would anger the working classes in Britain and play into Labour's hands in the upcoming election. Conservative losses in this election would undermine the support Baldwin was trying to build in the House of Commons for his rearmament plan. For this reason, he had informed the French government in February that the Rhineland was not a vital British interest (Schuker 1986, 312). This was in line with recommendations by Anthony Eden, the British Foreign Minister, who favored buying time for rearmament by appeasing Germany and hoped the Germans would move eastward (Adamthwaite 1977, 38; Sakwa 1973, 131–2). The British were willing to concede remilitarization because of doubts that it in any way reduced British security. In a document that was otherwise quite hostile in tone towards the Germans and which warned that Hitler would repudiate any treaty whenever it suited him, Eden argued that,

The German government, by the reoccupation of the zone effected on the morning of the 7th March, have thus not by that action produced a result, so far as the demilitarized zone itself is concerned, which we were not prepared to ultimately contemplate. It is the manner of their action ... which we deplore.

(Great Britain 1990 v. 47, 77)

As suggested by Eden's warning above that Germany would repudiate treaties at will, Britain's unwillingness to start a conflict with Germany in 1936 was not a result of underestimating the German threat. The British government was keenly aware that Germany posed a serious threat to British security, though not until Germany occupied the rump of Czechoslovakia in the spring of 1939 was it clear that Germany had essentially unlimited aims (Kaufman 1992, 431; Layne 2008, 427). Still, as early as 1933 Sir John Simon, Secretary of State for Foreign Affairs, was warning that Hitler's administration was "very dangerous" and would build up in a way that seriously threatened French security, making "the number of years for which real hostilities can be staved off ... doubtful" (Ripsman and Levy 2008, 159–60). In this view, Simon was strongly supported by Lord Viscount Hailsham, Secretary of State for War, and more generally by most of the other relevant officials and members of the government, including Eden and Neville Chamberlain. The British cabinet knew by late 1934 that Germany had over 300,000 men in military training and was creating an air force which would be capable of challenging Britain's (Ripsman and Levy, 160–6).

Given that British officials were not naïve about the German threat (Hughes 1988), why was Britain not more assertive? The answer is the Empire was badly overstretched and the Cabinet felt they lacked the economic and military resources, as well as allies, to act more aggressively (Kaufman 1992, 427–8). Understanding Britain's strategic position is crucial for grasping London's behavior during these crises. With a small military, a global empire to protect, multiple potential enemies – Germany in Europe, Italy in the Mediterranean, and Japan in the Pacific – Britain was seriously overextended. The Defense Requirements Committee was initially unable to determine whether Germany or Japan was the greater threat. The treasury made it clear that it was financially impossible to deal adequately with both threats (Layne 2008, 404–5). This ultimately led to a prioritization of the Nazi threat, in part because the British government believed Japan and Italy would attack as bandwagoners only after Britain became engaged in a war with Germany. The Defense Requirements Committee stated as much: "Japan may yield to the sudden temptation of a favourable opportunity arising from complications elsewhere. And elsewhere means Europe, and the danger to us in Europe will come only from Germany" (Layne 2008, 412). Thus, Britain opted to do nothing primarily because of beliefs about the balance of power rather than uncertainty over German intentions. This fits well with the model which predicts uncertainty over capabilities rather than intentions will be more problematic.

British officials also believed that it would be easier to oppose Germany in the future than in 1936. Britain's financial situation in the mid-1930s made it challenging to deal with the German threat. Chamberlain, both as Chancellor of the Exchequer and later as Prime Minister, believed the economy was sufficiently fragile that it was impossible to rearm rapidly without causing further economic collapse. This has led Ripsman and Levy (2008, 167–9) to conclude that London tried to appease Berlin in the 1930s in order to buy time for rearmament.[9] The financial situation was so tenuous that Chamberlain felt the British had to trade off current rearmament in favor of later rearmament (Layne 2008). In essence, if the British rearmed too rapidly, their finances would be exhausted, preventing them from building or maintaining an adequate military later when the threat materialized. Thus, timing rearmament just right became crucial. Certainly, the British did begin to rearm in earnest in 1936 and rearmament was rapidly accelerated in 1938 (Layne 2008, 429–35; Ripsman and Levy 2008, 176). In essence, there was significant uncertainty around the discount rate, δ, which the British and the French believed to be negative (i.e., that time was on their side). This is exactly the sort of behavior the discussion about the discount rate in the model predicts.[10]

Because of these beliefs, throughout both the Rhineland and Sudetenland crises London's main concern was to avoid being dragged into an ill-timed war by France over issues which in London's eyes did not threaten British security. Thus, during the Rhineland crisis, Eden's main worry was French overreaction. He argued that,

> We must discourage any military action by France against Germany ... The essential thing will be to involve or cajole France to accept [a new Locarno]. The trouble is that we are in a bad position to browbeat her into what we think reasonableness.
> (Great Britain 1990 v. 47, 81–2)

Eden need not have been so worried in 1936. Paris never formally asked Britain for support, likely out of a desire to avoid war until France's remilitarization was complete. Rather than using the crisis to draw Britain into war, it was hoped, especially by Gamelin, to use the crisis to gain British aid for French rearmament. This strategy proved to be a failure in the years between the remilitarization and the Sudetenland crisis (Adamthwaite 1977, 40; Alexander 1992, 259–69).

The Sudetenland crisis, 1938

While France and Britain struggled with rearmament, in 1938 Germany continued to alter the strategic balance by annexing Austria in the *Anschluss*.[11] Though this certainly concerned the French government, Paris felt popular support in Austria for unification with Germany justified inaction and London felt passivity was the best way to ensure German accommodation (Adamthwaite 1977, 79–81; Kaufman 1992, 432; Young 1996, 29). Also, since there was no chance Austria would fight, the crisis never contained the danger of a general European war, further encouraging British passivity (Newman 1978, 377–85). By this time the British had come to consider East Central Europe as outside their sphere of vital interests (Newman 1978, 372–3; Harinder 1983, 234). Essentially the British downgraded their view of the nature of the challenge, while staying concerned about Hitler's aggressiveness. They remained hard pressed to maintain their empire and particularly worried about the Japanese making a move in the Pacific (Adamthwaite 1977, 229). However, given that the Japanese were tied down in the Hanchow campaign in 1938, it is not clear that Tokyo was an immediate threat to British interests (Beck 1989, 175–8).[12]

The issue which did carry the risk of war was the Sudetenland crisis. The Sudetenland was an area of Czechoslovakia bordering Germany. It contained many ethnic Germans who had legitimate grievances against the Czechoslovak government. Bringing these ethnic Germans within Hitler's Reich had a strong appeal for the German people. Also, the region would add important heavy and light industries to the German economy, though it would increase the needs for food and raw material imports (*Science Letter* 1938, 213). More importantly the region was vital to Czechoslovak defensive preparations as it contained the Škoda munitions works and because the Czechoslovaks had fortified the mountains in the region in anticipation of war. The defense of Czechoslovakia would be nearly impossible if the Sudetenland was surrendered. To allow the Germans to occupy the Sudetenland was to write off France's alliance with Czechoslovakia and weaken ties with the Poles, who would then have little reason to trust French guarantees. Given the attractiveness of obtaining the Sudetenland, Hitler urged Konrad Henlein, the head of the Sudeten German party, to be as provocative as possible so as to bring about a pretext which Hitler could exploit (Craig 1950, 27). These provocations created a crisis in March 1938 which stewed through the summer until its autumn resolution at Munich.

Initially, the French stood firmly behind the Czechoslovaks and, in part due to the warnings of their ambassador in Prague, understood that the Sudeten Germans' demands were being orchestrated by Berlin in order to provide a pretext to threaten Czechoslovakia (Adamthwaite 1977, 61). In April, the French Prime Minister, Édouard Daladier, told the British that Hitler meant to destroy Czechoslovakia and that was but the first step. Chamberlain, now Britain's Prime Minister, remained unconvinced (Adamthwaite 1977, 180; Harinder 1983, 239; Lacaze 1998, 216; Steiner 2011, 565–6). The problem for the French was that they feared they could not win alone (Kaufman 1992, 423 and 433). A *Secréteriat Général de la Défense Nationale* memo emphasized French air and demographic weaknesses and raised the possibility of a war against both Germany and Italy. The memo observed that "France cannot resist forces three times as numerous" and concluded that in event of such a war "British support would be essential" (Steiner 2011, 566). Georges Bonnet, the French Foreign Minister, was particularly pessimistic (Young 1996, 30). In April, he had told the American ambassador that France could only expect "defeat and dismemberment" in a war with Germany (Haight 1960, 340–1). The chief of the French air force shared this assessment, warning that "French planes will be annihilated in fifteen days" after the onset of war (Haight 1960, 334).

Because of this, over the summer Bonnet sought aid in confronting Germany from the United States, Britain, Romania, Yugoslavia, the Soviet Union, and Poland.[13] Most remained non-committal at best in part because Paris' earlier capitulations made them doubt France's resolve and offensive capabilities (Adamthwaite 1977, 197; Thomas 1999, 130–2). As noted by the French military attaché in Vienna, "[T]he prestige of France in Central Europe, already gravely damaged by the events of 7 March 1936, has emerged from the Austrian affair ... almost completely annihilated" (Adamthwaite 1977, 77). The Romanian foreign minister drove this point home, telling the French in reference to the occupation of the Rhineland that "If on 7 March you could not defend yourself, how will you defend us against an aggressor?" (Steiner 2011, 160). Not surprisingly, throughout the crisis Paris had no confidence that it would receive assistance from Romania (Steiner 2011, 603). Of the leaders Bonnet pressed for assistance only Józef Beck, the Polish Foreign Minister, promised Bonnet he would go to war with Germany if France did (Cienciala 1999, 59).[14] The French were not convinced (Steiner 2011, 596). The US Ambassador to France, William Bullitt, was also skeptical of the Polish pledge. He argued that,

> "Poland would offer no resistance, either physical or diplomatic, to a German attack on Czechoslovakia" and would be glad "to see Germany control Austria and Bohemia, and to see Hungary walk off with Slovakia, while Poland got 'frontier rectifications' in the Teschen district."
> (Wandycz 1988b, 426)[15]

Such skepticism was warranted as Beck did not believe France would fight for Czechoslovakia and thus planned to use the crisis to extract exactly what Bullitt predicted (Steiner 2011, 572). Essentially, the Poles had concluded that an effective balancing coalition would not form against Germany and thus instead opted to bandwagon (see Chapter 5).

The Americans and Soviets were not much help either. Washington wavered between urging appeasement in March, followed by arguing that France should hold steadfast in June – though without offering actual support – and finally stating in July that it would not aid France (Adamthwaite 1977, 209; Marks 1985, 974–5; Offner 1977). Likewise, Moscow issued a series of non-committal statements over the course of 1938, leading the French to correctly conclude that the Soviets would remain aloof (Steiner 2011, 596). Prague had no better luck eliciting Soviet support. Moscow evaded requests for aid from Edvard Beneš, the Prime Minister of Czechoslovakia, on September 19 and 20 (Lukes 1999, 17–21). By September 21, the day the Sudetenland was essentially conceded, Moscow had still not made a definite commitment (Steiner 2011, 619–22). Though the Soviets ultimately mobilized over 40 divisions, the mobilization was kept secret until September 25 (Jukes 1991, 197–204). The Soviets did not offer unconditional aid until October 3 – after the Germans had already occupied the Czechoslovak defenses (Lukes 1999, 20). Presumably Moscow knew its offer was useless at such a late date and expected it to be refused. Even had the Soviets committed earlier, their ground forces would have had to move through Poland or Romania. Warsaw, worried the Soviets might occupy territory Poland had taken in 1919 and 1920, mobilized specifically to prevent the Soviets from moving through Poland (Cienciala 1999, 61; Jukes 1991,

199 and 205).[16] Going through Romania was no more practical (Kaufman 1992, 433). Its road and rail networks were in poor shape, making it difficult to transit with any speed (Thomas 1999, 147).[17] Furthermore, although the Romanian general staff had approved Russian overflights provided the planes had Czechoslovak markings, King Carol II had vetoed the plan (Jukes 1991, 199–200).[18]

By September this lack of support from France's potential allies, along with fears that Italy and Spain would bandwagon with Germany, caused Bonnet to favor peace at any price.[19] He told the British ambassador as much (Adamthwaite 1977, 207; Great Britain 1990 v. 49, 272; Haight 1960, 348). The French essentially ceded the diplomatic initiative to the British and agreed that the Czechoslovaks must make some concessions (Adamthwaite 1977, 67–70).

The lack of British support was particularly troubling to the French. Britain was inclined to appease rather than oppose Hitler and during the spring crisis Lord Halifax, the British Foreign Minister, wired Paris that London would not go to war over Czechoslovakia and that Czechoslovakia was indefensible (Adamthwaite 1977, 190; Steiner 2011, 654–5). Even when the crisis reached a boiling point in September 1938, the most the French ambassador could get out of Halifax was a statement that if France was forced to act that British public opinion would wish "[we] do our best to help" though Halifax was also keen to point out he did not believe "public opinion would be prepared … to enter upon hostilities with Germany" (Adamthwaite 1977, 208). This fit with Bonnet's impression based on conversations with the British ambassador over the summer "that in no case will the [British government] allow itself to be presented with a *fait accompli*" (Adamthwaite 1977, 197).

As in 1936, Britain's desire to avoid war derived in part from the need to buy time for rearmament (Hughes 1988, 866–7) and because London did not see the territory in question as crucial to its security. Certainly, as of late 1937, London still saw the military balance as decidedly unfavorable. A review by the British cabinet concluded that France's military was not yet ready for war and came down quite harshly on Britain's own readiness, stating that,

> Our Naval, Military, and Air Forces … are still far from sufficient to meet our defensive commitments … We cannot, therefore, exaggerate the importance, from the view of the Imperial defense, of any political or international action that can be taken to reduce the number of our potential enemies.
> (Adamthwaite 1981, 198)

Come September 1938 at the peak of the Sudetenland crisis, the War Office was still arguing that Britain needed to buy time for rearmament (Steiner 2011, 609).

Additionally, British diplomats worried that Hungary, Poland, and Italy would bandwagon with Germany or at least extend benevolent neutrality toward Berlin (Great Britain 1990 v. 49, 290–1). Consistent with these concerns, the Foreign Policy Committee was against a commitment to Czechoslovakia which it characterized as a "highly artificial" creation that caused instability and was beyond Britain's power to save anyway, especially after the *Anschluss* exposed Czechoslovakia's southern flank (Adamthwaite 1977, 86). Chamberlain concurred that the *Anschluss* had undermined Czechoslovakia's defenses (Hughes 1988, 866).

Also, throughout the crisis the Dominions were against war and during its final stage in September the Dominion high commissioners as well as the prime ministers of Australia and South Africa urged appeasement (Beck 1989, 174–5; Fry 1999; Weinberg 1999, 6–7). Even had they favored a more aggressive line, the Dominions had only just begun to rearm and were still quite poorly equipped (Fry 1999, 295). On August 30, the British cabinet unanimously voted to not fight for Czechoslovakia if Germany invaded. The British were willing to keep Berlin guessing as to their position in the hopes that Prague might get a better deal, but that was as far as London was prepared to go (Steiner 2011, 591). Britain's main worry, as seen by Halifax and Lord Stanley, the Secretary of State for Dominion Affairs, was that France might defend Czechoslovakia, compelling Britain to aid France (Harinder 1983, 234–5). From the British view, the key was not containing Hitler, but restraining France.

As in 1936, British policy was based on the belief that Germany's military was superior to its own. The British estimated that the Germans had 38 regular, 18 reserve, 24 Landwehr, and 9 Austrian divisions, for a total of 89 divisions all available for frontline deployment, while the allies had only around 60 divisions – 2 British, 53 French, but only 30 to 40 actually available in the field, and 21 Czechoslovakian divisions (Ben-Arie, 1990, 431–2). Especially important was that, due to the small size of the British army, Chamberlain was convinced Britain could not affect the military situation in East Central Europe (Goldstein, 1999, 286–7). He wrote to Beneš claiming that "[Resistance] must result in Bohemia being overrun and nothing that any other Power can do will prevent this fate" (Great Britain 1990 v. 49, 296). Chamberlain was not alone in this assessment. Shortly after the *Anschluss* the British Foreign Office had concluded that "neither we nor the French possess the offensive power to prevent Germany from working her will in Central Europe" (Hughes 1988, 866). Geography made aiding Czechoslovakia even harder. As Chamberlain wrote in his diary,

> You have only to look at the map to see nothing that France or we could do could possibly save Czechoslovakia from being overrun by the Germans, if they wanted to do it. The Austrian frontier is practically open; the Skoda [sic] munition works are within easy bombing distance of the German aerodromes, the railways all pass though German territory, Russia is 100 miles away.
> (Beck 1989, 183)

Nor was Chamberlain alone in these beliefs. So gloomy was the military's view of the situation that the British Chiefs of Staff had concluded that,

> No pressure that we and our possible allies can bring to bear, either by sea, on land, or in the air, could prevent Germany from invading and overrunning Bohemia and from inflicting a decisive defeat on the Czechoslovakian army.
> (Beck 1989, 182)

The British cabinet was fully persuaded by the Chiefs' views. Lord Halifax called the entire report "an extremely melancholy document" and Alexander Cadogan, the permanent Under-Secretary of the Foreign Office, concluded: "We must not precipitate conflict now. We shall be smashed" (Beck 1989, 183).

This despair rested in no small part on pessimism in regards to the relative balance of air forces. Throughout the late 1930s London was always more focused on home air defense – both in strategy and rearmament priorities – than in the military balance on the Continent (Steiner 2011, 604–7). This made the sad state of British air defenses all the more troubling and convinced Chamberlain that, even if the British army had been larger, it would not reach France rapidly enough to matter as German air superiority would quickly compel Britain to capitulate (Hughes 1988, 858). Britain had only 10 percent of the necessary antiaircraft artillery, and lacked sufficient water pumps, barrage balloons, and searchlights. Only one squadron of modern Spitfire fighters was in service (Steiner 2011, 607). Even Winston Churchill, then outside of the government and one of the most hawkish British politicians, believed the Germans had achieved parity with Britain in the air by 1935 and had then quickly surpassed the British (Churchill 1948, vol. 1). The British government believed itself to be outnumbered 3,200 to 1,606 in first line aircraft (Beck 1989, 184).[20] Nor did London expect much from the French air force as Gamelin had admitted to them in 1937 the even poorer state of France's air defenses (Alexander 1992, 161). These deficiencies were especially disheartening as the British government had spent much of the 1930s being truly frightened by the prospect of aerial bombardment. Chamberlain and many others in the British government and military believed the next war would be won in the air.[21] Baldwin had believed bombing to be nearly impossible to stop, claiming there was "no power on earth that can protect [the man in the street] from being bombed" (Freedman 2013, 126). Likewise, in 1937 Air Chief Marshal Hugh Dowdling, commander of RAF Fighter Command, had claimed that the bombing of London would cause such panic as to lead to defeat "in a fortnight or less" (Freedman 2013, 126–7). Years later Harold MacMillan, who was a Member of Parliament during the crisis, remembered that during the 1930s the British had "thought of air warfare rather as people think of nuclear warfare today" and that as late as June 1940 "the Prime Minister's office was comforting itself with the calculation that there might only be 18,000 deaths per day when the bombing of cities began" (Orange 2006, 1014). These beliefs fundamentally shaped British strategy in the late 1930s (Hughes 1988).

The French military also overestimated German strength (Ben-Arie 1990, 434). They assessed available German strength at 116 divisions and 2,760 first line aircraft of which 85 percent were of modern design with an ability to produce 1,000 planes per month. In fact the Germans had 72 divisions, 1,669 first line aircraft (out of a total of 3,267 planes, though with only enough pilots to fly 1,080 of them) of which only 50 percent were of modern design and only 450 planes per month could be produced (Ben-Arie 1990, 439–40; Jackson 1998, 236–7).[22] Certainly, a number of German generals did not share London's and Paris' view that any war would be a German walkover. Werner von Blomberg, the German

War Minister, Werner von Fritsch, the Commander in Chief of the German Army, and Ludwig Beck, the German Army Chief of Staff, all repeatedly warned Hitler in August and September 1938 that his actions were risking a serious defeat (Press 2005, 152–5). They pointed out that the planned invasion of the Sudetenland left only ten German divisions in the West to face 56 French divisions and that only 1,000 of the 10,000 planned bunkers of the Westwall were completed (Press 2005, 151). Yet, Paris seemed oblivious to these German weaknesses and rather focused on the French military's deficiencies.

The overinflated estimate of the Luftwaffe's abilities was particularly disturbing in light of the warnings from General Joseph Vuillemin, chief of staff of the French air force, that France had no bombers, that only 700 of its 1,126 planes were operational, and of those only 27 were "modern" (Steiner 2011, 597). Gamelin also deplored the state of French aviation, warning that it would be of little use after the war's initial stages due to "wastage". The supposed air discrepancy particularly worried the French cabinet which believed it needed at least 18 months of rearmament to close the gap (Alexander 1992, 165; Thomas 1999, 140–3).[23] Every war scare led to a financial panic which contracted lending further (Steiner 2011, 601; Thomas 1999, 122–39). Given the French believed time was on their side, but only if they could get the necessary loans for rearmament, avoiding war or even a crisis in 1938 seemed imperative. The American announcement on September 16 that, due to the Neutrality Act, the United States would not deliver the 200 planes France had ordered if war broke out could only have added to French fears (Haight 1960, 350).

The apparent imbalance in war materiel was not the only source of French military worries. Gamelin believed that the German annexation of Austria, by adding a new southern front had essentially undone the Czechoslovak defenses (Thomas 1999, 125). Certainly, Czechoslovakia's fortifications along the former Austrian frontier were weak (Steiner 2011, 596). Additionally, Gamelin argued that the decline of the Little Entente, Czechoslovakia's alliance with Romania and Yugoslavia, meant that there was no way for Soviet aid to reach Czechoslovakia. He also pointed out the weakness of Czechoslovak air defenses and concluded that Czechoslovakia would only be able to resist for a few days or weeks (Steiner 2011, 596–7). Further, France's continued lack of a mobile strike force meant it was only capable of defensive operations and not in a position to aid Czechoslovakia. Gamelin suggested the most France could due to aid Czechoslovakia would be to launch a limited offensive (Great Britain 1990 v. 24, 179–80). This was actually an improvement on his views shortly after the *Anschluss* when he had declared that it was "impossible for France to give military assistance to Czechoslovakia" (Steiner 2011, 596). Nor was Gamelin alone in the assessment. The Army Operations Bureau reflected a broadly held view within the French military when it concluded France was incapable of undertaking a swift offensive without "a complete reorganization of our army and the restructuring of our military policy" (Steiner 2011, 599).

On top of this, Gamelin correctly believed British military planning had not focused on how it could aid France, but had rather focused on aviation and naval needs, partially in response to Chamberlain's preferences (Alexander 1992, 246–8 and 271). British ground forces available to be deployed to France in the mid to late 1930s were estimated to be significantly smaller than those that had been sent in 1914 (Alexander 1992, 251–4). Indeed, during a Franco-British summit in April 1938, the British has insisted they would only send two divisions to France. Though Daladier knew the British were intentionally understating what they could contribute, it reinforced the existing French belief that the British army would be of little use if it came to war (Adamthwaite 1977, 230–1). Finally, the French were convinced that the still incomplete Westwall was a major obstacle which would hold up any French offensive designed to aid Czechoslovakia, though in fact it did little to slow Allied forces in 1944 when the wall was complete (Adamthwaite 1977, 234; Thomas 1999, 127–37). Thus, little could be done to aid Czechoslovakia and Gamelin expected its resistance to be brief (Adamthwaite 1977, 87–8 and 228; Alexander 1992, 281; Great Britain 1990 v. 49, 296). Daladier accepted Gamelin's analysis and repeated concerns about French aviation and Czechoslovakia's weakness to the American ambassador (Adamthwaite 1977, 231; Alexander 1992, 110–20 and 132).

The balance of forces, however, was much closer than the British and the French assumed (Overy 1999, 207). Less than a year later, France fielded 110 divisions, making the British estimate of 53 divisions seem almost deliberately low as France could not have created so many new divisions in such a short time. The estimates of German strength were equally suspect. The Landwehr and Reserve divisions were of poor quality and few of them were deployed. This left only 45 German divisions, three of which were to be deployed in East Prussia leaving only five assigned to the French frontier. Similarly, given that Czechoslovakia alone had 520 planes, the air war would not have been the walkover the French air marshals feared (Ben-Arie 1990, 434–40). Both the French and the British consistently overestimated how many planes Germany could keep operational and tended to look at their air forces in isolation against Germany rather than comparing the combined air forces of France, Britain, and Czechoslovakia against that of the Third Reich (Steiner 2011, 598 and 607).

However, it is not clear that France would have wanted to fight had they believed the military situation to be more sanguine. Daladier told the British at an April 1938 meeting that "the military situation was really determined by the political situation" rather than the other way around and in May, Bullitt observed,

> French and British action ... will be based on the assumption that the ultimate dissolution of Czechoslovakia is inevitable and that the best that can be hoped for is that such dissolution will take place without bloodshed in such a way as to save the face of France and England.
>
> (Adamthwaite 1977, 243)

Indeed, the British ambassador to Czechoslovakia repeatedly stated the same thing in confidential dispatches to London and argued that it was better for both Britain and Czechoslovakia to resolve the situation sooner rather than later while some sort of a deal could still be struck which might satisfy Germany and leave Prague in possession of most of Bohemia (Great Britain 1990 v. 49, 119–21). This belief as indicated above was shared by London and goes a long way to explain why over the summer of 1938 London focused more on convincing Prague to make concessions rather on deterring the Germans – a strategy Bonnet and Daladier agreed with for similar reasons (Great Britain 1990 v. 49, 150–2, 179, 211–13 and 216). In essence, much like with the Rhineland, both the British and the French saw the German move into the Sudetenland as both inevitable and not sufficiently harmful to their security to warrant fighting a major war to prevent its loss.

The crisis reached its boiling point in September. On September 7 the Germans rejected Czechoslovakia's offer to accept all of Henlein's demands and instead responded with increased demands and vulgar verbal attacks (Craig 1950, 31). Previously there had been hope in both France and Britain that the dispute could be mediated, especially if Prague was leaned on to make concessions, but the Germans simply upped their demands when concessions were made. Thus, it became clear that Hitler would not be content with any concessions short of the annexation of the Sudetenland. This behavior fit with intelligence reports the British cabinet had received in late August which claimed Germany intended to occupy the territory in four to six weeks (Walker and Watson 1994, 13).

Had France's inclination towards appeasement been based on uncertainty about German intentions, the new German behavior would have encouraged the French to stand firmly behind their commitments to Czechoslovakia – commitments which they had restated publically as late as early September. While on September 8 Daladier did threaten that France would march, he ultimately backtracked (Adamthwaite 1977, 210). While he was attempting to appear firm, Paris asked London to clarify how it would respond in the event France went to war with Germany. London's response was disheartening. On September 12 Halifax telegrammed: "While His Majesty's Government would never allow the security of France to be threatened, they are unable to make precise statements of the character of their future action, or the time at which it would be taken, in circumstances that they cannot at present foresee," leading Bonnet to inform the British minister in Paris on September 14 that, "France would accept any solution of [the] Czechoslovak question to avoid war" (Craig 1950, 32). Further communication indicated that while Britain was prepared to use its air and sea assets to aid France, it was only willing to pledge two divisions and would not even promise to institute conscription (Adamthwaite 1977, 219). This led three members of Daladier's cabinet, including Bonnet, to threaten to resign if Daladier continued to insist upon taking a hard line (Adamthwaite 1977, 220–1).

Thus, London and Paris decided to abandon Czechoslovakia to its fate and on September 19 convinced Prague in principle to cede the Sudetenland.[24] Though there was a brief period when war again seemed possible due to Hitler demanding on September 20 that the Sudetenland be turned over by October 10 (Steiner 2011, 616–24), the French and the British ultimately relented. During this period when war between France and Germany seemed possible Chamberlain made his personal intervention by bringing about a conference at Munich which he hoped would give Germany "all the essentials without war and without delay" (Adamthwaite 1977, 223). In reality, the game was up already as a French diplomatic demarche on September 27 showed France was willing to accept all of Hitler's demands at Godesberg (Craig 1950, 36). It is not clear that the French ever seriously considered fighting for Czechoslovakia. Paris never held military staff talks with Prague and when, after the Munich conference, Daladier expressed his disgust at the outcome, his lament was not that the military situation had forced France to avoid a fight, but rather it had prevented France from striking a better bargain (Adamthwaite 1977, 234). He told Bullitt,

> If I had a thousand bombers behind me ... I would have been in a much stronger position at Munich to resist Hitler's demands, and perhaps we would not have been forced to sign what we did sign.
>
> (Adamthwaite 1977, 243)

Ultimately, the French did not believe Hitler could be trusted, but they did not think they could win a war in 1938. Nor did they or the British think the Sudetenland was worth fighting for as neither saw Czechoslovakia as a particularly valuable ally. Daladier in particular was willing to sacrifice Czechoslovakia to help ensure that Britain would in fact be on France's side when war came (Steiner 2011, 603). There were hopes in some quarters that time was on France's side, but Daladier's dispirited view when he returned to cheering crowds in Paris suggests that he was not sure of even this. Without strong third party support France simply would not challenge Hitler until forced to do so. Given that Prague did not resist, Paris was able to delay war. London's thinking was similar, though the British were more sanguine about the prospects of rearmament and even less convinced of the value of Czechoslovakia.

The case shows that it is possible to have multiple countries that largely understand that they face a real threat but through doubts about the probability of third party support, beliefs that the military balance will improve, and beliefs that the immediate issue at stake is not worth the cost of war, end up all essentially passing the buck – not to another state as is often argued (Christensen and Snyder 1990), but to the future. France would have been more likely to fight if it believed it could count on robust British support, but the British consistently refused to make significant military commitments to France or allow French alliances to influence whether they would fight Germany. Prague may have been able to drag Paris to war had it insisted on armed resistance, though it is possible France would have abandoned Czechoslovakia to its fate. Given the irresolute commitments from London, Paris, and Moscow, Prague's decision seems justifiable. The main problem was that France could not be sure of British support and that Britain did not believe it had vital interests in East Central Europe nor that it could materially affect the outcome in that theater. The French knew they had much at stake in East Central Europe, but they also knew that given their defensive posture and the previous occupation of the Rhineland, there was not much they could do to relieve pressure on Czechoslovakia. That would take a major offensive, which as demonstrated by French inaction during the invasion of Poland in 1939, was something they had no intention of undertaking. Besides, Gamelin rated Poland far more highly than Czechoslovakia, so the loss of Czechoslovakia was less disconcerting. Ultimately, doubts that an effective balancing coalition could be formed in either 1936 or 1938 combined with doubts that either the Rhineland or Sudetenland was especially valuable led both Britain and France to favor appeasement over war.

Conclusion

Our theory predicts that uncertainty about capabilities is more of a problem in balancing calculations than is uncertainty about intentions. Furthermore, uncertainty about the actual balance of power is the most important and ultimately defines the importance of the other three uncertainties about capabilities: nature of the challenge; timing of balancing; and the necessary size of balancing coalitions. On the whole the case fits well with the model as uncertainty about capabilities, the impact of the changes to the status quo, and the value of strategic delay all played a role.

British and French reasons for not opposing Germany from 1936 to 1938 primarily lay with uncertainty about both capabilities and the benefits of delay. Both powers correctly believed they were lagging in rearmament, though crucially there was significant uncertainty and miscalculation as to the balance of forces. Both hoped that with sufficient time for rearmament they could rectify the imbalance. As mobilizations drained the treasury and there was some hope the contest would be more even in the future, delaying a confrontation with the Germans made some sense. More importantly the French did not believe they could stop the Germans on their own and never felt certain that the British would support them. This fits well with the problems associated with uncertainty about capabilities and the size of effective coalitions discussed in the model. If the French had a different view of the balance of power between the Wehrmacht and their own military, they would have been far more likely to challenge Hitler. Given their beliefs about German power, opposing the Germans alone made no sense. Given French uncertainty about whether Britain would fight, the French thus opted to kick the can down the road. The behavior of Poland and Czechoslovakia can be explained by the same logic which means French irresoluteness also cost them allies among the smaller powers.

Interestingly, and crucially for the ultimate outcome of this case, both the British and the French had a tendency to look only at their own forces, not their combined forces, in relation to the Wehrmacht and concluded that the balance was decidedly against them. How much of this was due to both states' uncertainty as to whether the other would join them in confronting Hitler or was due to leaders looking for reasons to justify inaction is debatable.

Likewise, the model also receives support in regard to its predictions about the importance of the nature of the move. Neither the British nor the French were convinced the relative gains at stake in each crisis were actually a threat to them or that they would be worth the cost of opposing the Germans. In particular, the British were focused on the relative balance of air power, and the occupation of the Rhineland, Austria, and Sudetenland did little to alter this balance. Given the belief that the seized territories did little to undermine British security and bought time for rearmament, short-term appeasement appeared to have few costs. Similarly, the occupation of the Rhineland did little to reduce France's security given the defensive posture of the French military and changes in military technology.

Finally, uncertainty about intentions played only a small role. Given the British were only willing to wage a war in Europe to save France and believed the Germans were focused on the east, the British had little reason to oppose German moves in the Rhineland, Austria, or Sudetenland. Indeed, to the extent they would further encourage the Germans to look east these outcomes were positive. Thus, there was some ambiguity about the strategic impact of German actions for the general European balance of power. The French viewed the remilitarization of the Rhineland similarly. Still, Paris largely saw the threat for what it was, and while there were some voices in Britain that argued Hitler was not a threat, most of the British government believed Germany was a long-term concern.

Of course, the case does not perfectly mirror the model. One element that does not fit is that both the British and the French took a middle approach to balancing. They opted to avoid provoking a war, but this is not the same as to claim they did nothing. Both were engaged in rearmament, though not at a full-bore rate until very late in the game. This differs from the model's requirement that states either decide to balance or do nothing. However, this is a result of simplification in the model and as long as it is remembered that reality is always more complex than any model, it is not a serious flaw. Additionally, the French reaction to the Rhineland remilitarization shows that militaries' preferred strategies need to be considered. The remilitarization strengthened German defenses and weakened French offensive options, but since France had ruled out an offensive this did not much matter and the territory did not make the Germans that much more of an offensive threat to France. Similarly, the case shows that domestic politics played a role; however, they are not included in our model. This was done not because we believe domestic politics to be unimportant, but rather so that we could focus on the role of uncertainty at the international level.

On the whole, the value of modeling and parsing out the various components of a threatening move is illustrated by the case. The model helps to better explain the dynamics of balancing and buck-passing. The model provides several insights into balancing and commitment problems and offers prospects for future developments in the research of balancing behavior. Of course, focusing solely on balancing leaves unanswered what states do when they do not balance. British and French behavior only partially answers that question. At times they both seemed to hide and hope the Germans would go east, but they never fully embraced this option. Rather they underbalanced rather than hid. Importantly, neither government ever considered bandwagoning with the Germans. Yet bandwagoning and hiding are real options for states. How states decide among these strategies will be explored in Chapters 4 and 5.

Notes

1. The Soviet Union was another important 'land force' based potential balancer. However, it was physically removed from these crises. The newly independent states of East Central Europe formed a barrier that made Soviet intervention, even if Stalin had been eager for such things, much more difficult. As we will see in this chapter and the next, this difficulty was exacerbated by the mistrust that these states had of Moscow. Of course, in addition to this physical distance, the ideological distance between Russia on the one hand and East Central Europe, Britain, and France also played a role (Haas 2014).
2. A similar situation was created after the Crimean War by the 1856 Treaty of Paris which demilitarized the Black Sea and the Åland Islands in the Baltic. Russia found these provisions both humiliating and constraining. St Petersburg pushed for its right to remilitarize the Black Sea during the Franco-Prussian War. Ultimately, Russia was able to sign a convention in London with Prussia, Austria, Turkey, Britain, and Italy reversing the Black Sea provision of the treaty. Efforts to obtain diplomatic support for the remilitarization the Åland Islands met with much less success as Russia was only able to remilitarize them during World War One.
3. The French army staff came up with an even higher number – 295,000 – and classified them all as fully trained soldiers, making the military balance appear far worse than it was (Alexander 1992, 259).
4. Churchill noted that a fortified Rhineland meant the Germans would have a free hand in the east during the British debate on the crisis. He did this twice: first on March 26, 1936 and again on April 6 (Churchill 1948, vol. 1, 204–5).
5. Given that none of France's East Central European allies were committed legally or in fact to aid France, maintaining their confidence in French strength was an important consideration (Young 1996, 18 and 66) and ultimately the remilitarization helped undo France's eastern alliances (Adamthwaite 1977, 41). See Chapter 5.
6. Since France preferred Germany to move east rather than west, allowing the remilitarization made some strategic sense (Sakwa 1973, 130).
7. Throughout the crisis the French government was convinced of German military superiority despite reasonably accurate military intelligence to the contrary (Wandycz 1988b, 434). The main intelligence breakdown lay in failing to identify crucial German shortages in war materiel which made a full German mobilization impossible (Steiner 2011, 138).
8. Such negotiations could have been analogous to those conducted by Russia in the nineteenth century as discussed in note 2.
9. Of course, one can question Chamberlain's underlying economic assumptions. Keynesians would argue that increased government spending would have been just what the British economy needed in the 1930s. Certainly, rearmament was an important part of the Nazi economic recovery plans.
10. The same is true for British and French concerns with upcoming elections in 1936. Both governments believed that delaying the start of rearmament until after the elections was the best way to ensure retaining political support for rearmament. These governments both feared that an earlier start to rearmament might cost the ruling governments seats in the 1936 elections or even lead to a change of government. This in turn would reduce support for rearmament within their respective parliaments.
11. Austria, like the Rhineland, had intrinsic nationalistic value to the Germans as well as relative gains value.
12. The belief that the Japanese were a medium-term threat was correct as evidenced by Japanese attacks on British possessions in Asia on December 8, 1941.
13. More will be said of Romanian, Yugoslav, and Polish policies in Chapter 5.
14. The US ambassador to Poland, Drexel Biddle, confirmed the existence of this promise to Washington.

15 Teschen is the German name for the city known in Czech as Těšín and Polish as Cieszyn.
16 In fact, the Soviet mobilization was mainly aimed at deterring the Poles from attacking Czechoslovakia (Steiner 2011, 619–22; Thomas 1999, 148–9).
17 Nicolae Petrescu-Comnène, the Romanian Foreign Minister, claimed somewhat unbelievably that the situation was so bad that no more than one Soviet division would be able to transit Romania every 20 days.
18 However, there is still some debate as to whether the Romanian general staff actually authorized these flights (Ragsdale 1998).
19 Hitler was not necessarily having much more success lining up his allies either. While the Hungarians coveted territory in Slovakia, they were not ready for war. Also, the Hungarians feared Yugoslavia and Romania would attack them if they attacked Czechoslovakia (Ádám 1999; Sakmyster 1973; Strang 1999, 167–8). Thus, the Hungarians were still hedging their bets (see Chapter 5). Italy, too, was not clearly committed. While Mussolini was fine with Hitler provoking a crisis, he was not ready to see Czechoslovakia entirely liquidated (Ádám 1999, 101; Strang 1999, 183). He did, however, pledge to fight with Germany if Britain declared war on Germany, though given the demands the Spanish Civil War was still placing on Italy, this promise was not worth very much (Strang 1999, 176 and 183).
20 Another British estimate had the disparity at a similarly dispiriting 2,909 planes to 1,550 (Steiner 2011, 607).
21 This focus on the air power helps in part to explain Britain's willingness to fight in 1939. While the overall military balance between Germany and Britain had widened between 1938 and 1939, Britain had significantly narrowed the gap in air power (Kaufman 1992, 435).
22 French estimates on the total number of German planes were reasonably accurate. It was the estimates of the planes' quality and what percentage of the planes were operational that were badly overstated (Steiner 2011, 598).
23 French industrial output in 1938 was at its lowest level since 1928 and was hamstrung by frequent strikes (Steiner 2011, 594).
24 Vansittart had opposed Chamberlain going to Germany to negotiate these concessions, likening it to Emperor Henry IV's trip to Canossa to submit to the Pope (Steiner 2011, 592).

4 To bandwagon or hide I

A theoretical examination of the alternatives to balancing

The preceding chapters examined why and when states balance against challengers of the status quo. Left unaddressed was what states do if they opt not to balance. Realists have long seen bandwagoning – aligning oneself with the threat to the status quo – as the opposite side of the coin to balancing, but as pointed out in Chapter 1 other options, most notably hiding, exist.[1] This chapter attempts to discern what factors makes states more likely to hide or to bandwagon if they opt not to balance. It does this by drawing inferences from the balancing models in the previous chapters. Specifically, the chapter will work through how uncertainty about the distribution of capabilities, the nature of the challenger, and the nature of the opportunity influence decisions to bandwagon or hide. Several new factors, including geography, institutions, economic ties, and the promise of spoils, will also be introduced.

In thinking about the implications of the model in Chapter 2 for whether states opt to bandwagon or hide, it will be assumed for the remainder of this section that states have already ruled out balancing. This is made for clarity and because the factors driving the decision to balance have already been thoroughly covered. Though such an order of decision-making may actually occur in some states, decisions about whether to balance, bandwagon, or hide are more likely reached as part of one ongoing process as will be evident from the cases below.

Before proceeding, it is important to recall that the literature posits two distinct types of bandwagoners. Walt (1985), in his Balance of Threat theory, argues states bandwagon primarily to protect themselves from a threat, while Schweller (1994) suggests states bandwagon because they are revisionist and bandwagoning offers them a chance to pick up spoils. These two ideal types of bandwagoners – in practice it may well be hard to sort out these various motives for at least some states – could value factors differently and therefore each type of bandwagoner as well as hiders will be considered. As will be seen below, despite their distinct motives the two types of bandwagoners should respond similarly to the various factors analyzed.

Role of material capabilities

The first factor to consider from the model presented in Chapter 2 is the benefit from common defense, $\frac{n_T}{N}(x)$, or more precisely the value of common defense relative to the strength of the challenger $\frac{n_T}{N}(x) - \alpha(\beta+\gamma)$. Obviously, once the decision to not balance is taken, no positive contribution to $\frac{n_T}{N}(x)$ is made. Yet, decisions taken thereafter also matter. Hiding does not further alter the value of common defense. Whether hiders would prefer a higher or lower value for $\frac{n_T}{N}(x) - \alpha(\beta+\gamma)$ is uncertain as it depends on whom they are hiding from: the balancers or the challenger. Presumably more revisionist states are more likely to be hiding from the balancers and more status quo states are more likely to hide from challengers. Of course, states may hide from both balancers and challengers hoping to avoid being entangled in a dispute that is not their own. Bandwagoning, as opposed to hiding, does alter the value of common defense relative to the challenger since bandwagoners contribute military assets to the revisionist side. For bandwagoners primarily driven by their own revisionism (Schwellerian bandwagoners) this is an unalloyed good. For bandwagoners driven primarily by fear of the challenger (Waltian bandwagoners) this is a mixed blessing. On the positive side of the ledger, it increases the odds that their side will win in any war between the balancers and the rising challenger, but on the negative side it also increases the bargaining position and threat posed by the rising challenger.

Despite these various preferences for the value of common defense, the effects on the likelihood of bandwagoning or hiding – once a decision to not balance has been made – all run in the same direction. The higher $\frac{n_T}{N}(x) - \alpha(\beta+\gamma)$ is the less attractive bandwagoning is and the more attracting hiding becomes. This is because the challenger is less likely to win any war and less likely to extract significant concessions from potential balancers to avoid war. Thus, the rewards of bandwagoning will be smaller and less certain while the risks of hiding from the challenger will be reduced.

The next material factor to consider is the benefit from national defense $(x - c_{bal})\delta^{t-1}$. As with balancing, states receive this regardless of what other states do. Its value should simply depend on the benefit of possessing those arms compared with the cost of acquiring them. The effect of this factor for both types of bandwagoners should be similar. Individual military strength should be useful for obtaining more spoils, being successful in any war with balancers, and protecting one's self from the challenger.

The implications of the national defense variable are much more complicated for hiders as the cost of acquiring arms for them is not exclusively financial. One might argue that states which are hiding would unambiguously benefit from a strong national defense and could engage in a sort of armed neutrality. This presumably is true for states that are of roughly the same power as the states from which they are hiding. For small states hiding from great powers, however, this may not be true. To the extent that a balancer or the challenger sees the hiding state's military buildup as a latent threat, the cost of acquiring said defense may not be worth it.[2] Yet, this does not tell us whether a state will hide, only that a relatively weak hider may prefer to not build its military as any security gains from greater capabilities would be more than offset by the greater animosity of its far more powerful potential enemies. Thus, while a higher value of common defense means states should be more likely to hide than bandwagon, a higher level of national defense does not affect the propensity to bandwagon or hide, though a preference for hiding could result in a weaker defense under certain conditions.

Nature of the challenger

Whether states opt to bandwagon or hide should also depend on their estimates of α, i.e., how revisionist the challenger is. At least initially, increasing estimates of revisionism in the challenger's nature, α, should encourage bandwagoning, both for more status quo and more revisionist non-balancing states. A challenger with a very low level of revisionism should be easy to hide from and is unlikely to provide much in the way of spoils anyway. Thus, there should be no need for and few rewards from bandwagoning. As the challenger appears to be more revisionist, the threat it poses and potential rewards it offers grow.

At some point, however, this relationship should break down. While an incredibly revisionist state should make hiding very unattractive, one could imagine that bandwagoning with such a state would also be frightening, especially for more status quo, Waltian type states. Most likely, more status quo leaning states would ultimately be forced into balancing by an extremely revisionist state, thereby preempting the question whether they would be more likely to hide or bandwagon.[3] If such states had determined balancing was a lost cause and yet believed the challenger to be so revisionist as to make bandwagoning also impossible, they likely would find it best to hide until the last possible moment hoping something would turn up and when that failed, to rely on their own insufficiently prepared defenses.

Even revisionist, 'jackal' type states in Schweller's framework might find partnering with such a state difficult and dangerous. Certainly, Hitler's allies ran risks of being dismembered or otherwise harmed by Germany – yet, Hitler did have allies. The same is true of Napoleon and many other highly aggressive conquerors in history – provided those states appeared likely to win. Still, it seems as though there must be a point at which even revisionist states would opt not to bandwagon. Yet, what is their alternative? Hiding is a poor option in the face of a sufficiently powerful state with nearly unlimited aims. True, some might be encouraged to balance out of fear, but this too could be a path to destruction. Why risk defeat and dismemberment to uphold a status quo it wishes to significantly alter? Surely, it is better to take what rewards are available and hope that they will not be swallowed up once they are no longer useful. Besides, being eaten last is better than being eaten first. Thus, increasing revisionism for the most part should increase the rate of bandwagoning and decrease the rate of hiding despite the inherent dangers involved.

Nature of the opportunity

The nature of the opportunity, γ, should also matter. The more the challenger's move threatens the status quo and is done for that purpose, rather than for the intrinsic value of the move itself, the more this should push states to bandwagon rather than hide. Revisionist states will be encouraged to seek spoils by a move which threatens to undermine the prevailing status quo and heartened that the challenger is unlikely to settle for limited gains. Bandwagoning states need much of the existing order to be upset for them to obtain spoils. Thus, a challenge which does not appear likely to alter the status quo in dramatic ways does not hold out much hope for significant rewards for bandwagoning.

Likewise, a limited move is unlikely to threaten more status quo states. Remember, we are thinking about states that have already decided not to balance or defend, so presumably the move is not aimed directly at them. Thus, an opportunity that seems unlikely to upset the overall power structure or which is being done because the challenger intrinsically values the move should make hiding appear more attractive. This should be true both for more revisionist states and more security seeking states.

Expected value of promised spoils

An obvious factor in determining whether states bandwagon or hide is the expected value of the spoils being promised. This depends on several things. First, the raw scale of what is being offered matters. What is the size and productivity of the territory being promised? How much economic or military aid is being offered? How valuable are other concessions like recognition of a government or the promise of a defensive pact? For all of these factors the more being offered, the better as far as the likelihood of bandwagoning is concerned.

Second, how credible are these promises? Can and will the offering state deliver? The more credible the offers, the more likely states will bandwagon rather than hide. Most obviously this depends on how trustworthy the state offering the spoils is. Of course, this may be unknown, but states must make efforts to guess at the likelihood that a state will renege on its promises and will base such estimates in part on the reputation the promising state has for following through on similar promises in the past. Just as important is trying to figure out whether the state can deliver its promises. Perhaps the most crucial element of this is whether the promised spoils depend upon winning a war – something that is generally true of territorial spoils. This is so because states usually offer the territory of other states rather than their own as rewards, though there are exceptions to this.[4] The outcome of the potential war of course almost always matters for states which are geographically proximate to the conflict as they risk being invaded. Such states, however, could conceivably be fairly confident of warding off attacks while being less sanguine about the prospects of conquering the promised territories. Yet, they may be able to retain territories given to them by their own allies regardless of the war's outcome. Non-territorial promises may be even less dependent upon the outcome of a war. For instance, Thailand, South Korea, and the Philippines all joined the US war effort in Vietnam in large part due to promises of economic and military aid from the United States (Shirkey 2009, 186–93). These states knew that the aid was guaranteed to arrive regardless of the outcome of the war.

The credibility of these promises is of course tied back to the relative power of the prospective coalitions. The more powerful the challenger's coalition, the higher the odds it will win and the more able it will be to provide spoils. However, a very strong challenger would not need to provide spoils as it would not need to attract bandwagoners to its side in order to win. Thus, the expected size of spoils should have a curvilinear relationship with the challenger's power, with the smallest expected spoils coming from either very weak or very powerful challengers.[5]

Other factors: The roles of geography, institutions, and economics

Three other factors merit consideration: geography, institutions, and economics. First, the geographic position of states should also have an impact on their decisions about hiding and bandwagoning. Smaller states that are geographically removed from potential aid from great powers have a harder time balancing against great power threats (Walt 1987). It is not just distance, but the nature of that distance. Is the great power challenger positioned such that it can block aid from reaching the smaller power? This was certainly true for the states of East Central Europe considered in Chapter 5. Germany was positioned between them and any potential assistance coming from Britain or France. This made their strategic environment fundamentally different from that of say Belgium. Thus, perhaps it is not surprising that few of these states opted to balance. Of course, a revisionist state could be in a similar predicament where it is cut off from aid coming from the challenger. Such a state would be unlikely to bandwagon out of fear of being isolated and defeated by balancers.

Yet as suggested above, simply knowing a state is unlikely to balance, does not answer the question of what policy that state will actually pursue. Geography again helps answer this question. The small European states which managed to hide *successfully* during World War II were all either on the periphery of Europe away from the most intense fighting (e.g., Sweden, Turkey, and Portugal) or were protected by extremely difficult, mountainous geography as in the case of Switzerland (Fox 1959).[6] Also, none were the focus of revisionist territorial aims, unlike several of the states covered below. This is not to claim such distance is necessary. Denmark and the Netherlands for instance both managed to hide successfully during World War One and many proximate states tried to hide in World War II, albeit unsuccessfully. Nor is it sufficient. Despite being fairly removed from the heart of the conflict, states such as Norway, Iceland, and Iran were all occupied during the war, the latter two by the allies. Still, favorable geography should encourage hiding. Thus, states should be more likely to attempt to hide if they are protected by their geography and can reasonably believe the fighting will pass them by, whereas states which are cut off from potential sources of aid are less likely to align with the coalition from which they are isolated.

Second, international institutions should affect the likelihood states would balance. Including the role of institutions is important as international relations is an institutionalized domain (Keohane, Haftendorn, and Wallander 1999). Such institutions could include not only multilateral international organizations, but also alliances.[7] Institutions matter because they can act as fora for communicating and coordinating with other states which face the same security challenges. Such institutions help reduce the diplomatic isolation that can prompt security seeking states to bandwagon or hide. States can find reassurance that they will not be alone in opposing the rising challenger nor the only one missing out on potential spoils. Also, organizations can help facilitate balancing by mediating disputes between potential balancers, reducing transaction costs, facilitating side payments, and coercing norm-breakers (Axelrod and Keohane 1985; Keohane 1982; Keohane and Nye 1974; Russett and Oneal 2001; Wallander and Keohane 1999). This latter factor matters because rising challengers often buck existing norms. The upholding of norms, therefore, could facilitate balancing. Finally, such institutions can act as a credible check on the aspirations of the rising state by reducing the odds that state will be able to provide significant spoils to states which bandwagon with it. This means even revisionist states seeking spoils should be less likely to bandwagon due to the presence of powerful multilateral organizations. Given that such revisionist states make up much of the pool of states which bandwagon (Schweller 1994), this effect of institutions is empirically important. Taken together, these independent effects of institutions add up to a considerable factor in determining the likelihood of whether states balance, bandwagon, or hide.

Finally, states which are economically dependent on the challenger and which lack credible substitutes for their economic relationships with the rising state – including trade, investment, and aid – are more likely to bandwagon with the challenger than are states which have a variety of important international economic connections, are economically interdependent rather than unidirectionally dependent upon the challenger, or have plausible substitutes for their economic ties with the challenger should those ties be severed (Hirschman 1980). Even if such states are not compelled to bandwagon with the challenger, they may opt to hide rather than balance in hopes of preserving their economic relationships. In effect, states which have multilateral economic ties and which are interdependent with a variety of states rather than economically dependent on the rising challenger are less constrained and have more foreign policy options available to them.

Transcending: The outside option

So far all of the policy options considered have taken the conflict posed by the rising challenger as given. In the face of the conflict, states can choose a side or try to stay out of it by hiding, but is this a realistic set of options? Can nothing be done about the conflict itself? Schroeder (1994) suggests states have another, if difficult, option: transcending. Often, taking either side or hiding from the conflict will appear unattractive, impossible, or both. For instance, Greco-Turkish disputes during the Cold War posed difficult challenges for their fellow NATO members who did not want to see a conflict between members weaken the alliance. Taking a side or hiding would have done nothing to resolve this issue. Likewise, during the run up to the Crimean War, Austria was faced with its closest ally, Russia, pursuing a policy in the Balkans that was highly inimical to Austrian interests. Neither opposing nor aiding Russia would help as either policy would weaken Austria's strategic position. The former would mean the loss of an ally and the latter the loss of Austrian influence among its neighbors (Schroeder 1972). Hiding ran the risk of both alienating the Russians while still losing out in the Balkans. Thus, all of the policies considered so far would have proven disastrous.

In such situations and indeed even at times when another option may be palatable but well short of ideal, states may try to transcend the situation by solving the conflict or radically reorienting political alignments. Obviously, this is difficult. Were it easy, there would be peace in the Middle East, no dispute over Kashmir, and no frozen conflict zones in the Russian near abroad to cite just a few examples. Still, states do often try to find ways out of what appear to be unavoidable conflicts and even sometimes succeed. Presumably, such successes should be more likely for powerful states dealing with smaller states than for states dealing with peers or small states trying to resolve conflicts between great powers. Returning to the examples above, the United States, as both Greece's and Turkey's strongest ally, had many economic and political levers it could use to tamp down the conflict between those states, whereas ultimately Austria lacked the necessary leverage to find a way to transcend the dispute between Russia on the one side and Britain and France on the other. Given the enormous pressures and often poor options the states of East Central Europe faced prior to World War II, it would not be surprising if they made attempts to find a way out of the apparently intractable bind posed by Germany's rise and Britain's and France's apparent weakness. Likewise, given these states' limited leverage, any such efforts would most likely fail.

Putting it all together: What factors matter for bandwagoning and hiding

Thus, several things should matter for whether a state opts to bandwagon or hide: the relative distribution of material capabilities between the challenger's coalition and any balancing coalition; the nature of the challenger; the nature of the opportunity; the expected value of promised spoils; international institutions; economic ties; and geographic position. The more favorable the distribution of capabilities is from the prospective of the challenger, the more likely bandwagoning is to occur. Likewise, the more disruptive to the status quo the nature of the opportunity is, the more likely bandwagoning is to occur. The nature of the challenger is more complex as an aggressive challenger is more likely to fully disrupt the status quo, but such aggression may be correlated with less believable commitments – both in regards to promised spoils and to not harming allies down the road. Still, it seems likely that a more aggressive and revisionist challenger should be more likely to prompt bandwagoning rather than hiding. Likewise, weak institutions should prompt bandwagoning. Finally, greater and more credible promises of spoils, greater geographic proximity to the challenger, and being economically dependent upon the challenger all increase the odds of bandwagoning.

Of these, the model in Chapter 2 suggested the relative distribution of capabilities should be the most important factor when it comes to balancing. This should be true for bandwagoning as well. If there is reasonable certainty about the distribution of capabilities, potential bandwagoners can make fairly informed choices about the likelihood of success of a revisionist coalition. Given that any proffered spoils would likely depend on such success, the balance of capabilities drives that factor as well. It also potentially influences geography as a successful challenger could draw closer to a state which is considering hiding if the challenger defeats and annexes parts of its opponents that lie in between it and the potential hider. Finally, Chapter 2 showed that uncertainty over the distribution of capabilities was far more problematic for the formation of a balancing coalition than was uncertainty over other factors. The more likely the formation of an effective balancing coalition, the less attractive bandwagoning, and the more attractive hiding, becomes. This is yet another reason the distribution of capabilities is crucial for understanding decisions about bandwagoning and hiding. Ironically, for small states, since they can do little to influence the relative balance of forces, these calculations end up hinging as much on estimates of the intentions of potential balancers as they do on estimates of capabilities directly, though of course as argued above and in Chapter 2 the potential balancers' intentions are driven in no small part by the balancers' own estimates of relative capabilities. Thus, states are most likely to worry about uncertainty over the distribution of capabilities and change behavior as their estimates of capabilities change. This is not to suggest that changes in the other variables would have no effect on a state's policy; they would. Rather it suggests that while changes in all of these variables would be reflected in the policies of states, the effects of changes in the relative distribution of capabilities would be the most pronounced. These hypotheses are explored in the next chapter in cases on Polish, Yugoslav, Romanian, and Hungarian foreign policy from the mid-1930s up to their entries into World War II.

Notes

1. Schroeder (1994) suggests states often try to hide from or transcend threats instead of balancing against or bandwagoning with them.
2. This is the central dynamic of the security dilemma (Herz 1950; Jervis 1978).
3. See Chapters 1 and 2.
4. For instance to induce Bulgaria to join the Central Powers in World War One, the Ottoman Empire ceded the Maritsa enclave to the Bulgarians (Holden 1976, 163–5). Despite being badly defeated in World War One, Bulgaria retained a small portion of the formerly Turkish Maritsa enclave.
5. Though the relationship should be curvilinear, there is no reason to expect that the value of spoils would be normally distributed.
6. Switzerland's long history of neutrality probably played a role as well, though such a history did not protect the Netherlands from occupation.
7. See Gelpi (1999); Richardson (1999); Tams (1999); and Tuschoff (1999) for examples of treating alliances as institutions.

5 To bandwagon or hide II

East Central Europe before World War II

The rise of Nazi Germany in the 1930s placed the states of East Central Europe in a difficult spot. A strengthened, risk acceptant, and highly revisionist Germany necessarily altered the security environment of the region and presented the states therein with both serious dangers and new opportunities. This chapter examines the foreign policies of four of those states: Poland, Yugoslavia, Romania, and Hungary. These states faced challenges and opportunities far different from those faced by Britain and France. They were far weaker vis-à-vis Germany, were in a quite different geographic position being sandwiched between two potentially hostile great powers,[1] and several were revisionist in their outlook. Thus, international relations theory and our models from Chapters 1 and 2 suggest they should be less likely to balance than the great powers covered in Chapter 3. In actuality these states exhibited a wide range of behaviors including balancing, bandwagoning, and hiding. All of them struggled mightily with which policy or policies to adopt and often shifted from one approach to another in the hope of finding a strategy that would work. In the end, the problems they faced proved insolvable. Poland and Romania lost significant territory as the result of the war. Worse, all four states were occupied by hostile powers and their regimes permanently overthrown.[2]

While the four states examined do not provide a comprehensive survey of the states in the region – the policies of Albania, Austria, Bulgaria, Czechoslovakia, and Greece are not examined – they are a reasonable sample. The four had a variety of relationships with the other states in the region, ranging from alliance to enmity. Likewise, their relations with France varied. Also, their proximity to and history with Germany differed. Finally, one of them was an early target of German revisionism, while the other three were potential allies of Germany. Two of the four did eventually become German allies, while the other two became victims of Hitler's aggression. Yet, these outcomes with the possible exception of the invasion of Poland were not forgone conclusions in the mid-1930s. None of the states fully trusted the Nazi regime. All felt threatened by German power and yet at one point or another each cooperated with Berlin. In other words, these four states allow for a variety of initial conditions, goals, and geo-strategic positions to be explored. Also, their stance toward Germany and their proclivity to balance, bandwagon, or simply hide shifted over time. As will be seen, these shifts in foreign policy fit well with the above hypotheses. The states will be addressed one at a time, beginning with Poland.

Poland

With the exception of small territorial disputes with Czechoslovakia, Poland in the 1930s was a status quo power, possessing significant territories which were claimed by the Germans and Soviets.[3] Obviously, Poland was too weak to confront both Germany and the Soviet Union alone and thus had formed an alliance with France in the early 1920s. Events from the mid-1920s onward, however, had led Poland to question the value of the French alliance. First, the Treaty of Locarno in 1925 had raised the possibility of the revision of Germany's eastern frontiers in return for an acceptance of its western frontiers (Sakwa 1973, 126). This, along with France's refusal to define the nature of the cooperation required by the Franco-Polish alliance, weakened ties with France and convinced Józef Piłsudski, the leading political figure in interwar Poland until his death in 1935, and his ideological heir, foreign minister Józef Beck, of the need for closer ties with Germany (Cienciala 1992, 80–2). Worse from a Polish perspective, the lack of French reaction to the remilitarization of the Rhineland by Germany in 1936 and the subsequent fortification of that region by the Germans raised questions both as to France's willingness to resist German revisionism and also the ability of the French army to launch successful attacks into Germany to relieve pressure on the Poles in the event of an eastward German move (Sakwa 1973, 129; Wandycz 1981, 560). The Polish ambassador to France, Alfred Chłapowski, argued that the remilitarization would force France to resign its

> historic role as a participant in the shaping of the destinies of Europe ... Central Europe and Poland would as a result of this be compelled to rely solely on their own strength; their position would be menaced as in spite of the manning of a defense line facing France, the Germans would still have enormous military units at their disposal which would be quite sufficient to attack other neighbours.
>
> (Sakwa 1973, 129)

During the Rhineland crisis Poland, along with Belgium and Czechoslovakia, declared fidelity to France and waited for Paris to act. Beck also tried in vain to use the crisis to reinvigorate and strengthen the Franco-Polish alliance (Wandycz 1988b, 435–44). When no action came, Franco-Polish relations suffered significantly (Sakwa 1973, 193).

After the remilitarization, Beck placed new emphasis on maintaining good relations with Germany. This did not reflect a naivety about German intentions. In a June 1938 conversation with the US Ambassador to Poland, Drexel Biddle, Beck expressed concerns that Berlin would seek to annex Gdańsk, the Polish Corridor, and Upper Silesia. He also expressed concerns about the effects of German control of Czechoslovakia should that come to pass. Rather, the emphasis on improving relations with Germany was a result of Beck's fear of Germany. Given the reduced likelihood of France protecting Poland, perhaps the tensions with Germany could be resolved through diplomacy. Still, throughout 1938, Beck remained willing to fight on the French side if it came to that. Biddle observed as much stating that,

> Beck, moreover, is aware that the combined armies of Poland, her ally Romania, possibly Yugoslavia and Hungary, and even Czechoslovakia, would potentially present an effective resistance to a German eastward military action, provided the British and French forces simultaneously engaged the Germans on the German Western Front. Though Poland and Czechoslovakia, fighting side by side might form incongruous military bedmates, their geopolitical positions are at least vis-à-vis Germany similar, and an actual German aggression might conceivably throw them on the same side, particularly if Poland were assured of synchronous [sic] forceful action on the part of Britain and France in the West. Besides, in such an event, Poland would march not for Czechoslovakia, but against Germany.
> (Cienciala 1992, 89)

If the French were unwilling to act, however, Beck saw no reason to further worsen relations with Berlin as this could only endanger Poland (Prazmowska 1986, 855; Sakwa 1973, 133–4). Beck had noted to Biddle that he believed Britain would seek a peaceful resolution and France would be forced to follow suit (Cienciala 1992, 87–8). By the time the Munich crisis came around in 1938, Beck was convinced both by previous British and French inaction and by their leaders' current statements that the western powers were unlikely to fight for Czechoslovakia (Sakmyster 1980, 153). Specifically, he was aware that Halifax had assured the Germans in November 1937 that Britain was not opposed to peaceful border changes in Central Europe – a position Chamberlain made public in March 1938 (Cienciala 1992, 84–5). He had also come to view the vacillating western powers with contempt (Wandycz 1988a, 25). Thus, he felt that he might as well use the crisis to extract territorial concessions from Czechoslovakia around the city of Těšín, especially as some of the territory Poland claimed was also claimed by Berlin and thus in danger of falling into German hands if Poland did not advance its claims. Beck did not present the Polish ultimatum to Czechoslovakia until after Britain and France conceded to German demands, thereby preserving Poland's freedom of action to fight the Germans alongside the western powers and Prague if it came to that (Cienciala 1989, 687–8; 1992, 82). Indeed, a member of Beck's staff told Sir Robert Vansittart, the British Permanent Under-Secretary of State for Foreign Affairs explicitly that Poland would fight alongside Britain and France if they resisted, but otherwise would annex the area around Těšín (Hitchins 1994, 90–1).[4] Similarly in April 1938, in a conversation with Léon Nöel, the French Ambassador to Poland, Beck had expressed both his worries about German expansionism after the *Anschluss*, his belief that only France could stop Germany, and his concerns that France would not act. Beck told Nöel that he believed there were three possible outcomes for the Sudetenland crisis. The best outcome would be for France and Britain to strongly back Czechoslovakia in which case Beck foresaw concessions to German and Polish minorities, but no territorial changes. Barring strong western action, however, Beck feared that the worst outcome, de facto German control of all of Czechoslovakia, was a distinct possibility. The most likely outcome in Beck's eyes was the total disintegration of Czechoslovakia, in which case Poland would attempt to obtain a common border with Hungary so as to coordinate with Hungary in containing Germany (Cienciala 1992, 86–8).[5] This desire for a common border with Hungary – a desire Budapest had long shared – led Poland to back Hungarian claims to the Carpatho-Ukraine,[6] though as discussed below in the Hungarian case nothing much came of this attempted coordination (Cienciala 1992, 83; Wandycz 1981, 556).

After Munich, Poland continued its attempts to resolve German claims on Gdańsk and the Polish Corridor through diplomacy, but with little success. The Poles offered to ease German transit across the corridor and to convert Gdańsk from a free city under the auspices of the League of Nations to a joint Polish–German condominium. The Poles also hoped, with German encouragement, that when the conflict between the Soviet Union and Germany materialized, the Germans would find the Poles a ready and useful ally (Herman 1980, 581; Prazmowska 1986, 857–9). The attitude of Józef Lipski, the Polish Ambassador to Germany, was typical in remarking that "the highest bodies in the Third Reich are well aware that in resolving the future Russian problem the Germans will not be able to take action without us" (Prazmowska 1986, 858).

Certainly, the British were of little help to the Poles in late 1938 and early 1939. London remained sympathetic to German aims of territorial revisions in the east. Beck correctly believed that Britain was trying to detach France from its Central European allies and hoped that Germany would move east rather than west (Prazmowska 1986, 860). Indeed, even after Britain guaranteed Polish territory on March 30, London still pressed Poland to negotiate over Gdańsk and refused to grant Poland a loan for rearmament (Prazmowska 1986, 867–8). The whole point of the guarantee seems to have been to encourage Berlin to negotiate rather than to actually contain the Germans (Cienciala 1989, 688). When newspapers owned by Lord Beaverbrook stated that the guarantee did not apply to Gdańsk or the Polish Corridor, the British Foreign Office rebutted the claim in only the weakest of terms, naturally infuriating Beck and casting further doubt on British resolve (Herman 1980, 589). Throughout the pre-invasion crisis, the British and French refused Polish offers of staff talks to coordinate military strategy and never would commit to attack the western German border (Prazmowska 1986, 869–70).[7]

Because of this noncommittal stance from Paris and London, as the crisis worsened over 1939 Beck seemed more intent to avoid angering the Germans than building up his alliances. Beck rebuffed the British suggestion of four-power cooperation (Britain, France, Poland, and the Soviet Union) out of fear any association with the Soviets would simply provoke Hitler (Prazmowska 1986, 862–5; Strang 1996, 737). In the end, Beck refused to make territorial concessions to the Germans and hoped staunch resistance would force them to back down. He stated that, "I consider that in the event of any attempt to barter our interest I will decisively take action against Germany, against the League of Nations and finally against any allied power which would participate in the deal" (Prazmowska

1986, 871). He was not alone in his determination to resist. Polish notes from one conference with the Germans read as follows:

> This enemy is a troublesome element, since it seems that he is losing the means of thinking and acting. He might recover that measure once he encounters determined opposition, which hitherto he has not met with. The mighty have been humble to him, and the weak have capitulated in advance, even at the cost of honour. The Germans are marching all across Europe with nine divisions; with such strength Poland would not be overcome. Hitler and his associates know that, so that the question of a political contest with us will not be like the others.
>
> (Prazmowska 1986, 863)

Thus, Poland moved from balancing against the German threat to limited bandwagoning as the odds of British and French aid diminished. Hiding was never much of an option due to geographic proximity and the fact Germany aimed to reacquire the Polish Corridor. Transcending was briefly attempted by suggesting the Germans focus on the Soviet Union which threatened both Poland and Germany. In bandwagoning, the Poles both hoped to satisfy limited revisionist aims and also to protect themselves from the German threat through a mixture of accommodation and making themselves useful to the Germans. When this too failed, the Poles fell back on grim resolve, poorly coordinated balancing, and ultimately a hopeless military defense. This failure to find a way out led to a half century of occupation – first by the Germans and then by the Soviets.

Yugoslavia

Yugoslavia entered the mid-1930s with a diplomatic orientation that seemingly would have disposed it to balance against a rising Germany. It had been allied to France since late 1927 and along with Czechoslovakia and Romania was a member of the Little Entente, an alliance created in February 1934 to prevent Hungary from retaking the territories lost to its neighbors at the end of World War I (Mirkovich 1941, 131). Yugoslavia along with Greece, Turkey, and Romania was also a member of the Balkan Entente which strove to preserve the territorial status quo in the region.[8] This pro-French, pro-status quo orientation was the preferred policy of King Alexander I. It was severely undermined by his assassination in Marseille on October 9, 1934 by the Bulgarian Vlado Chernozemski in league with Ustaše Croatian dissidents during a state visit to France.[9]

This involvement of a Bulgarian and Croats in the assassination was but the most visible sign of the ethnic divisions and regional tensions which weakened Yugoslavia in the pre-war period. Though the Serbs were strongly pro-French, the Croats and Slovenes were not. Even Croats and Slovenes loyal to the regime were far less willing to take risks in the name of confronting Germany and Italy than were the Serbs. Throughout the crises which led up to the German invasion in 1941 the Yugoslav government was aware that if it leaned too far one direction or the other, not only did it risk ruin at the international level, but it also risked civil war at worst or waging an interstate war without the support of half of its populace at best (Hoptner 1962; Mirkovich 1941, 141; Rothschild 1977, 264).

Alexander's death led to foreign policy being directed by the Regent, Prince Paul, for the remainder of the interwar period. Between June 1935 and February 1939 he was aided in this by Prime Minister Milan Stojadinović. Though political rivals, both Paul and Stojadinović favored a more neutral policy course than Alexander had pursued. However, they did so for slightly different reasons. While both were ultimately driven to this course by caution, Paul was favorably disposed to the Allies, and Stojadinović held a favorable view of Germany. Even before the Rhineland crisis, Stojadinović believed Yugoslavia was too weak to effectively oppose the rising revisionist powers in Europe. He told Paul on September 20, 1935 that Yugoslavia needed to lay low and should be "as wise as serpents and as harmless as doves ... So long as France does not decide which side it will go, we have no reason to run out ahead of the great powers" (Hoptner 1962, 36–7).

Both men perceived Italy as the greatest threat to Yugoslavia, but feared direct opposition to Mussolini would lead to ruin. For a time, Yugoslavia's difficulties with Italy further undermined relations with France. This resulted from France's efforts to build a Mediterranean coalition to oppose Germany. France attempted to mediate between Yugoslavia and Italy, but this resulted only in a growing distrust of France in Belgrade (Hoptner 1962, 24). This growing distrust was further reinforced by France's weakness exhibited during the Rhineland crisis (Kaufman 1992, 433). Yugoslavia, along with the other members of the Little Entente, had encouraged Paris to resist the remilitarization to no avail (Hoptner 1962, 44). The supine French behavior led Stojadinović to rebuff Leon Blum's attempts to strengthen the Franco-Yugoslav accord, complaining that, "We are compelled to reckon with the German danger which you have permitted to grow and flourish" (Hoptner 1962, 90). This worsening of relations was not lost on Paris. Daladier, at that time serving as the French Minister of Defense, noted that the French "attitude to the events of 7 March had shaken the Little Entente" (Alexander 1992, 81).

Discussions with Britain were at least as discouraging. In May 1936, Božidar Purić, the Yugoslav Ambassador to France, sounded out the British to see if they would be of more help in countering the Italian threat. The replies he got from Eden were so discouraging as to any role that Britain was likely to play in the coming struggle, he reported to Stojadinović that "certain circles in London have given up ... and liquidated the agreement with France" (Hoptner 1962, 51).

This downgrading of French and British support led Belgrade to try to assume a more neutral stance.[10] First, Stojadinović tried to reduce Yugoslavia's commitments to Czechoslovakia – most noticeably by rebuffing Beneš' attempts to turn the Little Entente into a general defense pact (Mirkovich 1941, 134). Second, hard on the heels of the Rhineland crisis, Yugoslavia and Italy signed several agreements in 1936 and 1937, including a non-aggression pact, a trade agreement, and a settlement of border disputes (Adamthwaite 1977, 46–7; Alexander 1992, 220–1; Hoptner 1962, 57–82). Finally, Stojadinović turned to Berlin for help in resisting the Italians. The Germans were eager to mediate the dispute and also offered an economic aid package. Stojadinović was relieved that aid could be found in Germany if needed, but declined the mediation for the present, preferring to chart a neutral course (Hoptner 1962, 46–7 and 87–8).[11] Stojadinović justified this more neutral course in a conversation with Purić in March 1937 by stating that given France's "lack of firmness in dealing with Germany on the question of the Rhineland ... one can understand why we want to achieve a policy of equilibrium in relations with all the great powers. A relationship which will not blindly bind us to any one of them" (Hoptner 1962, 91). In other words, Stojadinović now lacked confidence that France would effectively oppose Germany, and therefore Yugoslavia could not rely solely on the French alliance but rather must have a more independent stance so that it could reposition itself diplomatically as needed. He was not seeking an alliance with Germany.

The Germans made several efforts to turn this movement toward neutrality into a pro-Axis stance. Berlin hoped to be able to weaken Yugoslavia's ties to Czechoslovakia and France. As part of a diplomatic offensive in 1936 aimed mainly at winning over Romania, the Germans attempted to woo the Yugoslavs as well – even at the expense of German–Hungarian relations (Sakmyster 1980, 72–5). Ultimately, the Germans shifted tactics and tried to undo the Little Entente by bringing about Hungarian–Yugoslav rapprochement. Hermann Göring went as far as visiting Yugoslavia in November 1937 (Sakmyster 1980, 109). The effort bore limited fruit as the Stojadinović regime insisted on remaining neutral.[12]

The Germans were even less successful in getting Belgrade to abandon Prague. Even though Stojadinović had opposed Beneš' attempts to increase Yugoslavia's commitment to Czechoslovakia, his government was in no way favorable to the destruction of Czechoslovakia. The potential dismembering of Czechoslovakia posed a serious threat to Yugoslavia. Not only would the already threatening power of Germany grow, but also a strong Czechoslovakia was key to keeping Hungarian revisionism in check. Indeed, Hungary could potentially benefit directly from the division of Czechoslovakia by annexing parts of Slovakia. Nor was this all; Yugoslavia imported much of its military equipment from the Škoda munition works in Czechoslovakia (Rothschild 1977, 263; Wandycz 1981, 554). Finally and most ominously, the fragmentation of an ethnic polyglot state like Czechoslovakia would set a dangerous precedent for the even more ethnically diverse Yugoslav state (Rothschild 1977, 259–63).

Thus, prior to the Sudetenland crisis, Yugoslavia was neutral at best from a German perspective. Berlin was no doubt pleased that Yugoslavia, much like Poland, Hungary, and Romania, did not oppose the *Anschluss*, even though it brought the Germans up to the Yugoslav border and weakened Czechoslovakia's defensive position (Sakmyster 1980, 117–19). This equivocal stance on the *Anschluss* on Belgrade's part was due more to the fact that it meant Italy's influence in Austria was broken and the threat of a Habsburg restoration fully eliminated than to any skillful German diplomacy (Hoptner 1962, 110–12). The weakened Italian position led the Yugoslav General Staff to conclude that Germany and not Italy was now the biggest threat facing Yugoslavia (Hoptner 1962, 114).

When the Sudetenland crisis first erupted in the spring of 1938, Belgrade initially indicated a willingness to back Prague. During the May phase of the crisis, Stojadinović assured Kamil Krofta, the Czechoslovak Foreign Minister, that Yugoslavia would hold Hungary in check (Sakmyster 1980, 168). Yet, the Yugoslavs apparently continued to play both sides, saying one thing to the Czechoslovaks and Romanians and another to the Italians and Germans (Sakmyster 1980, 186). Contrary to Stojadinović's reassurances to the Czechoslovaks, both Göring and Count Galeazzo Ciano, the Italian Foreign Minister, in an attempt to get the Hungarians to pressure Prague, insisted Stojadinović had told them that if war resulted Yugoslavia would remain neutral (Sakmyster 1980, 174). The main problem was that Paul did not see how Yugoslavia could do much to help Czechoslovakia without Italian neutrality and robust French and British action, conditions that seemed less and less likely to be fulfilled as the crisis unfolded (Hoptner 1962, 114–17). Ultimately, as it became clear in the autumn that Czechoslovakia would be forced to concede, Belgrade did what it could to minimize the damage. On September 20, 1938, along with the Romanians, the Yugoslavs agreed to moderate improvements in the treatment of ethnic Magyars in their territories in the hopes of preventing Hungary from being allowed to annex the entire Felvidék region of Slovakia (Hoptner 1962, 113–17; Sakmyster 1980, 202–3). Even so, Belgrade never relented to Berlin's insistence that it declare itself neutral in the event of a war over the Sudetenland (Hoptner 1962, 117). The policy of steering a middle course continued.

The signing of the Munich Pact in October 1938 eliminated Czechoslovakia as a military power and thus completely undid the Little Entente. With one of its potential allies hopelessly crippled and it clear that France would not intervene effectively in the affairs of East Central Europe, any hope for Yugoslavia being able to balance against the rising Fascist powers was permanently removed. Purić in particular was now convinced that all British and French promises were worthless, making it vital for Yugoslav policy to remain flexible (Hoptner 1962, 119).

Stojadinović's instincts were to move closer to the Axis camp. In conjunction with the Romanians, he scrambled to make the Balkan Entente appear to be consistent with German aims (Mirkovich 1941, 135). Yugoslavia even slowed rearmament – in part because it no longer had a place to purchase arms from – but also out of fears that rearmament would provoke the Germans (Mirkovich 1941, 131). These pro-Axis policies, combined with the proto-Fascist orientations of Stojadinović's domestic supporters, led Paul to conclude Stojadinović was a danger that needed to be removed. Paul, therefore, replaced Stojadinović as Prime Minister with Dragiša Cvetković in February 1939 (Hoptner 1962, 120–2, 128 and 229).[13]

The strategic situation continued to deteriorate over the course of 1939. Italy occupied Albania in April and by June Paul was convinced a European war was inevitable. Growing German influence in the Balkans resulted in Belgrade striking a trade and military aid agreement with Berlin on July 5 (Steiner 2011, 953). Despite these closer ties, Belgrade resisted German pressure to leave the League of Nations and join the Anti-Comintern Pact. Instead, Belgrade declared to all the great powers that it would remain neutral and unarmed in any upcoming conflict (Hoptner 1962, 143 and 147).

Despite this professed neutrality, under Paul's direction Belgrade continued to try to find ways to productively cooperate with the Allies. Right after the German invasion of Poland in September 1939, Paul asked the French to occupy Salonika in Greece to preserve Yugoslavia's last remaining supply line to the West. The French declined, saying it would take three months to find the necessary troops, and the British opposed the move as they feared it would bring Italy into the war on the German side (Hoptner 1962, 170). Despite this setback, Belgrade continued inconclusive military talks with Paris right up to the French collapse in May 1940 (Hoptner 1962, 171–80).[14]

France's defeat was but the first of a series of events between May 1940 and March 1941 which made Belgrade's position increasingly untenable. In June 1940, the Soviet Union occupied Bessarabia and northern Bukovina in Romania, pushing Romania toward the Axis camp and opening up the question of further territorial revisions in the Balkans. This was quickly followed in August by the Second Vienna Award in which Hungary received Transylvania from Romania through the arbitration of Germany and Italy. Bulgaria knuckled under to German pressure and acceded to the Tripartite Pact in September. October brought the Italian invasion of Greece from Albania, potentially threatening Salonika. The German military moved into Romania in January 1941 and then into Bulgaria in early March, completing Yugoslavia's encirclement. The difficult position in which these events placed the Yugoslav government was aptly summarized by the Foreign Minister, Aleksandar Cincar-Marković:

> From the moment of the military action of Soviet Russia and the annexation of Bessarabia the difficulties of the Royal Government became apparent. This led to open territorial requests by Bulgaria and Hungary. The situation became worse with the Vienna arbitration and the German military penetration of Rumania, upon which Italy's war on Greece followed. It is clear that under those conditions we today are not in the position to lead any other policy but the policy of self-defense: our country is not in the position to carry on a war except in the case of foreign aggression. Our efforts to maintain peace in the Balkans were unsuccessful. Under present circumstances we are forced to find a solution bargaining with Germany on a diplomatic plan, a solution which will permit us to continue a policy of peace, safeguarding our vital national interests.
> (Mirkovich 1941, 136)

Yugoslavia's bind was equally apparent to outsiders. After Paul had refused to meet with Eden in January 1941 out of fear of provoking the Germans, Churchill commented to Eden that "Prince Paul's attitude looks like that of an unfortunate man in the cage with a tiger, hoping not to provoke him while steadily dinner-time approaches" (Churchill 1948, v.3, 158).

Given the increasingly deteriorating situation, much of the cabinet shared Cincar-Marković's outlook and began to favor some sort of accommodation of

Germany, though Paul remained inclined to support Britain (Hoptner 1962, 183). This led to a two-track policy. On the one hand, Belgrade was secretly supplying the Greeks with arms to fight the Italians, while denying the Germans the ability to ship armaments through Yugoslavia to the hard-pressed Italians (Hoptner 1962, 191–2). On the other hand, Belgrade initiated negotiations which appeared to be moving it toward the Axis camp. When pressured by Berlin to join the Tripartite Pact, rather than refusing outright Belgrade haggled over terms. In November 1940 the Germans offered Salonika and a guarantee of Yugoslav borders in exchange for demilitarizing Dalmatia and joining the Tripartite Pact. After cutting off aviation supplies to Belgrade, the Germans repeated the offer in February 1941. Both times the Yugoslavs declined without ending the negotiations. Indeed, they even offered to mediate the Greco-Italian dispute (Hoptner 1962, 189–92 and 208–9; Mirkovich 1941, 137; Rothschild 1977, 263). Belgrade appears to have known that entering the Pact would have been the end its freedom of action and a threat to its independence. The Yugoslav government was particularly insistent that in no circumstance would it allow German troops to transit through the country on the way to Greece, a condition Hitler was willing to accept (Rothschild 1977, 263). Paul stated this condition directly to Hitler and Cvetković reassured the American ambassador that Yugoslavia would never allow the German military to transit (Hoptner 1962, 204). While these talks were ongoing, Yugoslavia successfully negotiated a treaty of friendship and non-aggression with Hungary in December 1940. The deal had the virtue of accommodating the Axis powers without actually conceding anything (Hoptner 1962, 192).

By March, negotiations had consciously become a way to stall for time while hoping the situation improved. Given that Belgrade had intelligence – which they passed along to the British – that the Germans planned to invade the Soviet Union in May, stalling offered some prospect of success (Hoptner 1962, 225). Given that Paul and much of his cabinet believed the Allies would win in the end, the key was managing to not be invaded and overrun before the Germans were forced to turn their attentions elsewhere (Hoptner 1962, 235).

Frankly, stalling was the only option. Repeated attempts to sound out the British as to whether they would be able to deploy more troops to Greece and the Balkans in the event Yugoslavia joined the war on the side of the Allies were met with silence.[15] London promised financing and war materiel, but no troops, which given the speed with which and multiple direction from which Axis troops could pour into Yugoslavia was as good as promising nothing at all (Hoptner 1962, 211 and 224; Mirkovich 1941, 144).[16] The General Staff confirmed the grim situation in a report to an emergency session of the crown council on March 6. The military informed the gathered ministers that in the event of a German invasion the north of the country and major cities would be lost immediately. The army could retreat to the mountains in Bosnia, but had ammunition and provisions to last only six weeks. There was no hope of resupply. On top of this, the Croat and Slovene populations were known to favor concessions and were unlikely to resist except possibly against the most naked aggression. Rapid defeat was unavoidable (Hoptner 1962, 217 and 235).[17]

Given this, the council decided to join the Tripartite Pact provided the Germans accepted several conditions. One, that Yugoslav territorial integrity would be respected. Two, no Axis troops would transit through Yugoslavia. Three, the Yugoslav forces would not have to participate in fighting the Greeks. And four, Yugoslavia would be guaranteed access to the Aegean via Salonika (Hoptner 1962, 217). It was hoped that negotiations over these conditions would buy additional time, but the Germans derailed that hope by quickly agreeing to all four conditions on March 19 (Hoptner 1962, 233 and 240–1; Mirkovich 1941, 139).[18] Thus cornered, the government joined the Tripartite Pact on March 25, 1941.

This set off a chain of events which quickly and disastrously brought Yugoslavia into the war. The Pact was deeply unpopular amongst the Serbian portion of the population and on March 27 the predominately Serbian Air Force conducted a coup – ostensibly in the name of the young King Peter II – which brought to power a government headed by General Dušan Simović (Mirkovich 1941, 138–40). The new government repudiated the Pact, though it still naively hoped to avoid war. It refused to mobilize the military out of fear of provoking the Germans, unaware that Hitler had authorized the invasion of Yugoslavia within hours of learning of the coup (Hoptner 1962, 265–7 and 274; Mirkovich 1941, 144; Rothschild 1977, 266). The Simović government vainly looked for some formula to avoid war, even considering the policies of the previous government it had come to power in order to repudiate. Though it did manage to get the Soviets to sign a treaty of friendship (Hoptner 1962, 274 and 285), the die was already cast. The Axis powers invaded on April 6 and quickly routed the Yugoslav forces. The army unconditionally surrendered on April 17. As with Poland, Yugoslavia had failed to find a way to successfully navigate the shoals of the coming of World War II. Its government was overthrown never to return to power and its territory was occupied and divided amongst its enemies. Only after years of brutal guerilla warfare would Yugoslavia regain its independence albeit under a new regime.

Romania

Romania entered the 1930s as a status quo power. Having gained Transylvania from Hungary, Bessarabia from the Soviet Union, and southern Dobruja from Bulgaria between 1913 and 1919, Romanian officials simply hoped to hold onto what they already had. To this end, in the immediate post-war period Romania had formed the Little Entente with Yugoslavia and Czechoslovakia, which aimed at containing Hungarian revisionism, and had also developed close relations with France (Hitchins 1994, 427–8).[19] Still, Romania was far from secure and given that changes to the status quo risked the loss of territory, Bucharest could only see the rise of Nazi Germany as a destabilizing threat. These fears increased when Hungarian Prime Minister Gyula Gömbös began seeking closer relations with Germany in the early 1930s (Leitz 1997, 315). Officials in Bucharest were initially unsure how to react: King Carol II leaned towards improving relations with Germany to offset Hungarian influence while Foreign Minister Nicolae Titulescu favored strengthening the Little Entente and ties with France. Titulescu's views carried the day through 1934 (Leitz 1997, 314–15). Indeed, Romania backed the western powers in their confrontation with Italy over Ethiopia and Romania supported France during the crisis over the remilitarization of the Rhineland in 1936 (Hitchins 1994, 429–30).

Romania also took steps to strengthen its alliances. Between 1931 and 1934, Bucharest renewed its treaty with Poland aimed at the Soviet Union[20] and strengthened the Little Entente by transforming it into one trilateral treaty as opposed to three bilateral ones, though the opposition of Yugoslav Prime Minister Milan Stojadinović and the insuperable difficulties of getting military aid to Czechoslovakia in the event of a German invasion prevented Titulescu from turning the Little Entente into an anti-German alliance (Hitchins 1994, 430–3; Wandycz 1981, 561–2).[21] Under Titulescu's leadership, Romania also participated in the creation of the Balkan Entente which was aimed at curbing Bulgarian revisionism and consisted of Romania, Yugoslavia, Greece, and Turkey (Hitchins 1994, 430–3). Additionally, Bucharest attempted to bring Poland into the Little Entente by mediation of Polish–Czechoslovak grievances, but ultimately both the mediation and the attempt to bring Poland into the alliance failed, in no small part due to Poland's good relations with Hungary (Hitchins 1994, 430; Steiner 2011, 744–5). Likewise, attempts to sign a non-aggression pact with the Soviets at the urging of the French also ultimately failed (Hitchins 1994, 435).[22] Still, these efforts show that through 1936, Romania was solidly in the camp of balancing states and was actively trying to improve the odds that balancing would succeed by attempting to transcend the obstacles to broader and more effective alliances in East Central Europe. What happened?

Bucharest was repeatedly disappointed by the lack of French resolve and continued concessions to Berlin. As early as the Treaty of Locarno in 1925, Britain and France had shown a willingness to make concessions to German revisionist aims, especially in the east. By the mid-1930s, France was also having difficulty meeting Romania's armaments needs (Steiner 2011, 402). This, and even more so France's supine behavior in the face of the remilitarizations of the Rhineland, caused Bucharest to drift away from France and toward Germany, ultimately resulting in the dismissal of the pro-French Titulescu (Alexander 1992, 81; Hitchins 1994, 431 and 436–7; Rothschild 1977, 312). Whereas before Bucharest had sought to shore up alliances in the region, Carol now rebuffed Poland's attempt in April 1937 to create a Polish, Romanian, Bulgarian, and Hungarian bloc (Hitchins 1994, 438–9).[23] Additionally, a French effort to convert the Little Entente from an anti-Hungarian pact to a general defensive pact was rebuffed by all three members of the alliance (Adamthwaite 1977, 46–7). Still, Berlin's attempts in 1937 to get Bucharest to definitively move from the French to the German camp failed (Sakmyster 1980, 76). Romania was still hedging its bets.

The Munich crisis greatly altered the Romanian position. During the crisis Romania wavered from allowing Soviet overflights to aid the Czechs to ultimately disallowing them out of fear of Germany (Adamthwaite 1977, 204; Hitchins 1994, 439).[24] Romania's main concern, once it was clear Britain and France would not stand behind Czechoslovakia, was to limit any Hungarian gains in Slovakia.[25]

It was the effects of the crisis, however, which were vital. First, the German seizure of the Škoda munitions works removed the only serious alternative source of arms, making Romania dependent on Germany for armaments (Leitz 1997, 321–2; Wandycz 1981, 554). Roughly 70 percent of Romanian military imports had come from Czechoslovakia and imports from France were very slow in arriving (Adamthwaite 1977, 64). Second, and more importantly, the loss of the Sudetenland effectively removed Czechoslovakia from the military board and thus undid the Little Entente, Romania's surest protection against a revisionist Hungary. The Romanian general staff admitted as much on October 17, 1938, stating that while "the Little Entente is not officially dissolved, it is in practice now non-existent owing to the amputation of Czechoslovakia" (Leitz 1997, 322). Third, French influence in Romania in particular collapsed after Munich (Hoisington 1971, 470). Carol's visit to Paris and London in November 1938 did nothing to reassure Bucharest. It became clear neither western power would commit to military or economic aid for Romania. This in turn prompted Carol, who was now convinced only Germany could protect Romania, to make an unscheduled stop in Berlin on the way home, in hopes of improving relations and getting the Germans themselves to oppose Hungarian aims in the Carpatho-Ukraine. However, little came of the meeting and Romanian worries about the Carpatho-Ukraine only increased when Germany occupied the rump of Czechoslovakia in March 1939 (Hitchins 1994, 440; Leitz 1997, 322–4).

This, combined with stiffening French and British resolve in the face of obvious German aggression – notably the territorial guarantee to Poland in late March – in turn prompted Carol to appoint the pro-Western Grigore Gafencu as Foreign Minister and to accept a French and British guarantee of Romanian territory on April 13, 1939 (Hitchins 1994, 440–3; Leitz 1997, 325). However, rather than attempting to balance in conjunction with France or members of the Little Entente as before, Romania simply attempted to hide from the coming storm. Crucially, the guarantees required nothing from Romania. Had Romania needed to take pro-Western actions in return, it is unlikely that the Romanians would have accepted the guarantees. Neither Carol nor Gafencu believed the western powers could protect Romania but hoped the guarantees might increase Bucharest's leverage in negotiating with the Germans (Steiner 2011, 744–5). Therefore, in addition to accepting guarantees from Britain and France, Bucharest also signed an economic treaty with Berlin on March 23, 1939 (Hitchins 1994, 441). The treaty guaranteed a market for Romanian oil and agricultural products and contained German promises to deliver armaments and invest in Romanian mines and oil fields (Steiner 2011, 729). As Carol informed the German ambassador, Wilhelm Fabricius, Bucharest intended to remain neutral in the event of war and Romania refused to promise aid to Poland in the event of war with Germany (Hitchins 1994, 442–3; Leitz 1997, 325; Steiner 2011, 747). Additionally, Romania completed its abandonment of the Little Entente by signing a non-aggression pact with Hungary on August 24, 1939 (Hitchins 1994, 443).

Both German and Western protection proved illusory. The Molotov–Ribbentrop Pact shocked Bucharest and eliminated the chance Germany would protect

Romania from the Soviets (Hitchins 1994, 443). Likewise, the fall of Poland in September 1939 showed the impotence of French and British guarantees and removed yet another potential Romanian ally from the board. Worse, with the new German–Soviet coordination, Romania had nowhere to turn for allies as now all of the states which had revisionist claims on its territory had good relations with Germany (Leitz 1997, 327–8). The most the Romanians could hope for was that compliance with German wishes would convince Hitler to keep their enemies at bay. Thus, Bucharest increased oil exports to Germany in return for captured Polish war materiel, though the Romanians also let many Poles including members of the government flee into or through its territory (Leitz 1997, 328–30). Further, in December 1939, Romania adjusted its exchange rate with Germany so as to reduce the cost of its oil to the Germans (Hoisington 1971, 472). German successes over France in 1940 simply rammed home the obvious helplessness of the Romanian position and led to further increases in the amount of oil provided to the Germans (Hitchins 1994, 445). Still, Carol resisted joining the German camp.

Then on June 28, 1940 Hitler allowed the Soviets to occupy Bessarabia, as agreed to in the Molotov–Ribbentrop Pact, and northern Bukovina, which had not been agreed to.[26] This loss of territory turned Romania into a revisionist state. Joining the Axis now seemed the best way to recover the lost territories, so Romania took a dramatic series of actions in July. Bucharest renounced the clearly worthless British and French guarantee on July 1, left the League of Nations on July 11, and publically indicated a desire to join the Axis on July 13 (Rothschild 1977, 314). Yet, this did not prevent further dismemberment, this time by Germany's Balkan allies. As a result of the Second Vienna Award, Hungary occupied much of Transylvania in August and Bulgaria obtained all of southern Dobruja in early September. Both territories were transferred as a result of German "mediation" and as with the loss of Bessarabia and northern Bukovina, Romania failed to resist the transfers.

These territorial losses resulted in Carol being removed from power via a coup on September 6 and the installation of his son Michael as king. However, the real power lay in the hand of the military government of Ion Antonescu which quickly joined the Tripartite Pact on November 20, 1940 in hopes of currying favor with the Germans so that the lost territories could be won back (Hitchins 1994, 447–50; Rothschild 1977, 315–16). From the outset of the Antonescu regime Hitler was certain of Romania's allegiance as Antonescu had come to power to recover Romania's lost territories or acquire new territories as compensation. His regime's legitimacy and survival depended upon this and yet it could only be achieved if the Axis powers triumphed over the Soviet Union.[27] Ultimately, Romania would send more troops to the Eastern Front than any other of Hitler's allies and while the Germans were in ascendency over the Soviets, Bucharest did briefly recover Bessarabia, northern Bukovina, and was awarded Transnistria as compensation for the concessions it had to make to other German allies.

Thus, the Romanians moved from attempting to balance against German, Soviet, and Hungarian revisionism to hiding and then finally to bandwagoning with the German threat. A deep desire to recover lost territory played a major role, but by late 1940 all options other than suicidal military resistance were essentially eliminated. The shift occurred as it became clear the western powers lacked the resolve and then the ability to effectively balance. Romania attempted to hide for much of the period and never actively balanced after the Rhineland crisis, largely because British and French resistance to revisionism in East Central Europe was so weak. Certainly, after each display of weak resolve or military inaction by the western powers, Romania crept ever deeper into the German camp. Not being in any way territorial revisionist at the start of the 1930s, the Romanians did not actually bandwagon until after their territorial losses in the summer of 1940. Prior to that, bandwagoning offered little in the way of spoils as Romania was still a deeply status quo power. Western weakness ruled out balancing, but hiding remained more attractive than bandwagoning. Only after the severe territorial losses of 1940 did Bucharest decide to bandwagon. The hope was that allying with Germany would result in recovering territory not only from the Soviet Union via invasion, but also from Hungary as a result of German intercession. This latter hope was in vain and the territory recouped after the 1941 invasion of the Soviet Union was gained only temporarily. The Romanians ultimately shared in the Germans' total defeat. Bucharest once again lost Bessarabia and northern Bukovina to the Soviet Union and the Romanian regime was overthrown.[28] Bandwagoning proved to be as much of a failed strategy as balancing and hiding had been.

Hungary

Hungary entered the 1930s as a highly revisionist, but very weak state. At the end of World War I, the Treaty of Trianon had allocated lands which had been part of the Kingdom of Hungary within the Austro-Hungarian Empire to a variety of successor states. Yugoslavia, Czechoslovakia, and especially Romania were the primary beneficiaries of these territorial revisions. While borders had been drawn with ethnicity in mind, due to the complex and often intermingled geographic distribution of nationalities, many ethnic Magyars ended up as minorities in these successor states. Thus, throughout the period, Hungary's primary foreign policy goal was the recovery of these lands. Due to the restrictions on rearmament imposed by the 1920 Treaty of Trianon and the simple reality of Hungary's post-World War I demographics, Budapest was in no way powerful enough to defeat its neighbors. Even by 1938, after a modest effort at rearmament, Hungary had no large-caliber artillery, few planes, and only enough ammunition for two days of fighting (Sakmyster 1980, 66, 90, 115–16, and 178). Thus, Hungary could recover its lost territories only with great power help.

While this seemingly made Hungary a natural ally of Germany – and in fact it ultimately did – the Hungarian regime was quite politically conservative and risk averse. Budapest thus saw Nazi Germany as both a potential threat and a potential ally (Macartney 1938, 755–63; Sakmyster 1980, x–xi and 26). Miklós Horthy, the Hungarian regent and head of state, was an anglophile who ceded much of the direction of foreign affairs to his foreign and prime ministers (Sakmyster 1980, 28–40). Of these, only Prime Minister Gyula Gömbös was enamored with Nazism.

Had he lived past 1936, it is quite possible Hungary would have entered the German orbit earlier as he had been negotiating with the Germans behind Horthy's back in late 1935 (Sakmyster 1980, 46–50).[29] After Gömbös' death, control of foreign policy passed into the hands of Kálmán Kánya, the Foreign Minister. While he tended to be anti-Nazi – he referred to Adolf Hitler, Hermann Göring, and Joseph Goebbels as a "common rabble rouser", "a brute", and "a buffoon" respectively – he was willing to explore any angle which could achieve Hungary's irredentist aims as long as the risk was not too great (Sakmyster 1980, 54–7).

Beginning in 1936, international events slowly pushed Hungary into the German orbit. French acceptance of Germany's remilitarization of the Rhineland cast doubt in Hungarian eyes on France's willingness and military ability to uphold the post-war settlement in East Central Europe (Sakmyster 1980, 60). Hungarian and French relations were cool throughout the period, so a lack of French resolve did not reduce faith in an ally, but rather loosened a potential constraint. In general, Kánya was unwilling to commit Hungary in any direction lest it prove disastrous. He told his colleagues that he wanted to maintain Budapest's "freedom of maneuver" while one of Kánya's aides described him as wishing to "remain apart from the clash of interests of foreign powers, and, if a conflict broke out, to stay out of it if possible" (Sakmyster 1980, 85).

It is unsurprising then to learn that Kánya explored a variety of potential alliances. He made several efforts to coordinate his foreign policy with Poland, but despite Polish receptivity to the idea, this came to naught (Sakmyster 1980, 151–3). Budapest also dabbled in negotiation with the Soviet Union, which had been going on since 1935 initially in hopes of forming an anti-Romanian pact and then with the aim of containing German expansionism in Southeastern Europe (Pastor 2004, 732). In particular, Mihály Jungerth-Arnóthy, the Hungarian ambassador to the Soviet Union, told Maxim Litvinov, the Soviet Foreign Minister, that Budapest was against German expansion, but that if the Soviets refused to back Hungarian revisionism, Budapest would have no choice but to turn to Germany (Pastor 2004, 734). This effort was likely doomed from the start given Horthy's hostility to Bolshevism, but that the effort was even made suggests just how unwilling Budapest was to be tied to Berlin. Budapest even worked to reduce tensions with members of the anti-Hungarian Little Entente at a conference in Bled, Yugoslavia as late as August 1938 (Katona 1939, 603; Sakmyster 1980, 176).

Still, the drift was mainly in the German direction. By November 1937 Budapest and Berlin were already discussing the division of Czechoslovakia between them with Hungarian claims on Slovakia being recognized by Hitler. Crucially, however, the timetable remained unclear and the talks never got beyond generalities, though the talks did allow the Hungarians to learn Hitler desired to annex all of Bohemia and Moravia, not just the Sudetenland (Sakmyster 1980, 109–112 and 145).

As the Sudetenland issue began to heat up in the spring of 1938, Hungary still hoped to avoid being drawn into a European conflagration and was still distrustful of the Germans. Kánya reiterated this desire to remain neutral to both British diplomats and Hermann Göring as the crisis unfolded over the summer of 1938

(Sakmyster 1980, 173). Thus, while he rejected British suggestions to ally with Czechoslovakia, in part due to Hungarian irredentist aims, Kánya had also been quite displeased by the *Anschluss* in March 1938, telling neutral diplomats that he much preferred an independent Austria to a Germany of 80 million on Hungary's borders (Pastor 2004, 735; Sakmyster 1980, 93 and 131).

In August 1938, as Hitler was planning on making his move on Czechoslovakia, the Hungarian leadership was invited to Germany for a state visit which was attended by Horthy, Kánya, and Prime Minister Béla Imrédy. During the visit, Hitler detailed his plan for attacking Czechoslovakia and offered Slovakia to the Hungarians provided Hungary aided the effort. The offer was rejected for a variety of reasons. First, Imrédy, based on reports from the Hungarian embassy in Paris, believed the French would back Czechoslovakia (Pastor 2004, 736; Sakmyster 1980, 175 and 183). Imrédy was also concerned that Romania and Yugoslavia would honor their commitments to the Little Entente and attack Hungary if Budapest was in on the carve-up of Czechoslovakia (Steiner 2011, 588). Second, Horthy was convinced that British sea power would ultimately win the coming war (Steiner 2011, 588–9) and told Hitler so directly saying, "You can mobilize in five days and put thirty Army Corps here and forty there, while England will take perhaps five months to mobilize, but in the end she will inevitably win" (Sakmyster 1980, 179). Finally, the cautious Kánya was horrified by Hitler's willingness to gamble, stating in private of Hitler "that madman wanted to unleash a war, whatever the cost" (Sakmyster 1980, 184). As the visit unraveled, Hitler ominously warned the non-committal Hungarians that "he who wanted to sit at the table must at least help in the kitchen" (Sakmyster 1980, 180).

The Munich crisis, however, unfolded much differently than the Hungarian leadership had expected and they began to question the wisdom of their decision to not bandwagon with Berlin. Imrédy, originally an ardent anglophile, became irritated at London's tendency to ignore Hungary and both he and Kánya were furious that London was pressuring Prague to make concessions to Berlin but not to Budapest (Rothschild 1977, 178–9; Sakmyster 1980, 188–9 and 193). Kánya had little faith that Britain would take a strong stand in Central Europe ever since Lord Halifax's trip to Germany in November 1937 in which Halifax gave Germany a green light for peaceful border revisions in the east (Sakmyster 1980, 112). This led Hungary to take a more aggressive approach during the crisis than originally planned. Budapest promised the Wehrmacht overflight and landing rights in the event of war and along with Warsaw, insisted that any concessions to ethnic Germans must be made to all minorities in Czechoslovakia – essentially a demand that Polish and Hungarian areas be ceded (Sakmyster 1980, 195 and 200–1). The Hungarians also interrupted trade with Czechoslovakia, but refused German requests to create incidents outside of a small operation in the Carpatho-Ukraine (Sakmyster 1980, 202–5 and 209–14). Ultimately, this tentative bandwagoning obtained for Budapest several predominantly Magyar areas in southern Czechoslovakia through the First Vienna Award of November 2, 1938.

More importantly the crisis demonstrated to the Hungarian leadership, especially Imrédy, that Germany was the dominant power in East Central Europe and Britain would not project its power into the region (Sakmyster 1980, 208). In response to German requests, Imrédy forced the cautious Kánya from office and replaced him with István Csáky, who stated that Hungary needed to display "unshakable fidelity to the Axis Powers" (Sakmyster 1980, 222). Csáky quickly took the Hungarians into the Axis camp. In January 1939 Hungary joined the Anti-Comintern Pact, promised to leave the League of Nations (accomplished in April), and began discussions about dismembering the remainder of Czechoslovakia (Pastor 2004, 737; Sakmyster 1980, 222–4). When Hitler moved to occupy Bohemia and Moravia in March, the Hungarians duly occupied Carpatho-Ukraine which Hitler had allotted them (Pastor 2004, 740; Sakmyster 1980, 226).[30] Thus, Budapest's turn towards Germany after Munich was stark. Having decided that Britain and France would not build a balancing coalition against Germany in East Central Europe and seeing an opportunity to achieve many of their long-held irredentist aims, the Hungarians flung themselves into the Axis camp in early 1939 – a move which within a few years would of course prove disastrous.

This is not to say there were no bumps in the road between Munich and the Hungarians' decision to join the Germans in the invasion of the Soviet Union in June 1941; there were. The Hungarians were genuinely shocked by the Molotov–Ribbentrop Pact. Horthy and Pál Teleki, who had replaced Imrédy as Prime Minister in February 1939,[31] both remained long-convinced of Britain's potential strength and were offended by the destruction of Poland – a state with which Hungary had always maintained good relations (Steiner 2011, 954). The Hungarians refused offers of Polish territory to join the war, refused Germany the use of Hungarian rail lines for the duration of the campaign, let between 70,000 and 100,000 Poles flee across Hungary to continue the conflict in the West, and even allowed a small volunteer legion to fight on the Polish side (Rothschild 1977, 182; Steiner 2011, 956).

This, however, was but a temporary setback in the German–Hungarian relationship. In late summer 1940, German mediation granted Hungary the northern half of Romanian-held Transylvania in the Second Vienna Award. The Hungarians soon reciprocated the German aid by joining the Tripartite Pact in November. They also participated in the invasion of Yugoslavia in April 1941, receiving Prekmurje, Međimurje, and Bačka as spoils.[32] Thus, with the exception of the disagreement over Poland, from Munich onward Hungary was solidly in the Axis camp with the Hungarian leadership being committed to bandwagoning with Hitler both for spoils and because balancing options simply were not available given Horthy's antipathy for the communist Soviet Union.

Thus, the Hungarians, always highly revisionist yet fearful of Germany, moved from a wait-and-see approach to one of bandwagoning with Germany as it became clear Britain and France would not effectively oppose Germany's redrawing of the map in East Central Europe. As Hungarian aims could be achieved only with great power assistance, it was necessary for Budapest to either seize the opportunity or give up on its irredentist aims. Hungarian estimates of the distribution of forces moved favorably in the German direction, especially after the West abandoned Czechoslovakia at Munich. Also, given that the Munich settlement eliminated one of Hungary's main enemies, Czechoslovakia, and undid the Little Entente, the nature of the opportunity strongly favored Hungary shifting from neutrality to bandwagoning. Finally, as much of the territory Hungary sought had been held by Czechoslovakia, the nature of the opportunity was again inclined strongly toward bandwagoning. Overall, Hungary's actions fit well with the theory's predictions.

Conclusion

Polish, Yugoslav, Romanian, and Hungarian behavior all reflect the theory's predictions. Remarkably all four states had a fairly accurate view of Hitler's aggressive intentions. Decisions to move toward hiding or bandwagoning were not driven by changing beliefs about German intentions. Rather they were driven by changing estimates about the likely balance of capabilities. In turn, these estimates were largely driven by shifting beliefs about French and British intentions and also by the fact the remilitarization of the Rhineland, the occupation of the Sudetenland, and – in the cases of Romania and Yugoslavia – post-1939 German conquests, had placed the German military in a much stronger position than previously.

Poland entered the mid-1930s with a preference for balancing against Germany, especially as many of Germany's revisionist aims included Polish territory. Yet after the occupation of the Rhineland and the growing evidence that Britain and France were not going to take effective steps to confront Germany in East Central Europe, the Poles for a time moved away from balancing. At a couple points the Poles flirted with hiding, but given German intentions toward the Polish Corridor and Poland's proximity to Germany, hiding was never likely to succeed. The Poles also briefly tried to transcend by directing German aggression against the Soviet Union, but to no avail. When the West's fecklessness and weakness were made fully apparent at Munich, the Poles bandwagoned with Germany in order to pick up small enclaves of Czech territory. Ultimately, Warsaw returned to balancing as it became clear that Poland was to be Germany's next victim, even though Poland expected little effective help from France and Britain. Thus, as it became clear that it was unlikely that an effective balancing coalition would form against Germany and that the nature of the German move into the Rhineland had deeply disrupted the balance of power, Poland became less interested in balancing and flirted with other strategies. When none of these succeeded, since Hitler was determined to destroy Poland, the Poles returned to balancing.

Yugoslavia likewise began as a member of France's balancing coalition, but as with the Poles, the Yugoslavs moved away from balancing as it became apparent that the West was not going to effectively balance against Germany. Additionally, the nature of the German move into Czechoslovakia made it impossible for the Little Entente to function, further reducing the odds of successful balancing. Since Yugoslavia was not a target of Germany in the late 1930s, the Yugoslavs attempted to hide once they abandoned balancing. This was successful for a time until Italy's conflict with Greece drew Germany deeply into Balkan politics. By 1941, Germany bordered directly on Yugoslavia as did four other Axis states.

With Hitler no longer willing to countenance Yugoslav neutrality and with its military position being completely untenable, Belgrade opted to bandwagon with the Axis for its own safety. This was immediately undone by a military coup by individuals who could not stomach allying with the Axis. The new government attempted to return to hiding, but when it was obvious that hiding was impossible, they even considered bandwagoning. The Germans had already decided upon invasion, however, so whether the new government would have fully embraced the policy of the old will never be known. Still, it is striking that the pressures from the international environment were forcing the new government to contemplate a return to the policies it had seized power in order to stop.

Romania was also initially disposed to balance and even tried to transcend many of the divisions within East Central Europe to form an effective balancing coalition. Much like Yugoslavia, Romania abandoned balancing after Munich as that agreement undid the Little Entente and made it excruciatingly clear that the French and the British would not effectively balance against German aggression in the east. Romania then hid until 1940 when severe territorial losses due to the Molotov–Ribbentrop Pact and the Second Vienna Award turned Romania into a revisionist state. This combined with the military ascendency of Germany in East Central Europe led Romania to bandwagon with the Germans.

Hungarian behavior was fairly straightforward. Unlike the other three states, Hungary was always a revisionist power and thus never considered balancing. Rather it hid early on as it was too weak to do anything else. When the remilitarization of the Rhineland and more especially the resolution of the Sudetenland crisis made it clear Germany was ascendant in the east and that Britain and France were not likely to do anything about it, Hungary quickly moved to bandwagon in order to fulfill its irredentist aims. Thus, all four powers shifted strategies due to changes in their estimates that an effective balancing coalition would form.

Geography also played a role in each case. While Poland always shared a border with Germany – and a border largely free of natural obstacles at that – the other three states were initially physically buffered from German power by the presence of other states. After the *Anschluss*, Germany bordered directly on Hungary and Yugoslavia. Additionally, Germany was able to bring pressure on Yugoslavia and Romania as it gained allies which bordered these states. Recall that by 1941 Yugoslavia was essentially surrounded by Axis states. For these states, as the German threat grew nearer and the odds of receiving succor from other balancers grew dimmer, the will to resist diminished.

Likewise, the paucity and decline of effective international institutions made balancing less feasible and bandwagoning and hiding more realistic. Over the 1930s, the League of Nations proved to be feckless and the multilateral alliance structures within Southeastern Europe collapsed. As was seen above, both the Little Entente and the Balkan Entente were ultimately abandoned by their members. The French alliances with states in the region, too, were abandoned or weakened. This left the minor powers to deal with Germany bilaterally rather than multilaterally – a most uneven playing field for the small states studied in this chapter. Given this power disparity, these states were left with only two options: cozy up to Germany or try to lay low. Trying to balance could lead only to defeat and dismemberment. Obviously, there is an element of the classic chicken-and-egg problem here. Were these organizations and alliances abandoned because states opted against balancing or did states fail to balance because the institutions were weak? In truth, there are elements of both factors at work. Essentially, a vicious spiral was created. As states became less inclined to balance, they weakened institutions in part as a way to explore other options. As the institutions weakened, states became less confident that balancing would be successful, leading to them to invest even less in the institutions than before. This ultimately culminated in these states abandoning the post-World War I balancing institutions in favor of German-sponsored bandwagoning institutions.

Economic ties also played a role in pushing states from balancing toward bandwagoning and hiding. Though not covered explicitly in the cases above, trade relationships made it particularly difficult for states like Hungary, Yugoslavia, and Romania to balance, especially given the economic pressures brought on by the Great Depression (Wandycz 1981, 553). German trade policy during the 1930s favored bilateral relationships between Germany and the states of East Central and Southeastern Europe and undermined alternative trading relationships. For example, the Germans were willing to overpay for agricultural products from the Danubian basin. This meant that the agricultural sector in Southeastern Europe could remain profitable despite being inefficient. This resulted in Hungary, Romania, and Yugoslavia all becoming dependent on the German market for their agricultural goods (Hirschman 1980; Steiner 2011, 955). Furthermore, in order to deal with the scarcity of gold and hard currency to pay for its imports, the Germans set up a system of clearing houses that effectively limited these countries to spending their trade surplus on German goods. Also, German industry was set so as to be able to exploit low-grade mineral resources from Yugoslavia and Romania (Hirschman 1980) – resources that were not in demand elsewhere due to their poor quality. The Germans also bought these agricultural and mineral products in sufficient quantities to ensure price and quantity stability. This inefficiency and low quality meant that there was no ready substitute for the German market. When combined with the fact that these countries imported many of their finished goods and armaments from Germany, any political move that severed relations with Germany would have significant economic costs (Hirschman 1980).[33]

Events of the 1930s deepened this dependence. Yugoslavia's participation in the sanctions regime erected by the League of Nations against Italy after Mussolini's invasion of Ethiopia cost Belgrade one of its major markets (Steiner 2011, 152). Likewise, the *Anschluss* gave Germany control over Hungary's major source of iron and steel imports (Steiner 2011, 556). Similarly, Romania and Yugoslavia lost an important trade partner when Germany occupied Czechoslovakia. Even while Czechoslovakia remained independent, the Czechoslovak market was simply too small to replace the German market for agricultural goods (Wandycz 1981, 553). While this did not make balancing impossible, it was one more argument in favor of hiding or bandwagoning.

Of course, reality is usually more complex than theory. Most clearly, three of the four cases were somewhat complicated by domestic politics. While domestic politics played very little role in Polish foreign policy in the period covered, they did play a role in the other three states. Most clearly, Yugoslavia's response to Italian and German pressure was severely hampered by internal ethnic divisions. At times, however, it was decisions about how to proceed in foreign affairs which drove the domestic politics and not vice versa. Paul had Stojadinović removed from power largely to facilitate Yugoslavia pursuing a more neutral course. In a similar fashion, Imrédy removed Kánya from power to bring about Hungarian cooperation with Germany. Thus, the decision to change policies preceded the change in personnel. This was not, however, always the case. While it could be argued that the coup in Romania which overthrew Carol was somewhat similar in that it was done to bring about a shift in Romanian foreign policy, such extralegal actions are of a different character. Whether Carol could have kept Romania neutral for long is unclear, but certainly the coup sped up the shift to bandwagoning. The coup in Yugoslavia was similarly driven by a desire to change foreign policies, though of course the new regime did not last long prior to the German invasion. Perhaps the clearest effect of a state's policy taking a different path due to a domestic event was Hungary becoming far more cautious due to the death of Gömbös who may well have brought Hungary into the Germany camp more quickly had he lived. Nevertheless, the factors advanced by the theory such as the relative balance of capabilities and the nature of the opportunity clearly influenced state behavior even given the role played by domestic politics in a number of the states. Having shown in this and the preceding chapters that a variety of foreign policy behaviors in response to threats to the status quo including balancing, bandwagoning, and hiding can be explained during ante-bellum periods by the factors covered above, the next chapter will explore the nature of balancing and bandwagoning after the outbreak of war.

Notes

1 Of the four states covered, only Hungary and Yugoslavia entertained any hopes of a positive relationship with the Soviet Union.
2 At the end of the war Hungary ended up with its 1937 borders minus a few border villages lost to Czechoslovakia. Yugoslavia actually gained territory in Istria from Italy. All of the states' borders shifted considerably over the course of World War II. Hungary primarily gained territory while Germany was ascendant, while Romania both gained and lost significant chunks of territory due to Hitler's redrawing the map of Europe. After the war Poland lost territory in the east while gaining territory in the west. Both Poland and Yugoslavia were completely dismembered for a time during the war.
3 The territorial dispute with Czechoslovakia, while emotional, was not at the center of Polish foreign policy. It was, however, an insuperable obstacle to any Polish–Czechoslovak alliance (Cienciala 1992, 79–80).
4 After the war a member of Beck's staff claimed the Poles had even discussed mobilization plans to aid Czechoslovakia, but there is little extant paperwork to either substantiate or refute the claim.
5 These views of Beck's were also reflected in his instructions to the Polish ambassador to Romania.

6 This area, which comprised the far eastern tip of Czechoslovakia, is also known as Ruthenia or the Sub-Carpatho-Ukraine.
7 The British seem to have believed that given tensions with the Soviets, even if Poland was overwhelmed, Germany would be forced to keep many divisions in the east (Strang 1996, 741).
8 The alliance, also known as the Balkan Pact, was aimed to protect against the revisionist ambitions of a number of states including Hungary, Italy, Albania, Bulgaria, and the Soviet Union. Interestingly, a similar pact was signed between Yugoslavia, Greece, and Turkey in 1953 with the exact same aims. This later agreement would fizzle out due to the Soviet–Yugoslav rapprochement after the death of Stalin and the rising tensions between Greece and Turkey.
9 Chernozemski had joined the Internal Macedonian Revolutionary Organization in 1922 by which time the organization had aligned itself with Bulgaria. By the 1930s Chernozemski worked as an instructor in Ustaše training camps in Italy and Hungary.
10 The general staff also warned that Yugoslavia's position was "quite dangerous" and that Britain and France had failed to give any useful, concrete commitments to Yugoslavia (Hoptner 1962, 41–2).
11 This led to Stojadinović being seen by Germany as the best choice to head the Yugoslav government. Berlin repeatedly ordered the Volksdeutsch in Vojvodinia to vote for Stojadinović (Rothschild 1977, 259).
12 Throughout 1937 Belgrade strove to improve Franco-Yugoslav military coordination. Only when these attempts went nowhere and French weakness was made manifest by the Munich crisis, did the Yugoslavs begin to buy fewer armaments from France (Alexander 1992, 225–30).
13 Stojadinović's supporters had taken to wearing military uniforms and performing the Roman salute. Ultimately Stojadinović was encouraged to go into exile in March 1941 out of a fear that he could potentially become the focus of a German-led coup if he remained in the country.
14 Several feelers were also put out to the Soviets, but these went nowhere and ultimately the Soviets were scared off from pursing an aggressive policy in the Balkans by France's collapse. Talks with Turkey proved equally barren (Hoptner 1962, 206 and 225).
15 The British had dispatched a very small number of troops to aid the Greeks.
16 The hard-pressed British were not being stingy; they simply had no additional troops available to deploy to the Balkans (Churchill 1948 v.3, 94–110).
17 As it turned out, the Yugoslav army performed even worse than expected.
18 The Germans knew Yugoslavia was just stalling for time. Hitler had said as much to Mussolini back in December and had expressed the hope that future victories would push Yugoslavia into the Axis camp (Churchill 1948, v.3, 13).
19 Romanian contacts with Britain were generally limited throughout the period.
20 King Carol was deeply anti-Soviet and anti-Communist in outlook (Steiner 2011, 744–5).
21 Poland and the Soviet Union also worked to undercut Titulescu's efforts to strengthen the Little Entente. In general, Beck viewed the Little Entente with great skepticism because it strengthened Czechoslovakia at the expense of Hungary (Wandycz 1988b, 425).
22 Titulescu hoped that the Soviets would replace the Italians in helping to resist German pressure on Austria after the Italians had fallen out with the French in the wake of the invasion of Ethiopia (Wandycz 1988b, 422–3).
23 Admittedly, given the Hungarian and Bulgarian claims on Romanian territory, as well as Romania's existing commitments to Czechoslovakia, Yugoslavia, and Turkey, it would have been a tough sell even before the remilitarization of the Rhineland and fall of Titulescu.
24 The traditional explanation is that the government agreed to allow the overflights, only to be overruled by Carol. Some doubt, however, exists as to the veracity of the evidence on whether the government ever agreed at all (Ragsdale 1998).

25 Nicolae Petrescu-Comnène, the Romanian foreign minister, shared his concerns about Hungarian expansion into Slovakia with the Yugoslav Prime Minister, Milan Stojadinović (Hoptner 1962, 118).
26 Hitler did intervene diplomatically to prevent Stalin from also occupying southern Bukovina.
27 Hitler informed Mussolini of his belief in Antonescu's reliability as an ally for these very reasons during a meeting in December 1940 (Churchill 1948, v.3, 13).
28 After the war, Romania did get Transylvania back from Hungary, but never did reacquire Southern Dobruja from Bulgaria.
29 Gömbös had been promising to institute fascist reforms in exchange for German arms.
30 This involved limited combat with Slovak forces.
31 Imrédy had been forced to resign because of revelations he had Jewish ancestors.
32 Teleki opposed Hungary's participation in the invasion as going against Hungary's pledge of non-aggression toward Yugoslavia (see above), but was overruled by Horthy. Teleki committed suicide shortly after German troops began passing through Hungary on their way to Yugoslavia.
33 Changing arms suppliers has additional costs as it means a loss of access to ammunition and replacement parts for older equipment and requires retraining troops so that they can use the new equipment (Hirschman 1980).

6 Balancing and bandwagoning by other means

How the outbreak of war affects states' responses to threats

So far the discussion has centered on strategies that states employ when faced with an emerging threat. In general, the theory and cases have thought about how states respond to such potential and actual threats during periods of peace and during crises, especially those preceding a war. Only the case on Yugoslavia in Chapter 5 focuses on decisions *after* the outbreak of war, though the cases on Romania and Hungary also include some decisions after World War Two started. Yet, the outbreaks of wars by their very nature often threaten non-belligerent states by immediately or potentially altering the balance of power. How states respond to wartime challenges to the balance of power may be different from how they do so in peacetime. During peaceful and ante-bellum periods questions about whether threats are real can be particularly tricky as it is often difficult to answer questions about the relative balance of forces and intentions.[1] In order to draw sound inferences on such questions, states must focus on the diplomatic actions of their fellow states to gauge intentions and on military buildups in order to make estimates about capabilities. Given that diplomatic maneuvers are often intentionally duplicitous and determining the relative balance of capabilities between militaries that have not recently engaged in combat presents a thorny challenge, uncertainty and shifting estimates become a central part of the story.

Indeed, bargaining theories of war often point to this ante-bellum uncertainty as one of the more compelling explanations of why states wage war as opposed to striking a mutually acceptable bargain (Fearon 1995). It is possible that during wars the answers to both types of questions, as well as those about the nature of the opportunity, would be clearer as battles, strategic maneuvers, and the demands made by states – both diplomatically and tacitly through military maneuvers – would reveal states' capabilities and intentions (Slantchev 2004). This means that thinking about balancing and bandwagoning during wars – periods when new information is revealed about intentions and capabilities – could be fruitful as behaviors after the onset of hostilities may be different from those during peaceful periods.

Furthermore, in previous chapters it has been loosely implied that states which engaged in balancing or bandwagoning behavior would either be among the initial belligerents in a war caused by those behaviors or would join that war soon after it began. As the case of Hungary in the preceding chapter shows, this may not always be the case. Budapest's decision to bandwagon was made before the invasion of Poland in September 1939. Yet, Hungary did not become a belligerent until 1941 despite bandwagoning with Germany from early 1939 onwards.[2]

This calls into question the reasonableness of the belief that bandwagoners and balancers would quickly become active belligerents once war breaks out. Obviously, such immediate belligerency does occur. Balancers could join a war on the first day of combat and of course the initial parties to the war could be engaged in balancing. While the nature of bandwagoning requires the existence of a multilateral war for belligerents to bandwagon from day one (otherwise with whom would those states be bandwagoning?) such behavior does occur. However, states that balance or bandwagon during peacetime can have good reasons not to want to translate this policy into joining a war when it breaks out. Transforming a peacetime policy of balancing or bandwagoning into a wartime policy of balancing or bandwagoning requires states to take on additional costs and uncertainties. Similarly, a state that decided to respond to a peacetime challenge to the status quo by hiding may find this policy untenable during war even if it is not directly attacked by any of the belligerents. The question, however, is not whether rapid intervention occurs,[3] but rather is it reasonable to assume that intervening quickly is the norm?

First, we have to decide what we mean by quickly. A cutoff of 30 days from the outbreak of hostilities is probably reasonable in the modern era. Such a window gives states sufficient time to work through any domestic mechanisms for declaring war or deploying forces into combat.[4] It is also sufficient time for governments to receive and verify reports of the outbreak of hostilities and go through any last-minute diplomacy to avoid a wider war. The historical record offers support for such a cutoff. For instance, after the outbreak of hostilities between Serbia and Austria-Hungary in the late summer of 1914, many states quickly joined what became World War One. Russia, Germany, Belgium, France, Britain, and Japan all joined the war within 30 days. Yet though a further seven states would ultimately join, only one – the Ottoman Empire – did so between the initial rush in August 1914 and the spring of 1915. The remaining states would join slowly, one by one, over the course of the next three years. Therefore, a 30-day window seems reasonable, though of course other cutoffs are possible. However, in practice other cutoffs produce similar results. Using a 20-day cutoff, Japan ceases to be an early joiner during World War One. Using a 40-day cutoff, Finland becomes an early joiner in the 1920 War of Estonian Liberation and Canada becomes an early joiner in the 2001 Invasion of Afghanistan. No other military interventions into interstate wars are affected by such shifts in the cutoff point in the post-1816 period. Thus, the exact cutoff point is not crucial.

Of the 102 states in the Correlates of War (COW) Interstate War dataset version 4.0 (Sarkees and Wayman 2010) that joined ongoing wars, 29 did so in the first 30 days though four of these joined in what were also the last 30 days due to wars lasting less than two months. This means most states that ultimately intervene do not do so in the first 30 days. There are two possible explanations for this. First, states which employ bandwagoning or balancing strategies in the ante-bellum period often delay joining wars when they in fact break out. Second, states which join wars well after their initial outbreak may not have been engaged in balancing or bandwagoning in the ante-bellum period. Rather they may have only chosen to do so after events within the war led them to change their strategies. Each of these possibilities will be considered in turn, beginning with states delaying belligerency despite engaging in balancing and bandwagoning in the ante-bellum period.

Certainly there are some examples of such delayed belligerency, such as the Hungarian example discussed above. Indeed, states have a number of incentives to delay belligerency including waiting for potential opponents to exhaust themselves, waiting for opponents to move their forces away from the frontier, and waiting for their own rearmament to be completed. Recall, too, the discussion in Chapters 2 and 3 of the advantages of delaying balancing until some future date. Yet, there are reasons to think Hungary might be an exception. While states may want to delay entering wars until it suits them, it is not clear why potential opponents would allow a state to delay belligerency until a more favorable time provided that state's future belligerency was nearly certain. If it is optimal for one side to wait, presumably the other side has an interest in fighting now and would initiate a conflict regardless of its opponent's desire (Murray 1984, 314–15 and 362–3). Reiter (1995) finds that this sort of preemption is very rare, suggesting that states rarely delay entry into wars for these sorts of tactical reasons. Indeed, Hungary, even though it was already bandwagoning with Germany, delayed entry not for tactical reasons but for strategic ones. The Hungarian leadership had yet to be convinced that open belligerency was in their interest and opposed the destruction of Poland.

This leads directly to the second, more likely explanation that a late joiner's decision to balance or bandwagon is influenced by the war itself. While such states could have engaged in balancing or bandwagoning strategies in the ante-bellum period – much as Hungary did – many may have opted to hide or perhaps were not even concerned by the ante-bellum crisis.[5] One reason to think these later joiners would not have engaged in balancing or bandwagoning strategies prior to the war comes from the alliance literature. That literature shows that alliances, and in particular defense pacts, are good predictors of military intervention (Huth and Russett 1984; Most and Starr 1980; Raknerud and Hegre 1997; Siverson and King 1979; Siverson and Starr 1991),[6] but that alliances decline in predictive power the longer a war has lasted (Joyce, Ghosn, and Bayer 2014; Melin and Koch 2010). Indeed, Shirkey (2009) finds defense pacts are significant predictors of military intervention only during a war's first 30 days.[7] States which attempted to balance or bandwagon are likely to have formed alliances in the ante-bellum period. The fact that alliances are good predictors of intervention only early in wars suggests the intuition that states pursuing balancing or bandwagoning strategies prior to the war will join quickly, has merit. Presumably states which join later were not engaged in balancing or bandwagoning strategies prior to the war – at least not in relation to the states which composed the war's initial belligerents – and did not form alliances with future belligerents. Given that such states are the majority of interveners, it is important to think through what would prompt them to balance or bandwagon once a war is underway.

Such states should be responding to events within wars which create threats or opportunities prompting them to join (Shirkey 2009). They do so in hopes of altering the probable settlement of the war (Altfeld and Bueno de Mesquita 1979). Thus, these later joiners are engaged in balancing or bandwagoning and are prompted to do so by the course of the war itself. In other words, states learn from and adjust their strategies in response to events in wars.[8]

Since wars reveal information about states capabilities and intentions to both belligerent and non-belligerent states (Fearon 1995; Goemans 2000), this means wars affect states' estimates of the variables discussed in the models presented in Chapters 1 and 2: the relative balance of capabilities; the nature of the challenger; and the nature of the opportunity. For instance, battles may run contrary to a non-belligerent state's expectations, indicating that the war presents an opportunity for bandwagoning or a need to balance (Blainey 1973). Likewise, as belligerent powers make demands and threats – and quite possibly increase or decrease them in relation to events on the battlefield – it may become clear that the challenger is more or less revisionist than anticipated (Davis 2001; Werner 2000). Much as with learning about capabilities from battles, this learning should also cause some non-belligerent states to revise their strategies.[9] Finally, military successes (or defeats) by the challenger could change the nature of the opportunity presented to the challenger, once again potentially causing states to shift the strategy they have chosen. This logic should apply to belligerent states as well as non-belligerent states and could lead to peace (Slantchev 2004) or to states changing sides.

Finally, it is worth remembering that not all states join wars willingly. Of the states which joined ongoing interstate wars since 1816, 15 did so because their territory was invaded or their military forces were attacked (see Table 6.1). The table lists the state which joined, the COW War Number

Table 6.1 States which joined wars after being attacked*

Argentina (49) – balancing
Belgium (106)** – hiding
Greece (106) – bandwagoning and hiding
Australia (130) – balancing
Great Britain (130) – balancing
United States (130) – balancing
Canada (130) – balancing
Belgium (139) – hiding
Ethiopia (139) – defense***
Greece (139) – hiding
Netherlands (139) – hiding
Norway (139) – hiding
Soviet Union (139) – bandwagoning
Yugoslavia (139) – hiding
Angola (186)** – balancing

* World War Two is divided into two wars: one in Europe (139) and one in the Pacific arising from the Third Sino-Japanese War (130). Australia and Canada had troops in British possessions in the Far East which were attacked by the Japanese on December 8 along with the British forces garrisoning those possessions. Other states were occupied during both World Wars, but did not engage in sufficient resistance to be considered belligerent states by COW.
** Attacked during the first 30 days of the war.
*** Became a belligerent to expel existing Italian occupation.

for the war if joined (see Table. 6.5) and the state's ante-bellum strategy. Only two of these attacks happened within the first 30 days of the war: Belgium in World War One and Angola in the War over Angola (1975–1976). In the former, Belgium was clearly trying to hide. In the latter, Zairian and South African forces attacked Cuban troops in Angola prior to attacking Angolan troops.[10] Thus, it is a bit odd to see Angola as a joiner rather than as an original belligerent and the whole episode could be seen as an intervention into the Angolan civil war. There is no reason to assume the other states which were attacked much later were trying to balance or bandwagon. They may well have been trying to hide for instance. Table 6.1 indicates which of these behaviors best categorizes each state's ante-bellum strategy. Removing these involuntary joiners from the calculation leaves 27 states joining in the first month (still including four of which joined in what was also the last month) and 60 joining thereafter.

Motives for war and the timing of military intervention

It should be possible to deduce some patterns between why states join ongoing wars and when they are likely to do so over the course of a war. When a state joined can be thought of as falling into one of three broad categories: early (defined above as the first month); mid-war; or very late – likely after the outcome has been decided (herein defined as the last month of the war). States can also be thought of as joining for one of three reasons: balancing; bandwagoning for territorial spoils; and bandwagoning for non-territorial spoils.[11] This excludes states which joined wars because they were attacked or invaded as such states would be engaged in defense rather than balancing. Cross-referencing timing and state motives generates nine possible types of voluntary military intervention (see Table 6.2). Of these nine types, only five should be likely to occur as the mix of certain motives and timing does not make sense from a rational actor perspective.

Table 6.2 Types of joining, their likelihood, and underlying motives

	Balancing	*Bandwagoning – territorial spoils*	*Bandwagoning – non-territorial spoils*
First month	(A) *Likely to occur.* Motive: ante-bellum alliances	(B) *Should rarely occur.* Too soon to know which side to join. Motive for rare joiner: ante-bellum alliances	(C) *Should not occur.* Belligerents not yet seeking allies. Motive for exception: ante-bellum alliances
Mid-war	(D) *Likely to occur.* Motive: events in the war	(E) *Likely to occur.* Motive: events in the war	(F) *Likely to occur.* Motive: spoils offered by belligerents
Last month	(G) *Should not occur.* No need to or too late to balance	(H) *Likely to occur.* Motive: events in the war	(I) *Should not occur.* No reason for belligerents to seek allies

One other type should occur rarely and three should be very unlikely to occur. Why this is can be seen by going through each motive for joining.

First, there is little reason to expect balancers to join very late in a war (Table 6.2, Box G). If a non-belligerent was concerned that a belligerent was likely to alter the distribution of power in sufficiently unacceptable ways that balancing against that belligerent was attractive, the potential balancer would intervene as soon as this became apparent, well before the end of the war. In the last stages of a war it would be either too late to effectively balance or apparent that balancing was unnecessary. Even if a potential balancer waited until its prospective allies were on their last legs to join them and balance against their adversaries, this likely would not be the end of the war as successful balancing would likely take months or years. Thus, balancing is likely to extend wars, not rapidly end them. Only highly successful or highly unsuccessful balancing, combined with an extreme hesitation to balance even after the need to balance becomes apparent, would result in balancers entering in the last month of a war. Such a scenario is improbable.

Earlier balancing in either a war's first month or mid-war is likely to occur. Balancers joining in the first month of the war (Box A) should be doing so out of ante-bellum alliance commitments, while balancers joining mid-war (Box D) should be joining in response to information revealed by the war.[12] This is because if a potential intervener decides that its alliance is not a sufficient reason to balance initially, the alliance alone is unlikely to ever be sufficient by itself. Rather, information from the war itself would have to change the potential balancer's mind.[13] Furthermore, in the first month of the war, there is likely to be little information that was not already available ante-bellum about which side is likely to win and effects of such an outcome on the overall distribution of power.[14] Any information available ante-bellum should already have been factored into alliance structures; hence those structures should drive first-month balancing, but not later balancing. This fits with the previously discussed findings that alliances get honored early in the war or not at all, and thereafter, revealed information drives the timing of joining.

Bandwagoning for territorial spoils is likewise limited in when it should occur. Bandwagoners, like any rational actor, want to receive the maximum benefit for the minimal cost. Additionally, bandwagoners are often weaker states that can affect the outcome of a war only in limited ways. Thus, it is best for potential bandwagoners to wait to join a war until it becomes clearer which side will win. Events within a war should reveal information about which side is more likely to win. Additionally, bandwagoners would want to join closer to the end of a war than the beginning, as this would mean they would have to pay fewer costs. However, if potential bandwagoners wait too long to join, their services would be of less value to the belligerents and they may well receive fewer spoils.[15] This delicate act of waiting to determine which side to join if any and joining early enough to be rewarded, but late enough to limit costs means that bandwagoners seeking territorial spoils would likely join either mid-war (Box E) or in the last month of the war (Box H). They would be unlikely to join in the first month of a war (Box B) as it would not be apparent whether spoils would be available. Some states, however, may bandwagon this early in the hopes of spoils as the result of ante-bellum bandwagoning and ante-bellum alliances.

Similarly, potential bandwagoners seeking spoils not attached to the war would need to join early enough to receive substantial benefits. In the post-World War Two period, these sorts of bandwagoners have been sought by belligerents more so than they have sought out belligerents (see Shirkey 2009, Chapter 7). For example, the United States actively sought and obtained the aid of South Korea, Thailand, and the Philippines in the Vietnam War through offers of military and economic aid. For these reasons, bandwagoners seeking non-territorial spoils should be unlikely to join in the last month of a war (Box I), as belligerents on the winning side would be unlikely to seek assistance so late and the reward would likely be meager, making bandwagoning less attractive. The rewards would be low in part because bandwagoners seeking non-territorial spoils cannot simply seize what they want. This is distinct from territorial bandwagoners who can occupy the territory they desire in hopes of increasing their bargaining leverage through a *fait accompli*. Instead, non-territorial bandwagoners have to receive their rewards directly from more powerful states. Additionally, states on the losing side near the end of a war likely would be seeking a great deal of assistance – and non-territorial spoils are unlikely to be sufficient to motivate such efforts.

Non-territorial bandwagoners are also unlike to join early in a war (Box C) for two reasons. First, belligerents are unlikely to be seeking allies so soon, though it is not impossible that this could occur. Second, negotiations over non-territorial spoils should delay these bandwagoners' entries. This is because while such bandwagoners are still pursuing spoils, they are not seeking territory and cannot simply seize what they want. Such states may be seeking a better relationship with a powerful state or economic, military, technical, or diplomatic aid. Such an improved relationship could take the form of a new or strengthened military alliance or other diplomatic help. Also, states may bandwagon with a powerful state simply to avoid becoming a target of that state (Walt 1985). What is distinct about all of these benefits is they are not directly tied to the outcome of the war itself. A state which is rewarded financially receives that benefit regardless of the military outcome of the war. Additionally, states seeking better relations with a great power will likely retain the great power's goodwill regardless of who wins the war. Because the rewards are not tied directly to the war, the course of the war is not vital to their decision-making, though it should influence the size of rewards that the state they are bandwagoning with is willing to offer (Shirkey 2009). The only concern for such bandwagoners, beyond the direct costs of the war, would be a severe defeat that prevents their ally from providing significant aid – financial, diplomatic, or military – to the bandwagoning state. Thus, non-territorial bandwagoners are most likely to join mid-war (Box F), though their decision to join would likely not be tied to events within the war, but rather to negotiations with the stronger belligerents over spoils.[16]

It is also worth considering which of these types of intervention should be more likely to lead to joining the winning side. First, states joining in the last month of a war regardless of motive should be highly likely to win as in most cases the outcome of the war should be clear so close to the end of the war and states are unlikely to hitch their wagon to an obviously losing cause. Second, bandwagoners seeking territorial spoils joining mid-war should win at a higher rate than those joining in the first month. This is based on the same logic as for states joining at the end of a war as territory-seeking bandwagoners should aim to join the winning side. These mid-war bandwagoners, however, should win less often than those bandwagoning at the very end of the war. Third, states which join to balance mid-war should be less likely to win compared with balancers that joined immediately. This is because mid-war balancers would be joining as it became clear there was an increasing need to balance. In other words, they would be prompted to join by setbacks to their preferred side rather than by successes, meaning their odds of victory should be lowered. Fourth, there should be little relationship between winning and losing for states which bandwagon for non-territorial spoils as those spoils are unlikely to be connected to the outcome of the war. This means such bandwagoners may not consider which side is likely to win when contemplating intervention.[17] An exception would be those states which bandwagon for territorial spoils in the last month of a war, but this is a category of joining that as argued above is very unlikely to occur (see Table 6.3). Last, it is not clear whether joiners should win or lose more often than not, nor is it clear whether balancers will win or lose more often than bandwagoners.

Findings

These hypotheses are tested and the results presented in Table 6.4. Any state that voluntarily began its belligerency after the first day of the war is included in the table.[18] The state's name and the COW war number (the list of COW wars and their respective war numbers can be found in Table 6.5) are given as well as whether the state joined the winning or losing side according to COW. States which joined a given war multiple times are listed for each entry with a roman numeral after their name indicating which entry is being indicated. Only states which switched sides are considered as joining multiple times. States which simply exited for a time

Table 6.3 Types of joining and the likelihood of winning

	Balancing	Bandwagoning – territorial spoils	Bandwagoning – non-territorial spoils
First month	More likely to win than later balancers	Less likely to win than later bandwagoners	No relationship expected
Mid-war	Less likely to win than earlier balancers	More likely to win than earlier bandwagoners	No relationship expected
Last month	Highly likely to win; unlikely to occur	Highly likely to win	Highly likely to win; unlikely to occur

Table 6.4 Joining by type, belligerent, and war

	Balancing	Bandwagoning – territorial spoils	Bandwagoning – non-territorial spoils
First month	Two Sicilies (16)-W Austria (16)-W France (106)-W United Kingdom (106)-W Russia (106)-W Estonia (108)-W Germany I (108)-W Czechoslovakia (112)-W Australia (139)-W Canada (139)-W France I (139)-W Great Britain (139)-W New Zealand (139)-W South Africa (139)-W United States (151)-S	Modena (10)-L Tuscany (10)-L France (28)-W Italy (55)-W Romania (103)-W Japan (106)-W Germany (106)-L Jordan (181)-L	*Saudi Arabia (181)-L* *France (225)-W* *Australia (225)-W*
Mid-war	France (22)-W Great Britain (22)-W Peru (52)-W Peru (64)-L Portugal (106)-W United States (106)-W Finland (107)-W New Zealand (130)-W South Africa (130)-W United States (139)-W Great Britain (151)-S China (151)-S Canada (211)-W France (211)-W Great Britain (211)-W Italy (211)-W Oman (211)-W Qatar (211)-W Saudi Arabia (211)-W UAE (211)-W United States (211)-W	Bulgaria (106)-L Italy (106)-W Ottoman Empire (106)-L Romania (106)-W Germany II (108)-L Bulgaria I (139)-L Bulgaria II (139)-W Finland (139)-L France II (139)-L France III (139)-W Hungary (139)-L Italy I (139)-L Italy II (139)-W Romania I (139)-L Romania II (139)-W	Sardinia (22)-W France (130)-W Brazil (139)-W Australia (151)-S Belgium (151)-S Canada (151)-S Colombia (151)-S Ethiopia (151)-S France (151)-S Greece (151)-S Netherlands (151)-S Philippines (151)-S Thailand (151)-S Turkey (151)-S Cambodia (163)-L Philippines (163)-L South Korea (163)-L Thailand (163)-L Egypt (211)-W Morocco (211)-W Syria (211)-W Canada (225)-W
Last month		Ottoman Empire (103)-W Soviet Union (130)-W	*Mongolia (130)-W*

during a cease-fire or negotiations are not counted as rejoining when they reentered the conflict. For example, the second time France joined World War Two is listed as France II (139), but Bulgaria and Serbia are not counted as having joined the First Balkan War when their ceasefire with the Ottomans ended.[19] World War Two has been split into its European and Pacific theaters, with the Pacific theater being treated as a continuation of the Third Sino-Japanese War that began in 1937.

Table 6.5 List of COW interstate wars v.4.0

1	Franco-Spanish War of 1823	118	Manchurian War of 1929
4	First Russo-Turkish War of 1828–1829	121	Second Sino-Japanese War of 1931–1933
7	Mexican–American War of 1846–1847	124	Chaco War of 1932–1935
10	Austro-Sardinian War of 1848–1849	125	Saudi–Yemeni War of 1934
13	First Schleswig-Holstein War of 1848–1849	127	Conquest of Ethiopia of 1935–1936
16	War of the Roman Republic of 1849	130	Third Sino-Japanese War of 1937–1941
19	La Plata War of 1851–1852	133	Changkufeng War of 1938
22	Crimean War of 1853–1856	136	Nomonhan War of 1939
25	Anglo-Persian War of 1856–1857	139	World War II of 1939–1945
28	War of Italian Unification of 1859	142	Russo-Finnish War of 1939–1940
31	First Spanish–Moroccan War of 1859–1860	145	Franco-Thai War of 1940–1941
34	Italian–Roman War of 1860	147	First Kashmir War of 1948–1949
37	Neapolitan War of 1860–1861	148	Arab–Israeli War of 1948–1949
40	Franco-Mexican War of 1862–1867	151	Korean War of 1950–1953
43	Ecuadorian–Columbian War of 1863	153	Off-shore Islands War of 1954
46	Second Schleswig-Holstein War of 1864	155	Sinai War of 1956
		156	Soviet Invasion of Hungary of 1956
49	Lopez War of 1864–1870	158	Ifni War of 1957–1959
52	Naval War of 1865–1866	160	War in Assam of 1962
55	Seven Weeks War of 1866	163	Vietnam War Phase 2
58	Franco-Prussian War of 1870–1871	166	Second Kashmir War of 1965
60	First Central American War of 1876	169	Six Day War of 1967
61	Second Russo-Turkish War of 1877–1878	170	Second Laotian War Phase 2, 1968–1973
64	War of the Pacific of 1879–1883	172	War of Attrition of 1969–1970
65	Conquest of Egypt of 1882	175	Football War of 1969
67	Sino-French War of 1884–1885	176	War of the Communist Coalition of 1970–1971
70	Second Central American War of 1885	178	War for Bangladesh of 1971
73	First Sino-Japanese War of 1894–1895	181	Yom Kippur War of 1973
76	Greco-Turkish War of 1897	184	Turco-Cypriot War of 1974
79	Spanish–American War of 1898	186	War Over Angola of 1975–1976
82	Boxer Rebellion of 1900	187	Second Ogaden War Phase 2, 1977–1979
83	Sino-Russian War of 1900		
85	Russo-Japanese War of 1904–1905	189	Vietnamese–Cambodian War of 1975–1979
88	Third Central American War of 1906		
91	Fourth Central American War of 1907	190	Ugandan–Tanzanian War of 1978–1979
94	Second Spanish–Moroccan War of 1909–1910	193	Sino-Vietnamese Punitive War of 1979
		199	Iran–Iraq War of 1980–1988
97	Italian–Turkish War of 1911–1912	202	Falklands War of 1982
100	First Balkan War of 1912–1913	205	War over Lebanon of 1982
103	Second Balkan War of 1913	207	War over the Aouzou Strip of 1986–1987
106	World War I of 1914–1918		
107	Estonian War of Liberation of 1918–1920	211	Gulf War of 1990–1991
		215	War of Bosnian Independence of 1992
108	Latvian War of Liberation of 1918–1920	216	Azeri–Armenian War of 1993–1994
		217	Cenepa Valley War of 1995
109	Russo-Polish War of 1919–1920	219	Badme Border War of 1998–2000
112	Hungarian Adversaries of 1919	221	War for Kosovo of 1999
115	Second Greco-Turkish War of 1919–1922	223	Kargil War of 1999
		225	Invasion of Afghanistan of 2001
116	Franco-Turkish War of 1919–1921	227	Invasion of Iraq of 2003
117	Lithuanian–Polish War of 1920		

States were categorized by when the state joined and why the state joined, mirroring the structure of Tables 6.2 and 6.3. Motives for joining were coded as follows. States whose main reason for intervening was upholding the status quo in regard to the issues that were at stake in the war were coded as balancing. Likewise states whose main goal was trying to revise the status quo in regard to the issues at stake in the war and which were seeking territory were coded as territorial bandwagoners. Seeking territorial spoils includes bandwagoning in the hopes the winning side will not seize the territory of the state in question or at least will limit its annexations. In other words, pure Balance of Threat bandwagoners (Walt 1985) can seek territory – the retention of their own.[20] Bandwagoning states seeking both territorial and non-territorial spoils were classified as territorial bandwagoners. This is because the states in question tend to prioritize their territorial goals over their non-territorial goals. Finally, states whose main goal was extracting non-territorial spoils were coded as non-territorial bandwagoners. Such states often do have a clear preference for the outcome of a war, but that is not their primary reason for joining. Rather, they join in hopes of currying favor or securing rewards from a powerful state already in the war. Thus, non-territorial bandwagoners can end up allied with states engaged in balancing.

Timing of entry is broken down as joining in the first month, joining in the last month, and joining in any other month (mid-war). In wars lasting less than two months, it is possible for a state to join on a date that is both within the first and last month of the war. These interventions were coded as happening in the first month if they occurred closer to the war's onset and in the last month if they occurred at or past the mid-point of the war.[21] It is also indicated whether a state won (W) or lost (L) the war. Stalemates (S) are also coded. Entries which fit with the hypotheses outlined above in Table 6.2 are in the standard font; misses are in italics.

The actual distribution of joiners by time and motive fits the expected distribution fairly well. Early and mid-war balancing were both expected to be common behaviors. The data indicates they were: 15 states balanced in the first month and 21 did so mid-war out of a total of 87 cases of military intervention. That is 17.2 percent and 24.1 percent of the cases respectively. Of the early balancers nine (60 percent) had allies already in the war when they entered, consistent with expectations.[22] Nine mid-war balancers also had alliance obligations with active belligerents (42.8 percent), a somewhat lower percentage as expected. This does not count the three states that formed balancing alliances with one of the belligerents after the start of the war, but prior—often by days—to the state joining the war. This is because such alliances were caused by the decision to join the war, rather than decision to join the war being caused by the alliance.[23]

Mid-war bandwagoning for both territorial and non-territorial spoils were also predicted to be common behaviors; they were, with 15 (17.2 percent) and 22 (25.2 percent) instances respectively. As expected, mid-war territorial bandwagoning was influenced by alliances less than first-month territorial bandwagoning was. Only three states (20 percent) had alliances with belligerents – again not counting those that were created after the outbreak of war with active belligerents to facilitate bandwagoning.[24] Such last-minute alliances are clearly driven by events in the war, meaning both the alliance and belligerency are products of these events. The final behavior predicted to be likely, late territorial bandwagoning, had only two instances but this was 67 percent of the total instances of joining in the last month. Presumably many of the mid-war territorial bandwagoners hoped to end up in this box and simply got the timing wrong.[25] Also, as discussed below, a case can be made that Romania's intervention into the Second Balkan War belongs in the late rather than early territorial bandwagoning box.

Three behaviors were predicted as being very unlikely to occur: last-month balancing; last-month non-territorial bandwagoning; and first-month non-territorial bandwagoning. The evidence supports these predictions. There are no cases, one case, and three cases of these behaviors respectively. Additionally, one of these misses, Mongolia's (130) late non-territorial bandwagoning, is directly tied to the Soviet Union's joining of the same war (Third Sino-Japanese / World War Two in the Pacific) in a predicted box – last-month territorial bandwagoning. As Mongolia was a Soviet satellite state with a very limited freedom of action when it came to its foreign policy, the intervention makes sense. Mongolian participation lowered Soviet costs and Mongolia lacked the freedom of action to extract territorial concessions for its participation. Saudi participation in the Yom Kippur War and French and Australian participation in the Invasion of Afghanistan are misses for the theory, but all three were allied to states already in the war, as expected for early joiners.[26]

Last, early territorial bandwagoning was predicted to happen, but only rarely. Eight cases fall into this box (9.2 percent). This is somewhat more frequent than expected, but is certainly less common than first-month balancing and all forms of mid-war joining. Also, it was claimed that when such early territorial bandwagoning did occur, it would be the result of pre-war alliances. Of the eight states that exhibited this behavior, five had alliances with states that were either the initial belligerents in the war or that had already joined the war: France in the War of Italian Unification, Italy in the Seven Weeks War, Germany and Japan in World War One, and Jordan in the Yom Kippur War.[27] Of the other three states in this box, Romania in the Second Balkan War joined in the last month of that war, but closer to the beginning by four days. The Romanians were driven to enter by Bulgaria's obvious military collapse and the opportunity to pick up the southern Dobruja cheaply. Thus, Romanian motives look more like those of a last-month joiner, which in fact Romania was. The other two states, Modena and Tuscany, in the Austro-Sardinian War, did in fact have an ante-bellum alliance with Austria, but ended up joining the Sardinian side. This is because their ducal governments were overthrown in the revolutions of 1848 and the new republican governments threw in their lot with Sardinia against the conservative Austrians who were trying to restore the overthrown dukes to power. In other words, Austria and the ducal governments honored their alliances thereby naturally arraying the revolutionary governments on the other side. Thus, Modena's and Tuscany's behavior appears to be the exception that proves the rule.

Overall, the notion that there are distinct types of joining holds up well. Different motives led to different types of triggering events and different timings of entry. Balancers joined early out of alliance considerations and mid-war in response to revealed information. Bandwagoners seeking territory joined mid-war and occasionally very late and did so in response to revealed information. Bandwagoners not seeking territory joined mid-war in response to negotiations with alliance partners. There were a few misses but they were largely explainable and they do not undermine the overall value of our argument.

Interestingly, bandwagoning was more common overall than balancing (51 instances versus 36). This runs contrary to Waltz's (1979) expectations, but is consistent with Schweller (1994). Obviously, as a great deal and perhaps even the preponderance of balancing and bandwagoning would occur during periods of peace rather than war and given that other behaviors like hiding are possible, this is not a conclusive test of Waltz's proposition that states should tend toward balancing. Still, it fits with other studies that suggest Waltz's claim is likely incorrect (Rosecrance and Lo 1996; Schroeder 1994; Schweller 1994).

It is also striking that 23 of the 26 states which engaged in non-territorial bandwagoning joined coalitions led by the United States and that 25 of the 26 cases occurred from 1944 onwards. The former is consistent with McDonald's (2015) observation of the prevalence of US-led coalitions in the post-World War Two era. The latter is consistent with Shirkey (2009) which finds that such bandwagoning should be more common in the post-World War Two era given the norm of territorial integrity.[28] Presumably as one of the leading states of the post-World War Two era the United States is in a strong position to hand out such non-territorial spoils. Two of the three states not bandwagoning with the US – Mongolia in World War Two and Sardinia in the Crimean War – also allied themselves with leading powers. As mentioned above, Mongolia was a co-belligerent with the Soviet Union (and technically also with the United States) while Sardinia joined a Franco-British coalition.

Predictions that certain behaviors were more likely to result in a state being on the winning side of a war were also made. These predictions had mixed results. Faring well were the predictions that states that joined in the last month of the war would win at a high rate and that there would be little relationship between non-territorial bandwagoning and winning for states that joined early or mid-war. States won in all three of the last-month joining cases and early and mid-war non-territorial joiners won nine wars, lost five, and drew 11 (the draws are all a result of the Korean War), though three of these wins come from the Invasion of Afghanistan as COW counts that war as having ended when the Taliban fell and then later resumed as a new civil war. If those three wins are excluded, the record becomes six wins, five losses, and 11 draws. These outcomes fit well with the predictions.

The results for other predictions in relation to winning and losing were poor. Early balancers were also predicted to be more likely to win than mid-war balancers. In fact, they did exceptionally well, winning 14 times and drawing only once. However, mid-war balancers also did very well, winning 18 times, losing once, and drawing twice. The predictions fared equally poorly for territorial bandwagoners. While early territorial bandwagoners were predicted to be less likely to win, they in fact won four times and lost four times – a better record than mid-war territorial bandwagoners which were predicted to win more often. The mid-war bandwagoners only won six times compared with nine defeats. Thus, overall balancers went 32–1–3 while territorial bandwagoners went 12–13–0 when last-month bandwagoners are also included. The record for bandwagoning when non-territorial bandwagoners are included is little changed at 18–17–11 excluding the three wins from the Invasion of Afghanistan. Thus, the striking result is that states that intervene during wars out of balancing motives do far better than those that join for the purpose of bandwagoning. Given that balancing is often seen as the more difficult behavior this is initially surprising, but it is likely a result of the fact the bandwagoners are often less powerful states compared with the states already in the war and thus their entries are unlikely to significantly affect the outcome of the war. Balancers, other the other hand, are often powerful states whose contributions to the war effort can often turn a defeat into a victory. Indeed, that is precisely the point of interventions driven by balancing concerns.

Conclusion

Detailed cases studies would need to be performed on those states which intervened militarily mid-war and in the last month of wars to know for certain that their leadership's decision-making was influenced by estimates of the military balance, the nature of the challenge, and the nature of the opportunity. However, states' aggregate behaviors are consistent with what would be expected if they were indeed focused on those variables. The timing of states' entries is consistent with what one would expect given the broad motives of those states.

When this is combined with the fact that prior studies have found that military interveners are indeed influenced by battlefield results – in other words information about the military balance and the demands made and rewards offered by belligerent states (Shirkey 2009; 2012) – confidence in the conclusion that non-belligerent states are engaged in very similar decision-making processes as states in the ante-bellum period grows. Presumably states which choose to remain out of the fray often are making similar calculations. However, as with states that opt to hide prior to the war – i.e., neither balance nor bandwagon – they are concluding that hiding or another peaceful strategy is their best option.

Why does this matter beyond trying to explain non-belligerent states' behavior during wars? It matters in part because it suggests states are always engaged to some degree in these sorts of calculations. In other words, states are presumably worried about the relative balance of forces, the nature of threats, and the nature of opportunities, not only when wars are likely to occur in the near future or are already underway, but even when war is a remote or unlikely prospect. This means the theory and hypotheses developed in Chapters 1, 2, and 4 can be applied to help understand contemporary state behavior even if it is unclear that a war is likely to result. This is consistent both with realist theories that see balancing and bandwagoning as regular behaviors in both peace and war (Schweller 1994; Walt 1985; Waltz 1979) and bargaining theories that see state behavior as an endless string of bargaining (Blainey 1973; Fearon 1995; Powell 2012; Wagner 2004; 2007; Wolford 2014).

Chapter 7 attempts to apply the hypotheses from Chapters 1, 2, and 4 to a case of potential balancing, bandwagoning, and hiding during just such a peaceful period. It explores the contemporary case of assertive Chinese behavior in the South China Sea and the reaction of other states to that behavior. It also seeks to predict what alignments and state behaviors are likely and argues that tensions in the region are unlikely to lead to war in the near term.

Notes

1 How states answer these questions in large part determines whether a period remains peaceful or is but a prelude to further war.
2 This excludes the very small clash between Hungary and Slovakia – also a German ally – in March 1939.
3 The act of a state becoming an active belligerent in an existing war has been variously called diffusion, contagion, intervention, and joining in the literature. For objections to the use of diffusion and contagion see Shirkey (2009). For objections to the use of intervention outside of a humanitarian context see Finnemore (2003).
4 Certainly one can think of situations where it would be impossible to deploy troops into combat zones prior to the 30-day window expiring, but if a state had neither done that nor declared war, it is not clear why such a state should be considered to be at war.
5 The United States prior to World War One would be an example of such unconcerned behavior, while Greece is an example of a state that was trying to hide.
6 Of course this is only a general trend. For example, Italy famously decided not to join the Central Powers in 1914, with whom it had signed the Triple Alliance, but instead later joined the Entente in 1915.
7 There are a couple of other findings from the intervention literature which fit with the arguments made in the preceding chapters. First, geographically proximate states are more likely to join ongoing wars than are other states (Bremer 1982; Gleditsch 2002; Hammerström and Heldt 2002; Houweling and Siccama 1988; Leeds 2005; Most and Starr 1980; Pearson, Baumann, and Pickering 1994; Raknerud and Hegre 1997; Richardson 1960; Shirkey 2009; Siverson and Starr 1991; Starr and Most 1976; Wallensteen and Sollenberg 1998; Ward and Gleditsch 2002). This is consistent with, though not dependent upon, the notion that more distant states would be more able to successfully hide. Second, great powers are more likely to join wars (Altfeld and Bueno de Mesquita 1979; Pearson, Baumann, and Pickering 1994; Richardson 1960; Shirkey 2009; Siverson and Starr 1991; Wright 1965). Again, this is consistent with our previous arguments that smaller states should be more inclined to hide.
8 States should update their expectations in response to any bargaining between third parties (Iklé 1964).
9 Here Levy's (1994) definition of learning is used whereby learning is the updating of expectations in light of new information.
10 The Cuban forces were assisting the Angolan government in its civil war.
11 States could conceivably be seeking both territorial and non-territorial spoils. For the purposes of categorization below, such states are considered to be seeking territorial rather than non-territorial spoils. See Table 6.5 for a list of COW war numbers and the wars they indicate.
12 All balancers would be acting out of self-interest. Balancers are not less self-interested than bandwagoners.

13 In other words, a mid-war joiner could conceivably have an alliance with an initial belligerent, renege on those commitments by not intervening initially, and then join later due to information revealed by the war.
14 One possible exception to this is if all parties thought the war would be brief, early events could indicate that would not in fact be the case. It is unclear how this knowledge would trigger joining or how it would alter the way in which states honor ante-bellum alliance commitments. We are grateful to M. J. Peterson for pointing this out.
15 Even though bandwagoners cannot necessarily change the ultimate outcome of the war, they can reduce the costs borne by stronger states. Thus, bandwagoners are worth rewarding provided they join early enough to bear some costs even if they cannot alter the ultimate outcome of the war.
16 Territorial bandwagoners may also delay entry due to ongoing negotiations over spoils (Shirkey 2009, Chapter 5).
17 This is not to claim that non-territorial bandwagoners lack a preferred outcome for the war, just that their preferences and expectations for the outcome of the war are not central to the timing of their intervention.
18 Thus, Table 6.4 excludes initial belligerents and states that became a belligerent by being attacked or invaded.
19 Both states were among the initial belligerents in that war and are thus excluded from Table 6.4.
20 Such states are not balancing even though they want to preserve the status quo of their own territorial alignments as they are aligned with the side that seeks to alter the broader status quo. Obviously, states can mix Balance of Threat motives with revisionist aims where they seek the territories of other states in addition to hoping to preserve their own borders.
21 This results in Romania being coded as joining in the first month of the Second Balkan War, Jordan and Saudi Arabia being coded as joining in the first month of the Yom Kippur War, and the Ottoman Empire being coded as joining in the last month of the Second Balkan War.
22 Members of the British Commonwealth such as Canada, Australia, New Zealand, and South Africa were considered as allied to the United Kingdom for the purposes of World War Two, both in the Pacific and in Europe.
23 The three states are France and Britain in the Crimean War, both of which signed an alliance with the Ottomans days before joining the war, and Peru in the Chincha Islands War which became an ally of Chile but delayed declaring war so that it could legally take delivery of naval vessels it had purchased from Britain. At the time British law prevented exporting arms to belligerent powers (Burr 1980).
24 Bulgaria and the Ottoman Empire during World War One and Bulgaria, Hungary, and Romania during World War Two fall into this category of forming an alliance prior to belligerency but after the outbreak of war.
25 Italy and Romania in World War One both joined in response to successful Entente offensives and thought they were joining near the end of the war. See Renzi (1987) and Torrey (1998) respectively for the motives behind these states' interventions.
26 France and Australia are coded as winning the Invasion of Afghanistan because COW codes the war as ending when the Taliban fell from power in December 2001. The subsequent civil war is coded as another war entirely.
27 Alliance data was taken from the COW Alliance Dataset 4.1 (Gibler 2009).
28 See Zacher (2001) for evidence of the existence of this norm.

7 The rise of China
Will states balance, bandwagon, or hedge in the South China Sea today?

In 2012, Beijing released a new passport which included a map of China encompassing not only Taiwan, but also dozens of disputed islands in the South China Sea as well as territory contested with India. The passport provoked official protest by both the Philippine and Vietnamese governments. Border officials of the latter even refused to stamp the new passport. Indian officials responded by putting a map on visas issued to Chinese citizens featuring India's own version of the disputed border (Fisher 2012; Guinto and Heath 2012; *Dominion Post* 2012).

This is but one minor manifestation of China's increasing willingness to push its territorial claims and the responses this has provoked in its neighbors. One particularly contentious area for Chinese territorial claims has been the South China Sea. Beijing has aggressively asserted its fishing and hydrocarbon rights within the nine-dash line area it claims in the South China Sea (Wong 2015). This has led to regular clashes between Filipino and Chinese fishermen (Hernandez 2015). Chinese naval vessels have also plied waters near Malaysian offshore oil and gas facilities to the discomfort of Kuala Lumpur, though in general tensions between China and Malaysia are not as high since their claims overlap less with each other than with the other parties to these disputes (Chan 2016, 175–6; Perlez 2014b). More provocatively, China has engaged in extensive island building, turning small islets and submerged reefs in the Spratly Islands into full-fledged islands by pumping sand from the sea floor. From January 2014 to June 2015 the Chinese created 2,000 acres of new land in the Spratlys – most notably at Fiery Cross Reef and 200 miles east at the appropriately named Mischief Reef (Cooper and Perlez 2015a; Sanger and Gladstone 2015; Wong and Perlez 2015).[1] Though there has recently been a halt in island creation, this is a result of China's shift to building military facilities on those new islands, rather than a decrease in assertiveness from Beijing. These new facilities include a 10,000 foot runway on Fiery Cross Reef and hardened hangars large enough to accommodate a variety of military jets on Fiery Cross, Mischief, and Subi Reefs (Sanger and Gladstone 2016; Wong and Perlez 2015).[2] China has also invested considerable sums into upgrading its military capacities on Hainan Island – especially air and naval assets – and has established a missile battery on Woody Island in the Paracel Islands (Buszynski 2012, 145–6; Erickson et al. 2015; Landler and Forsythe 2016; Storey 2011, 91). These new military facilities have considerably extended the potential ranges of Chinese missiles, jets, radar, and naval patrols (Forsythe and Perlez 2016).

While it is natural that China's assertiveness would grow in line with increases in Chinese power resources (He and Feng 2012), such actions defy the spirit of a non-binding 2002 agreement signed by China and the members of the Association of Southeast Asian Nations (ASEAN) to avoid provocative actions in the South China Sea (Governments of the Member States of ASEAN and the Government of the People's Republic of China 2002). Unsurprisingly, these actions have led to tension between China and some ASEAN members and caused ASEAN to seek to deepen the agreement. In particular, ASEAN wants China to acknowledge full respect for the United Nations Convention on the Law of the Sea (UNCLOS), self-restraint, and the non-use of force to resolve disputes – concessions China has been unwilling to make (Browne 2015). Indeed, China has slowed negotiations with ASEAN on a more binding Code of Conduct for the South China Sea to a glacial pace (Browne 2015; Rapp-Hooper 2015b; Perlez 2016b). Beijing's actions in the South China Sea and unwillingness to make concessions in the Code of Conduct negotiations have led ASEAN to state in an official release that China's policies have "eroded trust and confidence and may undermine peace, security, and stability in the South China Sea" (Rapp-Hooper 2015a).

Chinese rhetoric has been equally tough. In May 2015 at a regional defense conference in Singapore, Admiral Sun Jianguo threatened that China may set up an air defense identification zone in the South China Sea similar to the one it has already established in the East China Sea (Wong 2015). That same month, embassy spokesman Zhu Haiquan articulated the Chinese legal position. He stated,

> China has indisputable sovereignty over the Nansha [Spratly] Islands and their adjacent waters. The relevant construction, which is reasonable, justified and lawful, is well within China's sovereignty. It does not impact or target any country, and is thus beyond reproach.
> (Entous, Lubold, and Barnes 2015)

Likewise, speaking to the media in March 2014 in reference to the South China Sea, Wang Yi, the Chinese Foreign Minister, insisted that,

> As for China's territorial and maritime dispute with some countries China would like to carry out equal-footing consultation and negotiation and properly handle by peaceful means on the basis of respecting historical facts and international law. There will not be any change in this position ... we will never bully smaller countries yet we will never accept unreasonable demands from smaller countries.
> (Wong 2014)

Given Chinese obstructionism on the Code of Conduct, unwillingness to recognize international courts' jurisdiction in territorial disputes (see below), and unorthodox interpretations of the rights conferred by exclusive economic zones

(Twomey 2014), references to negotiations and international law are less than fully reassuring. In particular, Chinese officials insist that since their claims precede the signing of UNCLOS, that treaty's provisions cannot be used to downgrade or limit their claims (Buszynski 2012, 140). China has also bristled at criticism from other states. Hua Chunying, a foreign ministry spokeswoman, reacted harshly in the spring of 2015 to US objections to China's land reconstruction program, arguing that,

> The US side made inappropriate remarks on China's longstanding sovereignty as well as rights and interests in the South China Sea to foment dissention and criticized China's normal and justified construction activities on islands and reefs.
> (Ministry of Foreign Affairs of the People's Republic of China 2015)

Still, the importance of recent Chinese actions should not be overplayed. The man-made islands are not easily defended and do not confer maritime control under UNCLOS.[3] Additionally, the South China Sea facilities are especially vulnerable to corrosion from sea water and the islets themselves are threatened with erosion. Most importantly, Chinese actions have done nothing to evict other claimants from the features they occupy. Doing so would require force and would be a significant escalation of current Chinese behavior (Erickson et al. 2015; Forsythe and Perlez 2016).

Also, the degree of change in Chinese behavior can be overstated. China has taken assertive actions in the past, especially prior to 2000 (Johnston 2011).[4] There were significant tensions between China on the one hand and Malaysia, the Philippines, and Vietnam on the other over features in the South China Sea during the early and mid-1990s (Acharya 2001, 135; Storey 2011, 112–14 and 255). This was followed by a lull in the late 1990s and early 2000s as China's leaders focused on improving relations with their Southeast Asian neighbors rather than aggressively advancing its territorial claims (Goh 2007; Li 2010; Lim 2014, 119; Storey 2011, 65–9).

Furthermore, from a Chinese perspective Beijing's actions can be seen as defensive. China's past has made both the government in Beijing and broader nationalist sentiment highly sensitive to perceived territorial encroachments.[5] China is also to some degree reacting to other states' attempts to bolster their own legal claims in the South China Sea and those states' moves to exploit the Sea's fishing and hydrocarbon resources. Also, the United States' alliances with Asian states are often seen as directed at China and as a potential form of encirclement (Storey 2011, 260). This makes any US involvement in the South China Sea dispute appear threatening to China. In no small part, this is because Beijing sees control of the South China Sea as vital for ensuring it can maintain navigation for its exports and oil imports through the Straits of Malacca (Storey 2011, 85–6). Thus, any powerful, foreign naval presence in the South China Sea can be construed as an implied economic threat. Finally, control of the South China Sea serves as a potential defensive shield against any military threats to southern China (Buszynski 2012, 141–6; Li 2010; Lim 2014, 117 and 130; Storey 2011, 91).

That said, recent actions do indicate a significant increase in Chinese assertiveness since 2007 (Storey 2011, 91) and raise an important question: how will China's neighbors in Southeast Asia react to the new policies that accompany China's rising power?[6] The previous chapters and international relations theory more broadly suggest at least three possibilities: bandwagoning, balancing, and hiding. Bandwagoners would befriend the rising power in hopes of obtaining rewards and increasing their security. Balancers would work to resist and hopefully block the growing demands of the rising state. States which hid would do so in the hope that by not interfering or cooperating with the rising power they would be left alone.[7] In practice, states may hedge by taking a mixed approach: working with Beijing on some issues while opposing it on others (Murphy 2010; Roy 2005). Indeed, some behaviors may defy traditional descriptions of behavior altogether. And of course, the various states in the region may pursue quite different policies from each other.

Still, it is worth considering whether there is a trend toward a given behavior. Which direction regional state behaviors lean is important not just within Southeast Asia but also globally as local behaviors structure the overall environment in which all states will interact with China. A region where many smaller states are actively bandwagoning with China would be far more threatening to outside states than one in which China's neighbors mostly balanced against it or even hid. We argue that due to the geo-strategic, economic, and institutional characteristics of the region, it is very unlikely that any of these states will choose to bandwagon with China. The states in the region have the capacity and ability to resist China in important ways. Significant shifts in the strategic, economic and institutional situation of the region would have to occur to induce widespread bandwagoning with China. While this is not impossible, it remains highly improbable for the foreseeable future. Of course, an absence of bandwagoning does not mean effective balancing either. First, the behavior of states bordering the South China Sea may vary significantly from those of Southeast Asian states that have no claims in that sea with non-claimant states being less likely to balance. Second, states may hedge or hide in the hope of passing the buck to other states or to the future. Finally, even states attempting to balance may fail to cooperate effectively with each other. Indeed, the large number of states in the region, and the fact that they face a single potential threat, makes collective action problems a real concern (Walt 2010).

The remainder of this chapter will be organized as follows. First, the theoretical implications for the three types of uncertainty – intentions, capabilities, and the nature of the move – are considered in relation to Chinese actions in the South China Sea. Second, the current problem facing the states in the region will be examined in light of the problems faced by states in East Central Europe in the 1930s. This comparative case study will examine the crucial differences between the geostrategic environment between the two regions and time periods and their implications for the likelihood of balancing are explored. Third, the behavior of states with territorial claims in the South China Sea plus that of the United States is described. Last, we discuss how closely the behavior of these states fits with the theoretical expectations derived from the types of uncertainty and the differences between East Central Europe and Southeast Asia.

Types of uncertainty

By restricting the case to states' actions in the South China Sea, the level of uncertainty is greatly reduced. If China's rise was examined globally or even just within the entirety of Asia, uncertainty about intentions, capabilities, and the strategic advantage obtained by various Chinese moves would be quite large. For our more narrow purposes, these very large uncertainties do play a role in influencing US behavior in the South China Sea and suggest it will be quite difficult for Washington to craft policy for the long run. Trying to determine Chinese intentions or relative military capabilities 20 or 30 years from now is most difficult. In the short run, however, the nature of these uncertainties vis-à-vis the United States is not that much different from the ones posed by action in the South China Sea. Thus, it will suffice to explore the more narrow case with the understanding that the conclusions drawn from it only apply locally and in the near to medium term.

First, there is very little uncertainty about the strategic value of the Chinese moves. While *de jure* control of the South China Sea would be quite valuable, as will be seen below, Beijing's actions are not significantly increasing the odds of such an outcome. And as far as *de facto* control goes, Chinese military installations on islets in the South China Sea – as opposed to those on Hainan Island – are quite vulnerable and do little to shift the military balance (Erickson et al. 2015).

Second, on the question of military capabilities there again is little uncertainty.[8] Chinese air and especially naval assets are far superior to those of any rival claimant and the gap is growing rather than shrinking. This would remain true even if the other claimants were to combine their forces. If the US Navy is brought into consideration, however, the balance of air and naval assets shifts strongly away from China. While the Chinese are developing significant sea-denial capacities, the US Navy remains much stronger than the People's Liberation Army Navy and could render decisive aid to the other claimants if it so chose (Lim 2014). Thus, much as in East Central Europe in the 1930s, the balance of forces hinges on an outside power's willingness to intercede. Therefore, any uncertainty about relative capabilities in the South China Sea boils down to uncertainty about US intentions and commitments.

Finally, there is uncertainty about Chinese intentions, but it is a limited sort of uncertainty. Beijing clearly intends to establish full Chinese control and sovereignty throughout all of the South China Sea that lies within its historical claim – the nine-dash line. On the other hand, Beijing has given little reason to believe it would seek territory beyond the line in the maritime areas of Southeast Asia. As will be seen below, China has successfully resolved several other outstanding territorial disputes with Vietnam. This helps to clarify the limits of Chinese aims. What is unclear is how many risks Beijing would be willing to run to achieve its goals. Would Beijing use large-scale military force and risk a serious confrontation or military clash with the United States? The possibility that China may escalate could make both its regional rival claimants and the United States wary about taking too firm a stand and makes the formation of a balancing coalition less likely. Thus, China's claims are limited but threatening nevertheless.

That said, the nature of uncertainty in the South China Sea suggests it should be possible to build a successful balancing coalition. The likelihood of balancing here depends on two factors. First, whether or not the United States is willing to provide both significant material support to states in the region and leadership around which a coalition can form. Second, whether or not the United States and the states in the region find taking a hard line against China's claims in the South China Sea is worth potentially damaging relations with Beijing. Neither of these necessary conditions is guaranteed, meaning states may try to hide, hedge, or transcend. As will be seen below, the differences between East Central Europe in the 1930s and Southeast Asia today also give reasons to think that a balancing coalition in the South China Sea could form. At a minimum, they suggest that bandwagoning with China is unlikely.

Key differences between 1930s East Central Europe and Southeast Asia today

Many scholars have previously debated whether balancing or bandwagoning in Asia is more likely (Acharya 2003; Christensen 2006; Friedberg 2000; Goh 2008; Kang 2009; Mearsheimer 2010). This chapter differs from previous analyses in that we use a specific comparative case of bandwagoning – that of East Central Europe in the 1930s which we developed in Chapter 3 – rather than looking at only Asia or at centuries-long sweeps of European history as a comparison. There are several uncanny similarities between contemporary Southeast Asia and 1930s East Central Europe which make the comparison relevant. First, each has a rising, revisionist great power with claims on territories held by its much weaker neighbors. Second, both China today and Germany in the 1930s had strong economic ties with the smaller powers in their region. Third, in both cases the rising power had significant co-ethnics abroad in the region. However, this last point is not as relevant as the first two since China's diaspora differs from German minorities in Europe. Namely, the Chinese diaspora is the product of emigration which started in the nineteenth century, not a humiliating loss of territory.[9] As a result, it is much less likely to be the cause of irredentist claims or to fuel popular nationalist demands.

Of course, the differences are equally striking and relevant. China is not seeking to export a doctrine of racial hatred and radical political reorganization and its leadership appears to be more risk averse than were the Nazis.[10] Also, the Chinese, unlike the Germans in the 1930s who threatened the existence of all of the states in East Central Europe, do not pose an existential threat to any of their neighbors with the exception of Taiwan. These differences are important as they make China far less threatening and far more attractive as a partner for neighboring states than was Nazi Germany. Yet, despite the concerns Germany raised, it was able to attract a great many states to its banner. Thus, it could be possible for China to do the same.

What would balancing or bandwagoning behavior among Southeast Asian states today look like? Balancers should not only resist Chinese claims diplomatically, but also engage in military buildups (internal balancing) and seek to forge and strengthen alliances to oppose China (external balancing). Bandwagoners on the other hand should seek closer political relations with Beijing including the formation or strengthening of military alliances. Such states should also move away diplomatically from the United States or other potential rivals of China. While closer economic relations with Beijing would be consistent with bandwagoning, increasing economic ties would also be consistent with a variety of other behaviors and could simply be the result of regional economic development and the global increase of international economic ties in general. However, closer economic relations with China which come very much at the *intentional* expense of economic relations with other states – i.e., trade diversion rather than trade creation – would be indicative of bandwagoning.[11]

Other behaviors are also possible. For instance, states could hide. These states would avoid taking stances on contentious security issues and maintain a low diplomatic profile. States could also oppose China on some issues while working with China on others. If these states attempted to maintain good relations with both China and the United States they could be seen as hedging, provided that the states in question saw such behavior as a way to keep future options open and risks low. Such behavior could also be consistent with attempts at transcending, provided the said states worked assiduously to reduce tensions and solve the underlying points of contention between China, the United States, and other regional players. Finally, such behaviors might not fit with any one dominant theme, but rather reflect a complicated basket of behaviors that vary based on the issue and context.

Four key differences between East Central Europe in the 1930s and Southeast Asia today suggest that the bandwagoning scenario is in fact very unlikely.[12] Differences in geopolitics, inter-regional disputes, regional organizations, and economic ties both inside and outside the region all reduce the odds of bandwagoning and point to the real possibility of balancing or hedging. Each of the four factors is explored in turn, showing first how they led to bandwagoning in the 1930s and then how the situation in Southeast Asia today is unlikely to lead to similar behaviors.

The geopolitics of great power military assistance

The geopolitics of East Central Europe in the 1930s greatly favored bandwagoning while those of Southeast Asia today do not. By the late 1930s Hungary, Romania, Finland, and Bulgaria all had bandwagoned with Nazi Germany. Even Poland and Yugoslavia, both of which Germany ultimately invaded, bandwagoned for a time. This outcome was helped by three aspects of the geography of Europe. First, East Central Europe was vulnerable to land invasion from Germany, while the sea provides a buffer for many Southeast Asian states, especially those with territorial claims in the South China Sea. Second, while Germany stood between the East Central European states and their potential great power allies, for Southeast Asian states the sea serves as a route for great power aid. Geography greatly constrained the ability of Britain and France to aid the states in the region due to Germany's central location. Chamberlain and Daladier, the British and French Prime Ministers, repeatedly emphasized that there was no way to get British and French forces to Czechoslovakia if war occurred. The western powers did have the ability to launch an offensive against Germany; however, given their belief in the superiority of defensive military tactics, this was unattractive. Furthermore, opening a "Western Front" was deeply unpopular at home given both the memories of World War One and the difficult economic situation (Shirer 1984). Indeed, in 1939 the western powers did little more than formally declare war and mobilize to defend the French frontier after Germany invaded Poland. A third obstacle to balancing was that the British and French had little desire to help. Neither was sure that protecting these states was worth the risk of war. The British were not even sure the survival of these states was particularly important. France had tried in the 1920s to create a string of alliances in the region to prevent German resurgence. However, by the 1930s the value of these alliances to France was in doubt, leading Paris to weaken its commitment to its erstwhile allies. Finally, the states of East Central Europe were also worried about the Soviet Union and some saw it as a greater threat than Germany. Thus, the Soviets remained an unknown quantity, further complicating the situation (Schweller 2006) and making strategic calculations more difficult than they are today in Southeast Asia.

As was seen in Chapter 5, the elites of Hungary, Poland, Yugoslavia, and Romania vigorously debated whether to bandwagon with, hide from, or balance against Germany (Cienciala 1992; Hitchins 1994; Sakmyster 1980; Lukač 1979). But ultimately they knew that opposing Germany without great power assistance was national suicide, especially since they could not count on a coalition of their neighbors. All this not only made bandwagoning more attractive than the alternative but also eventually made it seem like the only viable option available for many of the states in East Central Europe.

In contrast to 1930s Europe, the geography in Southeast Asia is far more favorable for balancing. First, of the states with claims in the South China Sea, only Vietnam shares a land border with China and it has resolved its land border disputes as well as those in the Gulf of Tonkin with Beijing (Storey 2011, 116–17). The rest – Malaysia, Indonesia, Brunei, and the Philippines – are all either offshore or significantly removed from China. This greatly reduces the immediacy and danger of any Chinese threats. Second, all have access to the sea, meaning China is unable to effectively block military aid from the United States. Indeed, the United States is a significant arms supplier to many of the states in the region (Roy 2005). The United States also has bases in Australia, Japan, and Guam which greatly increase its ability to project power into the region. Thus, the United States can offer effective military assistance in a way Britain and France could not in the 1930s. This is vital as the United States is the only plausible external, great power intervener in the South China Sea. Incidentally, this reduces the odds of buck-passing as the United States has no other great power to pass the buck to. It does not, however, eliminate the possibility as Washington could pass the buck to the future – a possibility that would align with British and French behavior in the 1930s.[13] These sea routes also allow states such as Australia and Japan to intervene, though any such intervention would most likely be in conjunction with, and certainly not in opposition to, the United States.

This argument runs contrary to some realist thought. Mearsheimer (2001) argues that common land borders promote balancing because a rising power presents a direct threat to those countries it borders. This is consistent with arguments that naval power and wealth are less likely to be balanced against than are land forces (Angell 1915; Levy and Thompson 2005; 2010; Parent and Rosato 2015). Of course, given the limited number of cases of rising powers and the Eurocentric bias of studies on balancing (Levy and Thompson 2005; 2010) it is possible that it is insular powers rather than any state projecting sea power that is unlikely to be balanced against (Blagden 2011).[14] Either way, this reluctance to balance against sea or insular powers derives from a belief about the stopping power of water (Blagden 2011; Levy and Thompson 2005; 2010; Mearsheimer 2001). In other words, it is harder for states to project military power across oceans than across land borders. However, while this is a reasonable conclusion for geographically proximate states – France can project military power into Germany more easily than it can into Britain – it does not hold for distant states. Over great distances, it is easier to project power across water due to the ease of shipping and the inability of other states to block that movement. For instance, in the 1930s, it was easier for Britain to project military power globally than it was to project power into the heart of Central Europe. This ability to project power by sea was a crucial factor in the creation and maintenance of the British Empire in the past and likewise is a vital aspect of the United States' position as the preeminent military power in the world today. Thus, our conclusion that the sea increases rather than decreases the odds of the United States providing assistance to regional actors, allowing Southeast Asian states to potentially engage in balancing in the South China Sea.

Mearsheimer (2001) also claims that sea borders require great powers engaged in balancing behavior to base military forces in the states of the smaller powers that are geographically proximate to the threat. Mearsheimer quite reasonably argues that small powers may, for reasons of sovereignty, be reluctant to allow foreign troops on their soil and that if the potential balancer shared a land border with the rising power, such basing would be unnecessary. However, if the balancer is physically separated from its potential allies by the rising state as France was in the 1930s, it may not be able to protect its potential allies. Furthermore, the threat to sovereignty may be reduced if the potential balancer is geographically removed and only naval and air assets are to be based on the smaller states' territories. Thus, again sea lanes may well facilitate rather than hinder balancing in Southeast Asia today.

Third, the United States is more willing to back the states of Southeast Asia today than Britain and France were to support the states of East Central Europe in the 1930s.[15] One factor strongly suggestive of how Washington would act in the event of a crisis in the region is that unlike Britain in relation to East Central Europe in the 1930s, the United States sees itself as having direct, national interests in the South China Sea. While Washington has no territorial claims in the region and does not officially take sides in territorial disputes in the South China Sea, it does insist on the freedom of navigation through that body of water (Entous, Lubold, and Barnes 2015). Given that $5.3 trillion worth of goods pass through the South China Sea and of that total $1.2 trillion are either exported from or imported into US ports (Erickson et al. 2015), this is not just a matter of principle but one of significant material interest as well.[16] Many of the goods not bound for the United States are headed to US allies such as Japan and South Korea (Kaplan 2011). Likewise, the distance that would need to be covered not only by merchant ships but also by US naval vessels passing from the Pacific to the Indian Ocean if the South China Sea were closed to international shipping would be significantly longer. Worse, if the sorts of maritime territorial claims China is advancing in the South China Sea were applied globally, a great many shipping lanes could be impacted. Washington has been careful to be consistent on freedom of navigation in recent years.[17] When five Chinese naval vessels appeared off the coast of Alaska, the US government confirmed their right to be there (Cooper 2015). These factors help to ensure Washington will see the region as strategically vital for decades to come.

Of course, it could be argued that France had a far greater interest in East Central Europe in the 1930s in that France's security rested in part on its alliances with states in that region. However, this is debatable as it also seemed possible that Germany might seek to redress its borders in the east while accepting those in the west (see Chapter 3). In any event, the fact that France did not adequately balance means even significant great power interests are not a guarantee of balancing behavior. Not surprisingly, many Asian states still question the extent of Washington's commitment, and therefore, have tended to hedge rather than depend fully on the United States (Sanger 2016). Even so, the contemporary geopolitical setting in Southeast Asia is far more propitious for effective great power aid overall than was East Central Europe in the 1930s.

Territorial disputes among potential balancers

Second, territorial claims between the states of Southeast Asia are much less divisive and more limited than those that plagued East Central Europe in the 1930s. Germany used the disputes of the 1930s to play one state off against another and impose itself as an arbiter of those conflicts. Today's disputes do not pose nearly as serious a barrier to cooperation and offer few opportunities to China for meddling.

In the 1930s almost all of the states of East Central Europe had territorial disputes with each other. Poland had territorial claims against Czechoslovakia. Hungary had claims against all of its neighbors (Austria, Czechoslovakia, Romania, and Yugoslavia). Bulgaria had claims against Romania, Yugoslavia, and Greece. Many of these disputes involved large amounts of territory, especially in the case of Hungary.[18] These were not peripheral issues, but often formed the core of states' foreign policies. In addition, these territories usually had important emotional and nationalistic significance to their populations which made them central to domestic politics. The very legitimacy of many states was questioned, most especially that of Czechoslovakia and Yugoslavia, as prior to 1918 they had either not existed or had been much smaller in scope. The territorial disputes threatened to either dramatically shrink or outright destroy these states – a far cry from the current situation in Southeast Asia where none of the relevant states' rights to exist are questioned and their mutual disputes are not central to states' foreign policies or domestic politics.

These various claims in East Central Europe greatly hindered cooperation (Kaufman 1992, 424). For example, if Poland had worked with Romania, it would have made coordinating with Hungary, a state with which Poland traditionally had warm relations, very difficult. While Yugoslavia, Czechoslovakia, and Romania could coordinate against Hungary, they could not bring Poland or Bulgaria into such a league due to Polish tensions with Czechoslovakia and Bulgarian tensions with Romania and Yugoslavia. Even when France negotiated alliances with many states in the region (Czechoslovakia, Poland, Romania, and Yugoslavia), those alliances had to remain bilateral pacts as multilateral agreements were simply impossible (Hitchins 1994). Thus, while these states were all threatened by Germany, they were also greatly threatened by each other, and therefore, unable to work together. Berlin exploited these divisions. Through its ability to arbitrate these disputes and the promise of territory taken from Czechoslovakia, Poland, Yugoslavia, and the Soviet Union, Berlin was able to induce states to bandwagon with it.

China lacks such inducements. While there are important animosities between several states surrounding the South China Sea, their territorial disputes are largely limited to offshore disputes in the South China and Celebes Seas. An important exception is the Philippine claim to Malaysian Sabah – the so-called Northern Borneo Dispute. However, this claim has not been pressed since the 1960s and full relations between the countries were restored in 1989. The stability of this situation is perhaps best demonstrated by a recent incident. In February 2013 several hundred armed militants acting under the direction of Jamalul Kiram III, a claimant to the defunct Sultanate of Sulu, left the Philippines and landed in Sabah with the stated goal of restoring the territory to the Philippines. While this led to a protracted and violent standoff between Malaysia and Kiram's followers, it did not trigger a dispute between the two countries (*BBC News Asia* 2013). Malaysia also has a border dispute with Indonesia, but the two states are working to resolve it diplomatically (Rapp-Hooper 2015a). These disputes are not insignificant, but compared with the territorial claims in East Central Europe in the 1930s, they are quite manageable and do not provide China with opportunities to exploit. Given the lesser salience of their territorial claims on each other, Vietnam, Malaysia, Brunei, Indonesia, and the Philippines should be able to focus on their shared dispute with China.[19] Simply put, contemporary Southeast Asia is not a powder keg of regional irredentism in the way East Central Europe was in the 1930s.

What could prove more problematic are the border disputes among other Southeast Asian states within ASEAN. Member states, such as Cambodia and Thailand, do have significant border disputes with their neighbors (Acharya 2001, 130). While such states are not party to the dispute in the South China Sea and their disputes do not rise to the level of the Eastern Central European disputes of the 1930s, they are important. To the extent that states that are party to the South China Sea dispute attempt to use ASEAN to resolve their dispute with China, these other disputes matter. These other ASEAN states with territorial disputes may not want to set precedents within ASEAN for how border disputes should be resolved which could prejudice their own claims. This could lead these states to limit ASEAN's role in producing a binding resolution in the South China Sea. This should be kept in mind when ASEAN is covered below.

The role of regional organizations

Third, the existence of regional organizations through which states can coordinate their responses to a local rising power enhances the likelihood of balancing. International institutions allow states to confront rising powers multilaterally rather than bilaterally, thereby reducing power imbalances. Regional organizations are crucial as it is difficult for small states to set the agendas of global institutions. Unlike East Central Europe during the 1930s, Southeast Asian states today have in ASEAN a regional organization they can turn to.

States in East Central Europe in the 1930s had no regional organizations through which to unite. True, the Little Entente between Czechoslovakia, Romania, and Yugoslavia tried for a time to act as a regional guarantor of the post-World War One settlement, meaning it was an obstacle to Hitler's ambitions. It had some early successes, such as preventing a Hapsburg from taking the vacant throne in Budapest. The alliance was even able to strengthen itself through increased institutionalization via the 1933 Reorganization Pact. By the mid-1930s, however, the Little Entente had become ineffective as a result of French neglect, German interference through the Stojadinović government of Yugoslavia, and increasing economic problems. As a result, by 1936 the institution began to regress and in 1938 it formally dissolved (Hitchins 1994; Krizman 1978). Turning to the notoriously ineffective League of Nations was not an attractive option. The League's dithering after Japan's invasion of Manchuria and Italy's invasion of Ethiopia, made it apparent that the League was ineffective at opposing aggression. Even had the League been better designed, its great power members tended to sacrifice the interests of lesser powers to their own agendas. Thus, the states of East Central Europe had no effective institutional vehicle for coordinating their response to Germany and ultimately were left to strike the best bilateral deals they could with Berlin. Usually this meant bandwagoning.

Contrary to this, ASEAN offers Southeast Asian states a forum through which they can negotiate with China simultaneously rather than in one-on-one settings where they would likely be overwhelmed. While China is more powerful than ASEAN, the imbalance is not as great as in bilateral relations. The body – though not entirely united on issues regarding the South China Sea – has diplomatically backed members in disputes with China over the South China Sea since a 1995 dispute between Beijing and Manila (Chan 2016, 175; Ott 2011). Also, when China participates in ASEAN summits, ASEAN members can and usually do invite other non-member states, such as the United States and Australia, to take part. This further offsets China's power. In fact, China, Australia, and the United States, as well as Japan and India, are involved in the ASEAN Regional Forum (ARF). The ARF is designed to facilitate multilateral discussions and negotiations between ASEAN members and other regional stakeholders. In 2010 it provided US Secretary of State Hillary Clinton with the opportunity to issue a statement supporting freedom of navigation in the South China Sea. Tellingly, Clinton was strongly encouraged to make such a statement by Vietnam (Ott 2011).

Additionally, global international organizations today offer more hope for ASEAN states than the League of Nations offered East Central European states in the 1930s. Even the staunchest critic of the United Nations will admit it is far more effective than the League ever was. Several ASEAN states have pressed their claims in the South China Sea at the UN, including an ongoing effort by the Philippines which has been supported by its fellow ASEAN members (Ott 2011). Given the difficulty small states have in driving the UN's agenda, however, ASEAN and the ARF will remain the more important venues for cooperation. Still, it is clear the UN offers more promise than the League did. Taken together, these regional and international fora have been so useful in resisting Chinese pressure that Beijing has discouraged their use and much prefers bilateral negotiations when addressing territorial disputes (Hemmings 2011).

Thus, ASEAN and the ARF provide states opposing China in the South China Sea with important tools for coordination which the states of 1930s East Central Europe lacked. Furthermore, ASEAN and the ARF, unlike the Little Entente, are not designed primarily as obstacles to China's foreign policy goals and in fact they have proved useful to China in furthering regional economic integration. As a result, ASEAN and the ARF are unlikely to become targets for dismemberment by China. For these reasons, regional organizations can potentially play an important role in allowing Southeast Asian states to balance rather than bandwagon if they so choose.

The nature of economic ties

The fourth factor decreasing the likelihood of bandwagoning is the nature of current economic connections as compared with those in the 1930s. Southeast Asia today is characterized by multilateral interdependence while East Central Europe in the 1930s was characterized by bilateral dependence. While there is debate about the extent to which economic interdependence can prevent conflict (Barbieri 1996; Gartzke 2007; Russett and Oneal 2001), there is agreement that unidirectional economic dependence often forces governments to avoid antagonizing the state upon which they are dependent (Hirschman 1980). As with the other factors, the economic relationship between Germany and the states of East Central Europe in the 1930s was more favorable to bandwagoning than is the relationship of China with Southeast Asian states today.

World War One had important economic consequences for the states of East Central Europe. Not only did it disrupt international trade flows which never fully recovered, but also the redrawing of maps in 1919 meant the balkanization of prewar economies, serious economic dislocations, and consequently a very slow economic recovery. By 1933 what international economic cooperation had emerged post-bellum was in severe decline because of the Great Depression and the resultant beggar-thy-neighbor policies. This robbed East Central European states of vital export markets. Germany took advantage of this situation to make the states of East Central Europe dependent upon it. Hjalmar Schacht, the Reichsbank President, adopted the "New Plan" which aimed to achieve autarky as far as possible and where necessary turned to Eastern European states for raw materials and markets. The end result was a series of disadvantageous trade treaties which put the East Central European states in a dependent economic relationship with Germany. These states simply had no alternative to this course given the loss of their export markets due to globally higher tariffs. This meant that crossing Germany on security issues would have serious negative economic impacts – impacts which would be more severe for the states of East Central Europe than for Germany (Hirschman 1980; Leitz 1997; Spaulding 1990).

The situation in Southeast Asia today could not be more different. First, the strong economic ties between China, the United States, and the states of Southeast Asia, while not balanced, form a web of mutual economic interdependence (Acharya 2014), not of particular dependence as in 1930s East Central Europe. Southeast Asia states do have important economic ties to China which make maintaining good relations with China important. For instance, Vietnam imports low-cost manufacturing parts from China and many poor Vietnamese agricultural workers live in southern China (Mullany and Barboza 2014). Such ties should limit the reaction of Southeast Asian states to Chinese provocations in the South China Sea. That said, these states are not unilaterally dependent upon China. Southeast Asian states have trading relations with many countries, both within Asia and globally. Intra-Southeast Asian trade doubled as a percentage of total trade for Southeast Asian states between 1995 and 2005 and is larger as a percentage of their total trade than NAFTA is for its member states (Acharya 2014). Thus, while these states benefit from trade with China, they have many trading partners and their relations are web-like rather than resembling a hub-and-spoke system.

Furthermore, these ties are important to China as well and severing them would cost China markets for its exports and suppliers for low-cost imports (Storey 2011, 134–44; 161; 172–5; 185–6; 224–7). Southeast Asian and Chinese trade is characterized by horizontal rather than hierarchical relationships (Men 2007) and regional trade is functionally integrative in nature (Dent 2008). There are also flows of foreign direct investment going in both directions between China and Southeast Asian states (Storey 2011, 203–4; 241–4). Crucially, China's economic ties with Southeast Asia are strongest with those states which are parties to the South China Sea dispute. Chinese trade ties to the maritime states of Southeast Asia are twice as large as Chinese ties to the mainland Southeast Asian states (Storey 2011, 85).[20] These economic ties to date have tended to dampen, rather than exacerbate, maritime disputes (Chan 2016, 56–7; Koo 2009). Therefore, while economic ties with China may reduce incentives to take a hard line, they likewise limit China's incentives to provoke a rupture and are structured such that these states can push back against Chinese claims without overly endangering their economies.

Of course, the importance of economic ties with China could also limit how outside parties respond to Chinese actions. Such ties make an open, explicit US policy of containment towards China – à la US policy toward the Soviet Union during the Cold War – unworkable and unappealing (Carpenter 2014). Other potential outside interveners in the South China Sea dispute have equally strong incentives to avoid antagonizing China. For example, Australia engages in significant trade with China. These economic ties induced Australia to join China's new Asian Infrastructure Investment Bank despite its concerns about Chinese assertiveness in the South China Sea and American calls to remain aloof from the Bank (Perlez 2015c). Yet, these broader economic ties also insure states will pay attention and react to Chinese moves in the Spratly and Paracel Islands. They also mean China has additional incentives to not provoke third parties as China benefits significantly from those relationships. Thus, while economic ties create incentives to mute responses to Chinese actions, they also create incentives to react to those actions and for the Chinese to limit those actions.

Second, while the Great Depression of the 1930s shattered the fragile economic ties that had been slowly reestablished in the 1920s, the financial crisis of 2007–09 and its global economic repercussions have not diminished international economic cooperation in the same manner or degree. Trade levels have remained high globally, giving Southeast Asian states many possible trading partners. This is neither to minimize the economic challenges which arose from the 2007–09 crisis nor to suggest all is well with the global economy today. Rather it is to point out that these economic dislocations did not lead to the increased trade barriers and beggar-thy-neighbor policies of the 1930s. Also, given that severing ties would significantly hurt China as well as ASEAN members and given that ASEAN states could find at least partial substitutes for trade with China, Beijing should be reluctant to sever trade in an attempt to gain political leverage. Doing so would weaken China's economy and the odds that it would induce Southeast Asian states to make political concessions are far lower than they were in Europe in the 1930s. Indeed, since the enactment of the ASEAN–China Free Trade Area in 2010 regional trade has grown significantly even as territorial disputes have heated up (Ott 2011; Storey 2011, 78–81). Thus, these trade ties have proven resilient and are unlikely to force ASEAN members to bend to China's will.

Third, continued Chinese economic growth depends on maintaining trading connections with the world at large. This in turn requires China to be seen as largely playing by the rules. This has led Beijing to back off from more provocative positions and not push as hard as one might otherwise expect. For instance, China relented by ending its restrictions on the export of rare earth minerals in order to comply with a World Trade Organization (WTO) ruling. To be sure, shifts had occurred in the rare earths market which made restricting exports less appealing in both economic and political terms, but nevertheless China was willing to play by the rules when the WTO court's ruling went against it (Gholz 2014).

This comparison between 1930s Europe and Southeast Asia today suggests that states bordering the South China Sea are unlikely to bandwagon with China. In fact, it would take a dramatic reversal in these four factors for this to become a likely foreign policy alternative: e.g., a major increase in Chinese power projection capacities; the collapse of ASEAN; the withdrawal of the United States from the region; and a dramatic breakdown of economic cooperation in the region and across the Pacific. Of course, these factors are interdependent and interactive. For instance, an increase in the level of territorial squabbling amongst Southeast Asian states would not only create an opening for China to become an arbitrator of those disputes, but it would also weaken ASEAN and possibly disrupt regional trade. Thus, deterioration in one of the factors could lead to deterioration in the rest. But this is not an inevitable slippery slope. Rather a series of sustained crises in each of these areas would be needed. Thus, contemporary conditions suggest that significant pressures to bandwagon are unlikely to form.

State behavior in the South China Sea today

Does actual state behavior fit with these predictions? Are states with claims in the South China Sea balancing, bandwagoning, hiding, or hedging? Do Washington's policies and actions support the contention that the United States is likely to aid states if they resist Chinese encroachments in the South China Sea? Is ASEAN playing an important and productive role? Each of these questions will be address below.

States with territorial claims in the South China Sea

States with claims to the reefs, shoals, and islets in the South China Sea have taken a series of actions to resist China's growing assertiveness in advancing its own claims to these features. The actions broadly fall into three categories: direct resistance within the South China Sea and modest increases in military budgets; attempts to draw closer to the United States; and the use of international institutions and legal instruments to challenge Chinese claims and actions in court. Each will be covered in turn.

China's occupation of reefs and islands in the South China Sea has not cowed its smaller neighbors. Rather they have matched the tactic. Vietnam has occupied twenty-nine such features and the Philippines, Malaysia, and Taiwan have occupied another fourteen features between them (Kaplan 2011; Rapp-Hooper 2015a). Manila has removed markers placed by Beijing on islets within the zone claimed by the Philippines (Buszynski 2012, 142). All of these states have built military facilities on at least some of the features they occupy and have engaged in limited land-reclamation efforts (Erickson et al. 2015; Rapp-Hooper 2015a).[21]

There have also been direct confrontations. Since 2005 there have been regular clashes between Chinese fishing vessels and those of Vietnam and the Philippines. In 2011, Chinese ships harassed Philippine and Vietnamese oil exploration vessels (Buszynski 2012, 141–4). More recently in May 2014, the Chinese attempted to advance their claims in the Paracels by deploying an oil exploration rig. This resulted in a series of confrontations over the course of several weeks between Chinese ships and Vietnamese Sea Guard ships and fishing vessels, with each side deploying water cannons and using ramming tactics. This resulted in the injury of several Vietnamese sailors and the sinking of a Vietnamese fishing vessel (Mullany 2014; Mullany and Barboza 2014; Perlez 2014a; Perlez and Bradsher 2014). The incidents resulted in anti-Chinese rioting in Hanoi and the self-immolation of a woman in Ho Chi Minh City in an attempt to pressure the government into taking an even stronger line with the Chinese (Bradsher 2014a; Perlez 2014a). In the same month, the Philippines detained eleven Chinese fishermen as a result of the dispute over Half Moon Shoal in the Spratly Islands (Mullany 2014; Mullany and Barboza 2014).[22] More recently, Chinese fishing vessels and Indonesian naval ships engaged in a series of confrontations between April and June 2016. These clashes resulted in injuries and the seizure of a Chinese fishing vessel (Cochrane 2016a).

Additionally, while these states cannot win a naval confrontation with China without US aid, they do seem willing to invest in their own security. Defense budgets on average have risen by a third over the last decade, with a focus on naval assets and aviation (Acharya 2003; Kaplan 2011). In October 2014, Malaysia decided to increase its defense budget by 10 percent and the Philippines has adopted a 15-year naval modernization plan focused on fast-attack craft, submarines, stealth frigates, and anti-submarine warfare helicopters. Manila has acted on this plan by purchasing a variety of transport and patrol vessels as well as two older US Coast Guard cutters (Green 2014; Rapp-Hooper 2015a). Likewise, Vietnam has recently purchased anti-ship and land-attack missiles from Russia (Rapp-Hooper 2015a). Discussions have also begun to create a joint training program between the Philippines, Malaysia, Indonesia, and Brunei (Rapp-Hooper 2015a).[23]

This is not to claim that Southeast Asian states seek military conflict with China. The vast majority of states in the region desire good relations with China in order to maintain economic cooperation (Rapp-Hooper 2015a). Compromise solutions such as negotiations or arbitration over the territorial disputes are possible and so are mixed approaches. Malaysia, for instance, allows American P-8 Poseidon surveillance and anti-submarine aircraft to take off from Borneo and is exploring further military cooperation with its neighbors and the United States, while simultaneously engaging in joint military exercises with China (Perlez 2014b; Rapp-Hooper 2015a).

Nor is it to claim that attempts by Southeast Asian states to resist Chinese claims have always been successful; they have not. For instance, the Philippines abandoned the rich fishing grounds around Scarborough Shoal to China after Beijing refused to abide by a US-brokered deal (Perlez and Bradsher 2014) and Manila's attempts to increase the US presence in the Philippines were tied up in court by Filipinos who still resent the former US occupation of and influence in the country (Hernandez 2015; Whaley 2014). Likewise, Vietnamese moves toward closer relations with the United States, while real, remain tentative to the frustration of some Vietnamese elites outside of the government (Perlez 2016d; Tuong 2014) and internal divisions about the wisdom of moving closer to the United States are shaping succession politics in Vietnam at the highest level (Ives 2016a; 2016b). Two manifestations of this reluctance on Hanoi's part for closer relations have been the limited scale of the annual joint military exercises with the United States Navy and the denial of US requests for access to Cam Ranh Bay (Perlez and Bradsher 2014).[24] Furthermore, despite spending increases, these states' defenses remain limited. The Philippine armed forces are especially weak, lacking both submarines and fighter jets. Its navy remains very small and consists mainly of vessels from the World War Two era (Bradsher 2014b; Hernandez 2015).

Also, the Chinese military is not standing still. For 2015, the military budget increased by 10 percent to $145 billion which is roughly in line with annual increases over the last 20 years (Twomey 2014; Wong and Buckley 2015; Wong, Perlez, and Buckley 2015). These budget increases have occurred while the People's Liberation Army (PLA) has been reducing its numbers. This is the result of the PLA's substantial modernization effort which focuses on naval and air assets – the very systems that would be relevant in any military conflict in the South China Sea – at the expense of infantry formations. Modernization is crucial, as only with modernization can China project force long distances from its shores.[25] Specifically, China has focused on sea control and sea denial capabilities rather than on abilities to project power past the so-called first island chain (Lim 2014, 94).[26] The Chinese have developed quite capable anti-ship missiles with impressive ranges and a reasonably capable submarine fleet (Buszynski 2012, 145–6; Lim 2014, 87–92). Such capabilities would be more than sufficient to defeat the navies of its Southeast Asian neighbors and greatly increase the risks for US Navy ships operating within the South China Sea.[27] What China lacks is a first class surface fleet and the supply and amphibious capabilities that would be necessary for projecting power past the second island chain into the open Pacific.[28] Beijing has done little to address these deficiencies. Thus, the modernization effort for the time being is aimed at shifting regional power realities rather than surpassing the United States Navy (Foot 2006; Lim 2014, 75–82).[29] Though by the PLA's own estimates such efforts would not make China a global military power until 2050 (Kroenig 2015), they would increase China's ability to project power off of its coasts much sooner. And of course, given China's size and growing wealth there is no way for its rivals in the South China Sea to match its might. Thus, while Vietnam and the Philippines have taken steps to resist Chinese moves, the local military balance remains decidedly and increasingly in China's favor.

The United States

The United States' role in the South China Sea is determined in part by the desire of regional actors for an increased US presence. The Philippines has lobbied the United States for support in their disputes with China (*Wall Street Journal* 2011). Manila's desire to bring in outside parties to the dispute is nicely illustrated by the Philippine Department of Foreign Affairs spokesman, Charles Jose's statement to the media in May 2015 arguing that "The Philippines believes that the US, as well as all responsible members of the international community, do have an interest and say in what is happening in the South China Sea" (Entous, Lubold, and Barnes 2015). Former Philippine President Benigno S. Aquino III was particularly strident in his calls for aid from the United States. He directly and rather hyperbolically compared his country's plight to that of Czechoslovakia in 1938 stating in a media interview,

> If we say yes to something we believe is wrong now, what guarantee is there that the wrong will not be further exacerbated down the line? At what point do you say, "Enough is enough?" Well, the world has to say it – remember that the Sudetenland was given in an attempt to appease Hitler to prevent World War Two.
> (Bradsher 2014b)

Philippine entreaties have had some success. Washington, via the Manila Declaration, renewed its commitment to the defense of the Philippines (Hemmings 2011) and US military aid doubled in 2015 to $50 million, with discussions of it rising to $300 million (Hernandez 2015). Washington has provided funds for the modernization of Philippine patrol ships and the acquisition of unmanned surveillance blimps (Whaley 2016a). Furthermore the Philippine government agreed in 2014 to allow the United States to station a limited number of troops and materiel at Philippine military bases. This agreement was expanded in April 2016 to allow the United States to base 200 servicemen and women at five Philippine facilities for the next ten years (Whaley 2016a; 2016b). Manila has even mulled over inviting the United States to return to Subic Bay (Hernandez 2015), though this seems unlikely to occur. Joint American–Filipino training exercises, as well as joint air and naval patrols, have become common (Whaley 2016b). Whether the recent election of Rodrigo Duterte, who has a well-known antipathy toward the United States and has said he is open to bilateral discussions with Beijing over the South China Sea, to the Presidency of the Philippines will derail these moves toward closer ties remains to be seen (Paddock 2016; Sanger 2016). Certainly, Beijing at least believes there is an opening to improve ties with the Philippines as China has slowed the planned construction of military facilities on Scarborough Shoal since Duterte's election (Perlez 2016b). Likewise, the election of Donald Trump as US president further complicates these relationships and deepens the uncertainty. On the one hand, Duterte has welcomed the election of Trump. On the other hand, Trump's willingness to challenge longstanding diplomatic understandings in order to 'get a better deal' could lead to questions about the solidity of US commitments in the region. Weeks before his inauguration Trump has already angered Beijing by accepting a phone call from the president of Taiwan on December 2, 2016 and openly questioning the One-China Policy on December 11, 2016.

US ties with other states in the region have also been strengthened. Washington has concluded medical and nuclear technology deals with Hanoi (Hemmings 2011) and the United States lifted the ban on the export of military hardware to Vietnam in 2014 (Kroenig 2015). The United States has also drawn closer to Singapore. In

2004, Singapore opened the Changi naval base which hosts a US Navy logistics unit, four US littoral combat ships on a rotational basis and can accommodate a US aircraft carrier (Roy 2005; Selden 2013). The United States is a major supplier of military hardware to Singapore and the government of Singapore generally sees the Americans as a stabilizing force in the region (Storey 2011, 235–7). Likewise, Washington lifted the ban on military-to-military contacts with Indonesia and its decades-old arms embargo on Vietnam (Buszynski 2012, 148; Harris 2016). The US Navy has also engaged in repeated joint exercises with Indonesia, Vietnam, and Malaysia and has at times deployed aircraft carrier groups to the region with the intent of influencing Chinese behavior (Perlez 2016c; Roy 2005; Rapp-Hooper 2015a; Storey 2011, 224–7; Whaley 2014).

Even so, many of these states still feel insecure. This insecurity no doubt arises in part from Washington's focus on maintaining the freedom of navigation rather than support for the smaller states' territorial claims. The United States does not recognize Manila's or Hanoi's claims to any features in the South China Sea and has been clear that it does not believe its defense pact with the Philippines covers the South China Sea (Buszynski 2012, 149). Crucially, while American officials have denounced Chinese actions – in 2014 then Secretary of Defense Chuck Hagel said China was engaged in "intimidation and coercion" and had "undertaken destabilizing, unilateral actions asserting its claims in the South China Sea" (Cooper and Perlez 2014) – their rhetoric has mainly reflected the focus on US navigation rights rather than states' territorial claims. For instance, US Secretary of State John Kerry, in a meeting with his Chinese counterpart Wang Yi, emphasized concerns about land reclamation and called for the security of sea lanes and fishing grounds to be managed in accordance with international law (Gordon 2015). He did not weigh in on the merits of Hanoi's and Manila's claims. US President Barack Obama reiterated these concerns about reclamation and free navigation in November 2015 at a Pacific Rim economic summit (Shear 2015).

American actions have likewise focused on navigation rights. The United States has engaged in overflights of Chinese reclamation projects, insisting they are in international air space (Cooper and Perlez 2015a) and sent a guided missile cruiser within twelve miles of the Chinese-occupied Subi Reef in October 2015 (Cooper and Perlez 2015b).[30] This reef was carefully chosen as before Chinese reclamation projects it was submerged at high tide and therefore is not entitled to the twelve-mile limit under UNCLOS (Cooper and Perlez 2015a).[31] Washington has regularly conducted similar patrols throughout 2016 (Cooper 2016). These actions were clearly chosen for their legal implications and focus on the right of navigation rather than on who controls various features in the South China Sea. In defending the patrol, US Admiral Harry B. Harris, Jr. indicated that it was in line with global US policy, stating that, "We've been conducting freedom of navigation operations all over the world for decades, so no one should be surprised by them. The South China Sea is not, and will not, be an exception" (Perlez 2015b). The US legal position is such that it runs counter to the maritime territorial claims of any state which would use reclaimed land or partially submerged features to assert sovereignty over what Washington sees as open water.

Consistent with this, US commitments to aid the Philippines in the South China Sea have remained limited. After Obama was rather vague in May 2014 on whether the US would defend the Philippines against a Chinese attack, the farthest US Deputy National Security Advisor Ben Rhodes would go in reassuring Manila was to state,

> We have reaffirmed our support for mutual defense treaties with allies in the region and have supported the efforts of the Philippines to pursue international arbitration to resolve maritime disputes.
>
> (Perlez and Bradsher 2014)

Given the United States' view of what its defense pact with the Philippines requires, this statement did not commit the United States to action in the South China Sea. Even Rhodes' limited reassurance was undercut a few weeks later when clashes occurred between Chinese, Vietnamese, and Philippine vessels. An anonymous US official, rather than denouncing Beijing's actions, instead stated that "None of the countries are helping matters" (Cooper and Perlez 2014). Understandably, Filipino officials remain unsure as to the reliability of US security guarantees.

Partially in response to Washington's less than certain commitment, states in the region have attempted to strengthen their relations with other potential interveners in the conflict. For instance, the Philippines has engaged in joint military exercises with Australia and Japan and worked to obtain diplomatic support from India. Likewise, Vietnam has undertaken military exercises with India and has improved ties with Japan (Rapp-Hooper 2015a). These efforts have borne some fruit. Japan is considering aerial patrols in the South China Sea. Australia has publically stated its opposition to recent Chinese actions. Finally, India has declared its support for freedom of navigation in the South China Sea and signed an agreement with the United States in 2015 to keep sea-lanes open (Buszynski 2012, 143; Rapp-Hooper 2015a).

Regardless whether Washington wants to increase its commitment to Vietnam and the Philippines or remained more narrowly focused on the issue of the freedom of navigation, it faces several thorny challenges in crafting a response to Chinese maritime claims and land reclamation. First, it faces a problem of dual deterrence (Crawford 2003; Jervis 1994). While Washington wants to keep China from taking aggressive actions and effectively asserting sovereignty over the South China Sea, it also wants to discourage allies such as the Philippines from taking actions which could lead to a militarized dispute.[32] As Vikram J. Singh, the former US Deputy Assistant Secretary of Defense for South and Southeast Asia, said after encounters between Vietnamese and Chinese vessels in May 2014,

> Wars start from small things, often by accident and miscalculation – like dangerous maneuvers by aircraft that result in a collision or aggressive moves that lead to an unexpected military response.
>
> (Cooper and Perlez 2014)

In other words, Washington fears that states may take overly risky actions if they are assured of US support in any military confrontation that may follow. Some observers argue US actions have already emboldened Hanoi and Manila (Wu 2014). Thus, though the Americans want to deter China, they also want to restrain other parties and avoid entrapment. When the challenge of dual deterrence is combined with Chinese salami-slicing tactics where each move is calculated to be below the threshold which would warrant an armed response (Browne 2015; Schelling 1966), Washington faces a particularly thorny problem when it comes to designing responses to Chinese assertiveness. It is easy to do too little and also easy to do too much.

Second, the United States is unable to focus squarely on the South China Sea or even Asian matters more broadly. Washington is often distracted by events in the Middle East or Eastern Europe and it is particularly difficult to confront Chinese and Russian aggressiveness simultaneously. Furthermore, even within Asia the Americans often want or need Chinese cooperation – for instance in dealing with North Korea (Choe 2016; Christensen 2011; Green 2014). On top of this, it is not at all clear that public support exists within the United States for a policy of containment (Green 2014, 206). Finally, if Chinese moves are driven in part by defensive motives as some argue (Twomey 2014), US actions which aggressively counter Chinese moves could make matters worse by aggravating the security dilemma (He and Feng 2012). Beijing is well aware of these tensions and has attempted to exploit them. Chinese officials have tried to signal that any US action challenging Chinese sovereignty in the South China Sea would result in worse relations. As Hugh White, a former Australian defense official observed in relation to Beijing's island building and oil exploration,

> China is deliberately doing these things to demonstrate the unsustainability of the American position of having a good relationship with China and maintaining its alliances in Asia, which constitute the leadership of the United States in Asia.
>
> (Cooper and Perlez 2014)

Of course, the Chinese have much the same problem as the Americans. Beijing wants to maintain good economic relations with Southeast Asian states and with the United States (Wu 2014) just as much as Washington wants to maintain ties with China. Beijing certainly does not want to provoke a US policy of containment that mimics US policy toward the Soviet Union during the Cold War. Neither Beijing nor Washington wants the South China Sea to become the main issue in their relationship.

When combined with the fact that military balancing is inherently costly, a third challenge arises: free-riding. An overly robust US response to Chinese assertiveness could convince US allies and other states that they do not need to do the heavy lifting (Carpenter 2014). Many Asian states see the United States as a public good provider – specifically as a provider of stability and security (Goh 2011, 387). This has led states in the region to welcome the US's presence, but also to underinvest in their own defense. For instance, even Japan – one of the few states in the region with the economic resources to confront China – spends very little on defense in relative terms when compared with the United States. Japanese defense spending remains quite low and seems unlikely to increase substantially in the near future. Even marginal increases have encountered significant domestic resistance (Holmes 2012; Scanlon 2014; Spitzer 2013).[33] Likewise, as discussed above, Philippine defenses remain anemic. Given that ASEAN states have economies and populations far smaller than China's and cannot unilaterally confront China, they face strong temptations to pass the buck. Of course, this limited capacity also reduces the inherent problems associated with free-riding as the contributions of many of the states bordering the South China Sea are not strictly necessary to construct a successful balancing coalition. Still, burden-sharing is always useful and to the extent that local actors know they would have to pay costs, it may restrain them and help avoid some of the problems of dual deterrence discussed above. These challenges have likely contributed to the murkiness of the US position in regards to the South China Sea.

At the end of the day, how much help these states can expect from third parties is an open question. Washington has been vague about its stance when it comes to potential clashes over disputed territory in the South China Sea. When queried whether Washington would aid Manila if push came to shove in the South China Sea, US Admiral Jonathan W. Greenert quickly responded "Of course, we would help" before adding "I don't know what that help would be specifically" (Sanger and Landler 2014). Furthermore, as suggested above there are limits to how much regional actors want the Americans to do. As Rhodes put it, "The countries in the region want the United States to be present and to be a stabilizing force, but they also don't want tension between the United States and China, certainly not at a high pitch" (Sanger and Landler 2014). Such views undoubtedly reflect Washington's preferences as well.

The role of ASEAN and international law

Another avenue of resistance to Chinese territorial claims is through regional institutions and international law. Such an approach is useful as not only can institutions and law help smaller states resist great power pressure, they can also allow states to resist in ways that limit the severity of the confrontation. While the use of law and institutions do not make war unthinkable, they do constrain Chinese power and militate against the likelihood of war (Acharya 2014). Furthermore, Southeast Asian states, even those with good relations with the United States, do not want Washington to force them into choosing between China and the United States (Wu 2014, 210). States in the region wish to retain flexibility and many of them engage in hedging behavior (Acharya 2001, 180; Goh 2011, 387). For example, Singapore – a state with excellent relations with Washington – prefers cordial relations between Beijing and Washington and also wants to retain diplomatic room for maneuver (Storey 2011, 238–9). Its government's main fear in regards to the South China Sea, given that Singapore has no territorial claims, is that disputes there could destabilize the entire region (Storey 2011, 245–6). Thus, any solution to the overlapping territorial claims which heightens rather than reduces tensions is counterproductive in Singaporean eyes, no matter which states end up possessing the various features in the South China Sea. Such a view is hardly limited to Singapore, but rather is common among Southeast Asian states that do not have claims in the South China Sea. Thus, resolving the disputes through mediation – something both intergovernmental institutions and international law are explicitly designed to do – appeals to many Southeast Asian states.

ASEAN has played the main role in regional efforts to address the competing claims in the South China Sea. Since its creation, ASEAN has been seen as a potential vehicle for resolving regional disputes without the use of force and as a means to "enhance the bargaining power of small and weak states in their dealings with the Great Powers" (Acharya 2001, 52). None other than Lee Kuan Yew, the now deceased long-time Prime Minister of Singapore, stated that ASEAN would help to ensure that smaller powers in the region would "have their interests taken into consideration when the great powers make their compromises" (Acharya 2001, 52). Thus, ASEAN would seem well suited to deal with a territorial dispute which involves several smaller states and two great powers either directly or indirectly.

Certainly, ASEAN has tried to resolve the dispute. It has taken a number of steps over the last two decades to address the South China Sea dispute, though it has moved in its customarily slow manner much to the frustration of the Americans (Acharya 2001, 132 and 178). Much of ASEAN's efforts to mediate the South China Sea dispute have been through the ARF which was created in 1995. The ARF includes not only ASEAN members, but also many other states which are stakeholders in various regional issues, including China and the United States. This allows the various stakeholders in the South China Sea dispute to meet in a forum of which they are members and it also ensures through the inclusion of the United States that China cannot simply overpower ASEAN in the negotiations. Not surprisingly, China has resisted the use of the ARF for addressing territorial disputes in the South China Sea. Initially, Beijing opposed any inclusion of the South China Sea dispute on the ARF's agenda, claiming that the ARF is "not an appropriate place" to resolve the dispute and that "the most effective way to handle this dispute is through bilateral negotiations" (Acharya 2001, 177). While Beijing ultimately relented to talks within the ARF, it still insists the ARF cannot have a managerial role in resolving the dispute and has yet to feel constrained by the ARF's norms when it comes to the South China Sea (Goh 2011, 380–2). The main effect of the ARF may well be to grant legitimacy to the United States' role in the South China Sea dispute and perhaps ultimately to cloak Chinese power (Goh 2011, 381).[34]

Given the weaknesses inherent in the ARF and ASEAN's past difficulties in getting participants in negotiations to come to agreement, it is unsurprising that these efforts have borne limited fruit. The main achievement was the 2002 non-binding agreement to avoid provocative actions in the South China Sea (Governments of the Member States of ASEAN and the Government of the People's Republic of China 2002). As discussed above, China's actions since

2007 have run contrary to the spirit of this accord. ASEAN's efforts to mediate the South China Sea dispute through the ARF have largely failed for several reasons. First, ASEAN emphasizes member sovereignty and non-interference, meaning ASEAN, by design, has very limited abilities when it comes to forcing compromise on states. This non-threatening aspect makes ASEAN negotiations attractive, but it also limits their effectiveness (Acharya 2001, 57; Ba 2010; Emmers and Tan 2011; Goh 2011). Second, China has consistently resisted multilateral approaches to the South China Sea dispute (Storey 2011, 90). Third, ASEAN is not a vehicle for regional military cooperation (Acharya 2001, 61). Fourth, historically ASEAN has served as a vehicle to promote bilateral talks rather than as a multilateral forum. Yet, on the issue of the South China Sea member states wish to proceed multilaterally to increase their leverage vis-à-vis China (Acharya 2001, 178). This has required ASEAN to develop new ways of doing business, further slowing its actions. Finally, as long as China can pursue a forward agenda in the South China Sea without prompting serious ruptures in its relations with the United States and members of ASEAN, Beijing has little reason to desist and accept ASEAN mediation.

Parties to the South China Sea dispute have not limited their appeals to institutions and international law to ASEAN. The Philippines in particular has made use of legal instruments to resolve their disputes with the Chinese, though at times this has backfired. As discussed above, the Philippines accepted US mediation over Scarborough Shoal and withdrew from the disputed area with the understanding China would do the same. Instead China assumed control of the shoal, leaving then President Aquino at pains to emphasize that Manila has not renounced any of its territorial claims in the South China Sea (Bradsher 2014b).

Despite this setback, Manila has sought a variety of legal means to pursue its territorial claims in the South China Sea. For example, Manila has appealed to the United Nations, albeit to little effect (Whaley 2014). More importantly, in its dispute over South Johnson Reef, Manila has pursued a lengthy legal route. It formally protested to China in April 2014, then raised the issue at an ASEAN summit in May 2014, and finally took the case before the Permanent Court of Arbitration in The Hague which agreed to hear the case in late October 2015 (Deutsch 2015). The Court ruled in Manila's favor, concluding that Chinese actions near Scarborough Shoal had caused environmental damage, that the feature was too small to be used for a territorial claim, and that therefore the area lay within the Philippines' exclusive economic zone, meaning that Chinese fishing activities there were illegal (Permanent Court of Arbitration 2016). Importantly, the Court's ruling did not give sovereignty of Scarborough Shoal to the Philippines and if the Court's logic was applied to the rest of the South China Sea, it likely would mean that none of the features would be large enough to serve as bases to claim the surrounding waters as sovereign territory.[35] There are indications that other parties to the South China Sea dispute may attempt to use the case to their advantage given the ruling in Manila's favor (Escritt 2015; Harris 2016).[36]

That said, Cambodia – a state with close ties to China – blocked an attempt by the Philippines to have ASEAN release a joint statement which referenced the ruling (Mogato, Martina, and Blanchard 2016). There are also concerns that the ruling may cause China to become more assertive in advancing its territorial claims rather than less. Some have even raised the possibility of China establishing an air defense zone over the South China Sea, though that has yet to happen (Hunt and Jiang 2016). Thus, though the ruling puts pressure on China it will not necessarily cause states to shift their positions on the disputes in the South China Sea.

That said, exactly what result the ruling will produce on the ground is unclear given that China has refused to recognize the Court's jurisdiction and has said it will ignore the ruling (Bradsher 2014a; Hernandez 2015; Perlez 2015a; 2016a; 2016b). This is consistent with China's resistance to the application of UNCLOS to any of its maritime disputes (Bradsher 2014b). To the extent that China does not want to be seen as an outlaw state – Beijing wants to be able to use international law and international institutions to advance its interests in other issue areas – these lawsuits do apply real pressure even if they are unlikely to halt Chinese assertiveness by themselves (Browne 2015).

Thus, Southeast Asian states have turned to institutions and international law in their dispute with China over the South China Sea. While these mechanisms appear unlikely to bring about a resolution to the issue anytime soon, they do appear to enhance those states' abilities to confront China in ways that are less likely to provoke a serious rupture.

Conclusion

There is little reason to believe Southeast Asian states would feel compelled to wilt in the face of Chinese territorial claims. Outright bandwagoning with China is unlikely. States with claims in the South China Sea will continue to resist Chinese territorial aspirations, albeit while simultaneously continuing to engage in mutually beneficial economic cooperation with Beijing. The main elements of uncertainty that exist are to what degree the United States would intervene in any conflict in the South China Sea and how aggressively China will pursue its territorial claims in the future. There is little uncertainty about the nature of the Chinese moves. They do very little to shift the balance of power or even improve China's legal claims. Likewise, there is no uncertainty about the military prowess of China relative to the other claimant states. China's military is vastly superior. While there is some uncertainty as to how well the US Navy would be able to cope with China's newer sea denial technologies, it is still quite clear that the US Navy outclasses the PLA Navy in general. Thus, the sort of uncertainties covered in Chapters 1, 2 and 4 suggest US policy is crucial for determining whether a balancing coalition will emerge in the South China Sea. Given that neither the United States nor most Southeast Asian states favor poor relations between Washington and Beijing, it seems likely that American policies will continue to attempt to straddle the fine line between clearly opposing China's claims while not provoking a crisis. This in turn would make it challenging for Southeast Asian states to do more in opposing China's actions in the South China Sea than what they are already doing.

In other words, an outright balancing coalition targeting China is unlikely to emerge. Rather states are likely to hedge through a mix of strategies and attempt to avoid being forced tightly into any camp.[37] Hanoi's and Manila's resistance to Chinese claims while engaging in limited military buildups and tentative alliance formation is consistent with this. So is Manila's preference for resolving disputes through multilateral organizations and international law. These methods pose less of a risk of a serious rupture in relations and the negative economic and security consequences which would follow such a rupture. Indonesia and Malaysia have been even more cautious, though given their efforts to improve ties with the United States and uphold their claims they also appear to be hedging rather than hiding. Such a mixing of strategies is not paradoxical, but rather aligns with the interests of these states. Claimant states are likely to continue to seek closer economic ties with China, while looking to keep open the option of military cooperation with the United States. Hiding is unlikely as states have strong incentives to stand firm in the face of territorial demands in the South China Sea. Finally, even though Singapore has no territorial claims to uphold, it is not hiding either. Instead, Singapore has sought to keep the United States engaged in the region while supporting ASEAN's efforts to mediate disputes in the South China Sea. Singapore has also sought to avoid an outright confrontation between the United States and China. These attempts at mediation and problem-solving are consistent with transcending rather than hiding or hedging.

As one pulls back and looks at ASEAN members that do not border the South China Sea, balancing seems even more unlikely. Such states have few incentives to anger China and risk losing the benefits of cooperation. They are not faced with a direct threat and have little ability to contribute to a balancing coalition. That said, the same logic also suggests that such states have little incentive to bandwagon with China and balance against the United States. The recent policies of Burma and Thailand are illustrative. Burma has recently moved to improve relations with the United States and lessen its dependence on China while still remaining on good terms with Beijing. Thailand has moved in the other direction. Bangkok has sought to improve relations with Beijing while moving somewhat away from the United States.[38] Even states such as Laos that have little to gain from closer relations with the United States may hedge or hide so as to remain on good terms with both Beijing and Hanoi. Thus, again hedging is a likely policy, though hiding is also a plausible option for states not bordering the South China Sea.

Our conclusions fit closely with those of Goh (2008). She suggests most ASEAN states have a profound ambivalence toward China. They want to benefit economically from China's development, but do not want to be forced into a tight alignment with China. Likewise, most ASEAN states welcome a US presence in the region, but hope to avoid a serious confrontation between Beijing and Washington. Goh argues this leads ASEAN states to pursue two mutually supportive policies. First, ASEAN states generally attempt to enmesh China and the United States within institutional frameworks such as the ARF and multilateral economic ties. Second, most ASEAN states pursue some form of hedging. This allows them to acquire the benefits of friendly ties with both Washington and Beijing and avoid picking sides.

Returning to the new Chinese passport, the response of China's neighbors is telling. It does not indicate coming military conflict. Rather, it suggests that states will hedge by upholding their territorial claims while simultaneously cooperating economically with China and the United States. This tendency to pursue a mix of strategies will shape the strategic environment in which outside powers craft their strategies in Asia and characterize the policies of Southeast Asian states in the years to come.

Notes

1 Mischief Reef, which is claimed by Manilla, was occupied by Beijing in 1995 (Storey 2011, 255).
2 This gives China a total of three airfields on manmade islands in the South China Sea (Hernandez 2015).
3 The new facilities on Hainan Island, however, are more easily defended and do somewhat alter the local military equation.
4 For instance, China seized full control of the Paracel Islands from the Republic of Vietnam as the result of a naval clash in 1974 (Lim 2014, 122).
5 This sensitivity comes from a long history of being victimized by the territorial encroachments of other powers: the late nineteenth century and early twentieth century creation of European and Japanese spheres of influence which involved extraterritoriality, British and American gunboats patrolling several of China's rivers, and finally a full-blown Japanese invasion in the 1930s and 1940s.
6 Obviously, the reaction of other Asian states to Chinese assertiveness is important. Of special concern is Japan's reaction to China's territorial claims in the East China Sea.
7 A case could be made that hiding carries the least risk of war in the South China Sea in the short run as it would neither trigger a local war nor speed China's rise. Whether this is also true in the long term is less clear.
8 This is true even though Beijing is notoriously opaque when it comes to its military capacities. This lack of transparency may be a deliberate attempt to hide Chinese vulnerabilities (Mastro 2016).
9 Some ethnic Germans did reside outside of Germany or Austria as a result of earlier migrations. They were not, however, as significant politically in the 1930s compared with those ethnic Germans that ended up residing in non-German states because of the Central Powers' defeat in 1918.
10 This still leaves substantial room for risky behavior as Hitler was exceptionally tolerant of risk.
11 Given the nature of economic substitution, closer economic ties with one state can result in reduced ties with another as there is only so much economic activity to go around even with economic growth. For instance after the adoption of the North American Free Trade Agreement, US trade with the Caribbean decreased as US trade shifted toward Mexico and Canada. This was not the intent of the agreement and the United States subsequently took steps to reinvigorate trade with the Caribbean.
12 See Chapters 3 and 5 for elaboration about the diplomacy of 1930s European states discussed in the sections below.
13 Passing bucks to the future, while potentially rational, is also consistent with construal level theories in psychology which suggest that individuals have difficulty conceptualizing events far in the future. Such theories suggest states would balance against rising challengers far later than is optimal (Krebs and Rapport 2012).
14 It is unclear how strong the reluctance to balance against sea or insular powers really is. For instance, the United States and Britain balanced against a rising Japan in the

late 1930s despite Japan being an insular and predominately sea power. Of course, Japan was projecting power onto the Asian continent via its invasion of China.
15 Much like France in the 1930s in relation to East Central Europe, US alliances with Asian states tend to be bilateral rather than multilateral (Mastaduno 2002).
16 Some estimates put the amount of commerce flowing through the South China Sea as equal to one third of global trade and half of the global trade in oil and natural gas (Chan 2016, 46).
17 Of course, this has not always been the case post-1945 when US actions have at times run contrary to the principle. For instance, in the 1986 case, Nicaragua vs. United States, which was heard before the International Court of Justice, the Nicaraguan government successfully sued the US for, among other breaches, mining its harbors in violation of peaceful maritime commerce. Still, freedom of navigation has been a core principle of US diplomacy for most of American history (Bemis 1977, 571), perhaps making the current American insistence upon the principle more credible.
18 The Soviet Union also had territorial claims against Poland and Romania.
19 Whether this in fact will happen is another matter as China may be able to split off individual states from the potential coalition. For instance, Chan (2016, 176) argues that in return for Chinese acquiescence to its oil exploration in the South China Sea, Brunei has tacitly agreed to resolve its territorial disputes with Beijing bilaterally rather than multilaterally.
20 Storey counts Vietnam and Malaysia as maritime states for this calculation.
21 The four states have reclaimed a total of 125 acres over the previous 30 years whereas China has reclaimed 2,000 acres in one year alone. While the Philippines has offered to halt its reclamation efforts if China does so as well (Gordon 2015), this offer is unlikely to be accepted as Philippine reclamation efforts pale in scale to those of China.
22 The overlap between these incidents is likely a result of Hanoi's and Manila's efforts to coordinate their responses to Chinese moves (Rapp-Hooper 2015b).
23 Not all regional military cooperation is aimed at China. For instance, Indonesia, Malaysia, and the Philippines recently agreed to coordinate their naval patrols to reduce piracy in the region (Cochrane 2016b).
24 Vietnam has allowed Singapore and Japan to use the naval facilities at Cam Ranh Bay (Perlez 2016d).
25 The effort is not aimed solely at projecting force into the South and East China Seas, but rather is aimed at modernizing the Chinese military as a whole. For example, China has recently developed the ability to deploy multiple independently-targeted reentry vehicles on its nuclear weapons which could significantly strengthen its nuclear arsenal (Sanger and Broad 2015).
26 The first and second island chains are from China's perspective looking out into the Pacific. The first chain runs from Japan, through Taiwan and the Philippines, to Borneo. The second chain runs from Japan, through the Bonin and Marianas Islands, to Palau and New Guinea.
27 There is some question as to whether China has sufficient real-time detection and targeting capabilities to make its missiles as effective as they could be (Lim 2014, 87–9).
28 China's supply and amphibious capabilities are sufficient for a regional conflict (Lim 2014, 80–2).
29 The modernization effort has included political and organizational reforms as well as the acquisition of new technologies. President Xi Jinping has attempted to tackle entrenched interests among the ground forces in the PLA and reshape the military's organizational structures. As Xi told a committee of Chinese Communist Party leaders, "There cannot be modernization of national defense and the military without modernization of the military's forms of organization … There has to be thoroughgoing reform of leadership and command systems, force structure and policy institutions" (Perlez and Buckley 2014).

30 It appears the United States may have mishandled the passage and acted in a way that did not uphold US claims as clearly as intended (Weinberger 2015).
31 Land reclamation does not change the status of the reef in international law.
32 The same dynamic exists with Japan in the East China Sea.
33 This resistance is not based solely or even primarily on economic considerations. Japan has a long-standing debate between those that believe that Japan needs to take a more proactive military posture in the region and those that feel it is vital to maintain the more passive defensive policy that Japan has maintained since the end of the Second World War and which is still enshrined in its constitution.
34 Goh references the English School's notion that raw power is less effective than power which is cloaked in legitimacy by operating through rules, institutions, and other accepted forms of behavior. See Bull (1977) and Watson (1992).
35 Such a view closely mirrors the United States' position on the features in the South China Sea.
36 Prior research has found that unambiguous legal principles can help peacefully resolve territorial disputes especially when those principles clearly favor one side over the other (Huth, Croco, and Appel 2011). This suggests that the Court's ruling could be an important first step toward resolution, though China's refusal to recognize the Court's jurisdiction makes that outcome less likely at least in the short run.
37 It could be argued that Manila and Hanoi are engaged in defense rather than balancing or hedging as China's threat to their claims in the South China Sea has been actualized to some extent. However, China has not tried to take any features held by these states by force. Also, both Hanoi and Manila have been quite assertive in defense of their claims and seek to draw in outside players. Both seem to be concerned with the long-term threat China poses to their South China Sea claims. Thus, their thinking and actions are more consistent with the logic of balancing than a more narrow conception of defense.
38 In both cases, domestic politics have also played an important role in shaping foreign policy.

Conclusion

This chapter summarizes the book's major findings and explores several policy implications that stem from them. We have made three claims. The first, and primary, claim is that various types of uncertainty affect the likelihood of balancing in different ways. Second, a number of other factors are crucial in determining whether states are more likely to hide or bandwagon once they have opted not to balance. Third, these decisions continue to be made even after war has broken out but they play out in slightly different ways. Once the chapter has summarized our findings on these three points, it will derive several policy implications for potential balancers and bandwagoners that come out of these findings.

Review of the book's main findings

States' propensities to balance, bandwagon, or hide can be explained by a number of factors. In particular, we argued that uncertainty about states' relative capabilities, the offensive nature of the challenger's move, and the challenger's intentions were crucial to whether or not a successful balancing coalition was likely to form. Further we argued that uncertainty about relative capabilities was especially devilish and could often prevent states from balancing. This uncertainty about capabilities was more important than uncertainty over the offensive nature of the challenger's move against the status quo and both were more important than uncertainty over intentions. We also argued that states which fail to balance may pass the buck not only to other states but also to the future. Such states may engage in delay out of myopia or out of hopes that they will be better able to meet the threat posed by a rising state in the future.

These hypotheses were supported by the cases in Chapters 3 and 5. British and French behavior discussed in Chapter 3 fit particularly well with expectations. The leaders of those states were discouraged from balancing against Germany because they did not believe they had sufficient forces available to deter or defeat Germany and they hoped to push any confrontation, up to and including war, off until after they rearmed. Where intentions did play a major role in the case was not in wondering what the rising state intended, this was clear to most statesmen of the period, but rather, in uncertainty over whether other states would help balance against Germany. The French were unsure that they could count on British support, leading Paris to favor appeasement. Likewise, the states of East Central Europe became less disposed to balance as they became convinced that neither Britain nor France would effectively oppose Germany. This implies that states with territorial claims in the South China Sea are likely to base their decisions about balancing against China on their expectations about US policy toward China.

We also argued in Chapters 5 and 7 that geography, divisions between potential balancers, the nature of economic ties, and the presence of international institutions should influence whether or not states bandwagon. First, states which had access to military aid from other states, especially from great powers, were more inclined to balance than those which were geographically isolated from their potential allies. Second, when *substantial and politically significant* territorial disputes exist between potential balancers this naturally makes cooperation between then almost impossible until these territorial disputes are solved. This made it less likely that a successful balancing coalition would form in the 1930s, reducing the appeal of balancing. It also allowed the rising challenger to exploit its ability to resolve these disputes in favor of one state. In fact, it was Hitler's willingness to change the post-World War One settlement to reward cooperation and punish obstruction or opposition in the late 1930s that made his policy so successful. This even made hiding dangerous and pushed states to bandwagon with the rising power in hopes of currying its favor and avoiding its wrath. Such incentives played a major role in moving both Hungary and Romania into the Axis camp. Third, states which were economically dependent upon the rising challenger were more inclined to bandwagon with that challenger than were states which had multilateral economic ties and potential substitutes for their relations with the rising power. This also was true for states which relied on the rising challenger for military hardware. Fourth, effective global and especially regional institutions reduced temptations to bandwagon. Without effective institutions smaller powers can become diplomatically isolated. Such states have difficulty bargaining bilaterally with threatening great powers in the security realm and get pushed toward bandwagoning. The presence of effective institutions allows such states to proceed multilaterally thereby increasing their power. Institutions also create venues through which smaller states can oppose rising powers in less confrontational ways. This makes confrontation more palatable as it contains less risk of war. Again the cases in East Central Europe in the 1930s and Southeast Asia today supported this claim.

Also, all of the cases in Chapters 3, 5, and 7 showed that states do not make a single decision to balance, bandwagon, or hide but make these decisions repeatedly. States often changed strategies as their estimates about the likely costs and benefits of any given strategy changed. This is rational and to be expected, but is often forgotten. Chapter 6 showed that these calculations do not end when war begins. Rather states on the sidelines continue to make decisions about balancing, bandwagoning, and hiding. Their estimates about the relative distribution of capabilities, intentions, and the offensive nature of the challenger's moves are all shaped by events within the war. Battles and wartime demands – much like arms races and crisis diplomacy – help answer questions about and reduce uncertainty surrounding the three key types of uncertainty discussed above. Chapter 6 also showed that both balancing and bandwagoning are common strategies even after the outbreak of hostilities. Additionally, that chapter found that balancers tended to end up on the winning side of a war more often than bandwagoners. Likely this happens because great powers balance more often than they bandwagon. Such powerful states have a large effect on which side will win a war. Less powerful states, though at times balancers, make up a larger percentage of bandwagoners. This is likely because such states could do little to ensure the formation of a successful balancing coalition and because revisionist smaller powers have few ways to achieve their goals other than bandwagoning with revisionist great power challengers.

Last, many states, especially the smaller states of Southeast Asia today and to a lesser extent those of East Central Europe in the 1930s, pursued mixed strategies. Such states often consciously hedged their bets. This was especially true for states such as Poland in the 1930s and Vietnam and the Philippines today which cannot hide given that they had or have territorial disputes with a rising challenger. While other smaller states could potentially lay low diplomatically and avoid harm, these states were or are by their very location a focus of the foreign policy of the rising state. Such states cannot hide and cannot benefit much from bandwagoning either. That leaves balancing as an option, but if balancing is too costly or ineffective, it, too, becomes an unattractive strategy. Hence the result is a mix of strategies and an ongoing search for a policy that will work. Taken together these findings go a long way towards furthering our understanding of how states respond to threats in the face of uncertainty. They indicate what types of behaviors states are likely to engage in and illuminate the factors that influence when and how states will act.

Policy implications

These findings have several policy implications. Among these is that states which aim to balance need to make it clear to prospective allies that a successful balancing coalition can, and likely will, form. This requires not only resolute actions to demonstrate the intent to balance, but also the display of sufficient capabilities on the part of the state or states to defeat or deter the challenger. Failure to do this leads to potential allies hiding from or even bandwagoning with the challenger. As seen in Chapters 3 and 5, British irresolution and weakness led in part to France's under-balancing and attempts to delay. Further, the combined weakness and irresolute behavior of both France and Britain influenced many of the states of East Central Europe's decisions to hide or bandwagon with Germany. Uncertainty about which states would likely balance led to each state comparing its military might with Germany's in isolation rather than comparing the combined power of the potential anti-Nazi coalition with Germany's power. This reinforced notions of weakness and reduced the odds that states would balance.

Conversely, challengers need to do one of two things to avoid being confronted by a balancing coalition. First, rising challengers can attempt to achieve a position of strength by significantly increasing their own capabilities and exploiting divisions between and sowing dissention among potential balancers. If the challenger can make balancing appear to be a costly and futile exercise, states are far less likely to engage in it. Each state that abandons balancing as a policy reduces the incentives for others to balance as the odds that a successful balancing coalition would form decrease as the potential coalition gets smaller. Therefore, challengers can create virtuous cycles (from their point of view) where the discouragement of one potential enemy leads to the discouragement of other potential enemies. The challenger should also attempt to exploit any potential divisions among likely balancers. It could offer to take the side of one potential balancer against another in any ongoing disputes – especially territorial disputes. The challenger could also make it appear that the likely burden of balancing or war would fall more heavily upon one of the balancers, making that state inclined to cut a deal to avoid the excessive costs. Thus, a mix of increased military spending, the offering of spoils to buy off potential enemies, and moves designed to illustrate the fecklessness of potential great power balancers to their likely allies can discourage balancing coalitions from forming in the first place.

Second, challengers could demonstrate that they are not a significant threat to most states' interests, thereby encouraging appeasement and conciliation. The problem is that quite likely the actions necessary to demonstrate relatively benign intent cut in the opposite direction from those which would demonstrate the low likelihood of the formation of a successful balancing coalition. As argued above, military buildups, if they are sufficiently large relative to the military capabilities of potential balancers, help to convince states that balancing is impossible, thereby deterring those potential opponents from balancing. Yet, buildups also likely heighten those states' perceptions of threat and reduce the odds of accommodation. Thus, challengers likely have to ultimately choose between scaring potential opponents into hiding or bandwagoning and finding ways of convincing those same states that the threat is sufficiently limited, making balancing an unnecessary expense. The only alternative to this choice – and one Hitler managed to pull off exceedingly well during most of the 1930s – is to simultaneously convince states that a successful balancing coalition is unlikely to form and that the brunt of the challenger's demands are going to fall elsewhere. Certainly British and to a lesser extent French leaders were convinced of this during the Rhineland and Sudetenland crises. Both believed that confronting Germany was futile until after rearmament was complete and London believed that Berlin would turn east away from Britain and France, meaning time could be purchased at the expense of other states. In other words, London hoped that temporary accommodation was possible even though Germany posed a very real and obvious threat. Of course, as is well known this hope was soon to be dashed.

This jockeying between potential balancers and challengers continues after the outbreak of war. Both balancers and challengers continue to have strong incentives to encourage states to intervene militarily on their side. They can do this by offering spoils, but just as importantly by demonstrating an ability to win the war by winning battles. This is akin to demonstrating during peacetime that a potential balancing coalition is likely or unlikely to form. Third parties to the conflict will likewise continue to evaluate their options. The actions of the belligerent powers may threaten them or provide them with opportunities. Thus, during the course of wars neutral third parties will continually have to make decisions about balancing, bandwagoning, hiding, or transcending.

Last, given the central importance of uncertainty over capabilities and whether or not states are able to construct a successful balancing coalition, investments in intelligence gathering are crucial. As shown in Chapter 3, the British and the French consistently overestimated the German military's abilities between 1936 and 1938. This was not a result of their intelligence services miscounting German hardware and men under arms. British and French estimates of the number of soldiers and planes in the Wehrmacht were relatively accurate. Rather they overestimated the quality of German planes and how many could be sent aloft at any one time, counted reservists as equivalent to first line troops, and missed crucial German materiel shortages. In other words, the intelligence errors were in estimating the quality of the German forces and in estimates about logistical challenges the Germans would face rather than in counting observables such as planes. These failures point to the importance of analysis as well as information collection. Recent US intelligence failures prior to the invasion of Iraq also suggest that simply throwing money at the problem is insufficient as US intelligence services are generally quite well funded. In fact, it is interesting that in 2003 Washington and London seem to have suffered from a problem similar to that which afflicted London and Paris in the 1930s. Namely, despite having reasonably accurate assessments of the capabilities of Hitler's Germany and Saddam's Iraq respectively, these decision-makers chose to exaggerate the strength of their opponents. The key difference was one of motive: in the 1930s France and the UK were doing this to talk themselves out of acting whereas in the early 2000s the US and the UK we doing this to justify intervention (Committee of Privy Counsellors 2016). Thus, states faced with threats must ensure that they not only invest in the collection of sufficient intelligence, but also that their analysis of that intelligence is accurate and not distorted by the biases and preferences of intelligence officers and high-ranking government officials. Obviously, this is far easier said than done.

In this book we have attempted to find regularities in how states deal with the inherent uncertainty that surrounds potential threats. While we certainly have not exhausted the subject, as suggested above we have offered a number of explanations for how states address these uncertainties and why and when they chose to balance, bandwagon, hide, hedge, or transcend. Recent events in the Middle East, the Russian near abroad, and Asia all suggest that states will continue to face these sorts of challenges for a long time to come. This means that how states should respond to potential threats will continue to bedevil governments. We therefore feel this will remain an important area of research in international relations for many years to come.

References

Acharya, A. (2001), *Constructing a Security Community in Southeast Asia: ASEAN and the problem of regional order* (London: Routledge).
Acharya, A. (2003), "Will Asia's Past Be Its Future?," *International Security* 28:3, 149–64.
Acharya, A. (2014), "Power Shift or Paradigm Shift? China's Rise and Asia's Emerging Security Order," *International Studies Quarterly* 58:1, 158–73.
Ádám, M. (1999), "The Munich Crisis and Hungary: The Fall of the Versailles Settlement in Central Europe," in Lukes, I. and Goldstein, E. (eds) *The Munich Crisis, 1938, Prelude to World War II*, Portland, OR: Frank Cass.
Adamthwaite, A. (1977), *France and the Coming of the Second World War, 1936–1939* (London: Frank Cass).
Adamthwaite, A. (1981), *The Lost Peace: International Relations in Europe, 1918–1939* (New York: St. Martin's).
Alexander, M. (1992), *The Republic in Danger: General Maurice Gamelin and the politics of French defense, 1933–1940* (Cambridge: Cambridge University Press).
Altfeld, M., and Bueno de Mesquita, B. (1979), "Choosing Sides in War," *International Studies Quarterly* 23:1, 87–112.
Angell, N. (1915), *The World's Highway: Some Notes on America's Relation to Sea Power and Non-Military Sanctions for the Law of Nations* (New York: Doran).
Art, R., Brooks, S., Wohlforth, W., Lieber, K., and Alexander, G. (2006), "Correspondence: Striking the Balance," *International Security* 30:3, 177–96.
Axelrod, R. and Keohane, R. (1985), "Achieving Cooperation Under Anarchy: Strategies and Institutions," *World Politics* 38:1, 226–54.
Ba, A. (2010), "Regional Security in East Asia: ASEAN's Value Added and Limitations," *Journal of Current Southeast Asian Affairs* 29:3, 115–30.
Barbieri, K. (1996), "Economic Interdependence: A Path to Peace or a Source of Interstate Conflict?," *Journal of Peace Research* 33:1, 29–49.
BBC News Asia. (2013), "Malaysia rejects ceasefire offer from Filipino group," 7 March.
Beck, R. (1989), "Munich's Lessons Reconsidered," *International Security* 14:2, 161–91.
Bemis, S. (1977), *John Quincy Adams and the Foundations of American Foreign Policy* (Norwalk: Easton Press).
Ben-Arie, K. (1990), "Czechoslovakia and the Time of 'Munich': the Military Situation," *Journal of Contemporary History* 25:4, 431–46.
Biddle, S. (2001), "Rebuilding the Foundations of Offense–Defense Theory," *Journal of Politics* 63:3, 741–74.
Blagden, D. (2011), "Sea Powers, Continental Powers, and Balancing Theory," *International Security* 36:2, 190–202.

Blainey, G. (1973), *The Causes of War* (New York: Free Press).
Bradsher, K. (2014a), "Philippines Challenges China Over Disputed Atoll," *New York Times*, 14 May.
Bradsher, K. (2014b), "Philippine Leader Sounds Alarm on China," *New York Times*, 5 February.
Bremer, S. (1982), "The Contagiousness of Coercion: The Spread of Serious International Disputes, 1900–1976," *International Interactions* 9:1, 29–55.
Brooks, S. and Wohlforth, W. (2011), "Assessing the Balance," *Cambridge Review of International Affairs* 24:2, 201–19.
Browne, A. (2015), "Beijing Wary of Political Toll of Aggression at Sea," *Wall Street Journal*, 14 May.
Bueno de Mesquita, B., Morrow, J. and Zorick, E. (1997), "Capabilities, Perception and Escalation," *American Political Science Review* 91:1, 15–27.
Bueno de Mesquita, B., Morrow, J., Siverson, R., and Smith, A. (2004), "Testing Novel Implications from the Selectorate Theory of War," *World Politics* 56:3, 363–88.
Bull, H. (1977), *The Anarchical Society: A Study of Order in World Politics*. (New York: Columbia University Press).
Burr, R. (1980), *By Reason or Force: Chile and the Balancing of Power in South America, 1830–1905* (Millwood: Kraus Reprint).
Buszynski, L. (2012), "The South China Sea: Oil, Maritime Claims, and US–China Strategic Rivalry," *The Washington Quarterly* 35:2, 140–56.
Carpenter, T. (2014), "Obama's China Strategy is Doomed," *National Interest*, 16 August.
Chan, S. (2016), *China's Troubled Waters: Maritime Disputes in Theoretical Perspective* (Cambridge: Cambridge University Press).
Chiozza, G., and Goemans, H. (2004), "International Conflict and the Tenure of Leaders: Is War Still *Ex Post* Inefficient?," *American Journal of Political Science* 48:3, 604–19.
Choe S. (2016), "US Weighs Tighter Sanctions on North Korea if China Fails to Act", *New York Times*, 20 January.
Christensen, T. (2006), "Fostering Stability or Creating a Monster? The Rise of China and US Policy toward East Asia," *International Security* 31:1, 81–126.
Christensen, T. (2011), "The Advantages of an Assertive China: Responding to Beijing's Abrasive Diplomacy," *Foreign Affairs* 90:2, 54–67.
Christensen, T. and Snyder, S. (1990), "Chain Gangs and Passed Bucks: Predicting Alliance Patterns in Multipolarity," *International Organization* 44:2, 137–68.
Churchill, W. (1948), *The Second World War* (Cambridge: Houghton Mifflin).
Cienciala, A. (1989), "Essay and Reflection: The Munich Crisis Revisited," *The International History Review* 11:4, 684–8.
Cienciala, A. (1992), "A View From Warsaw," in Latynski, M. (ed.) *The Munich Pact: Continental Perspectives* (Washington: Woodrow Wilson Center).
Cienciala, A. (1999), "The Munich Crisis of 1938: Plans and Strategy in Warsaw in Context of Western Appeasement of Germany," in Lukes, I. and Goldstein, E. (eds) *The Munich Crisis, 1938, Prelude to World War II*, Portland, OR: Frank Cass.
Claude, I. (1962), *Power and International Relations* (New York: Random House).
Cochrane, J. (2016a), "Indonesia Confirms Seizing Fishing Boat in South China Sea, Defying Beijing", *New York Times*, 20 June.
Cochrane, J. (2016b), "Indonesia, Malaysia and Philippines to Bolster Security at Sea", *New York Times*, 5 May.
Committee of Privy Counsellors. (2016), *The Report of the Iraq Inquiry* (London: Government of the United Kingdom).

Cooper, H. (2015), "In a First, Chinese Navy Sails Off Alaska," *New York Times*, 2 September.

Cooper, H. (2016), "Patrolling Disputed Waters, US and China Jockey for Dominance", *New York Times*, 30 March.

Cooper, H. and Perlez, J. (2014), "US Sway in Asia is Imperiled as China Challenges Alliances," *New York Times*, May 30.

Cooper, H. and Perlez, J. (2015a), "US Flies Over a Chinese Project at Sea, and Beijing Objects," *New York Times*, 22 May.

Cooper, H. and Perlez, J. (2015b), "White House Moves to Reassure Allies With South China Sea Patrol, but Quietly," *New York Times*, 27 October.

Copeland, D. (2000), *The Origins of Major War* (Ithaca: Cornell University Press).

Craig, G. (1950), "High Tide of Appeasement: The Road to Munich, 1937–38," *Political Science Quarterly* 65:1, 20–37.

Crawford, T. (2003), *Pivotal Deterrence: Third Part Statecraft and the Pursuit of Peace* (Ithaca: Cornell University Press).

Croco, S. (2011), "The Decider's Dilemma: Leader Culpability, War Outcomes, and Domestic Punishment," *American Political Science Review* 105:3, 457–77.

Cusack, T. and Stoll, R. (1991), "Balancing Behavior in the Interstate System, 1816–1976," *International Interactions* 16:4, 255–70.

Danilovic, V. (2001), "The Sources of Threat Credibility in Extended Deterrence," *Journal of Conflict Resolution* 45:3, 341–69.

Davis, J. (2001), *Threats and Promises: The Pursuit of International Influence* (Baltimore: John Hopkins University Press).

Dent, C. (2008), *East Asian Regionalism* (London: Routledge).

Deutsch, A. (2015), "In defeat for Beijing, Hague court to hear South China Sea dispute," *Reuters*, 30 October.

Dominion Post. (2012), "Vietnam Passport Map Controversy," 27 November.

Edelstein, D. (2002), "Managing Uncertainty: Beliefs about intentions and the rise of great powers," *Security Studies* 12:1, 1–40.

Elman, M. (1995), "The Foreign Policy of Small States: Challenging Neorealism in its Own Backyard," *British Journal of Political Science* 25:2, 171–217.

Emmers, R., and Tan, S. (2011), "The ASEAN Regional Forum and Preventive Diplomacy: Built to Fail?," *Asian Security* 7:1, 44–60.

Entous, A., Lubold, G., and Barnes, J. (2015), "US Military Proposes Challenge to China Sea Claims: Moves would send Navy planes, ships near artificial islands build by China in contested waters," *Wall Street Journal*, 12 May.

Erickson, A., Strange, A., Cheng, D., Ratner, E., Brimley, S., Haddick, R., Rapp-Hooper, M., and Cooper, Z. (2015), "China's Menacing Sandcastles in the South China Sea," *CSIS Asia Program*, 2 March.

Escritt, T. (2015), "Philippines take South China Sea claim to Hague court," *Reuters*, 24 November.

Fearon, J. (1995), "Rationalist Explanations for War," *International Organization* 49:3, 379–414.

Fey, M., and Ramsay, K. (2007), "Mutual Optimism and War," *American Journal of Political Science* 51:4, 738–54.

Finnemore, M. (2003), *The Purpose of Intervention: Changing Beliefs About the Use of Force* (Ithaca: Cornell University Press).

Fisher, M. (2012), "Here's the Chinese Passport Map That's Infuriating Much of Asia," *The Washington Post*, 26 November.

Foot, R. (2006), "Chinese Strategies in a US-Hegemonic Global Order: Accommodating and Hedging," *International Affairs* 82:1, 77–94.
Forsythe, M. and Perlez, J. (2016), "South China Sea Buildup Brings Beijing Closer to Realizing Control", *New York Times*, 8 March.
Fox, A. (1959), *The Power of Small States: Diplomacy in World War II* (Chicago: University of Chicago Press).
Freedman, L. (2013), *Strategy: A History* (Oxford: Oxford University Press).
Friedberg, A. (2000), "Will Europe's past be Asia's future?," *Survival* 42:3, 147–60.
Fry, M. (1999), "Agents and Structures: The Dominions and the Czechoslovak Crisis, September 1983," in Lukes, I. and Goldstein, E. (eds) *The Munich Crisis, 1938, Prelude to World War II*, Portland, OR: Frank Cass.
Gaddis, J. (1997), *We Now Know: Rethinking Cold War History* (Oxford: Oxford University Press).
Gartzke, E. (1999), "War is in the Error Term," *International Organization* 53:3, 567–87.
Gartzke, E. (2007), "The Capitalist Peace," *American Journal of Political Science* 51:1, 166–91.
Gelpi, C. (1999), "Alliances as Instruments of Intra-Allied Control," in Haftendorn, H., Keohane, R., and Wallander, C. (eds) *Imperfect Unions: Security Institutions over Time and Space* (Oxford: Oxford University Press).
Gholz, E. (2014), "Rare Earth Elements and National Security," *Council on Foreign Relations Energy Report* October, 1–13.
Gibler, D. (2009), *International Military Alliances, 1648–2008* (Washington: CQ Press).
Glaser, C. (1992), "Political Consequences of Military Strategy: Extending and Refining the Spiral Model," *World Politics* 44:4, 497–538.
Glaser, C. (1997), "The Security Dilemma Revisited," *World Politics* 50:1, 171–201.
Glaser, C. (2011), "Why Unipolarity Doesn't Matter (Much)," *Cambridge Review of International Affairs* 24:2, 135–48.
Gleditsch, K. (2002), *All International Politics is Local: The Diffusion of Conflict, Integrations, and Democratization* (Ann Arbor: University of Michigan Press).
Goemans, H. (2000), *War and Punishment: The Causes of War Termination and the First World War* (Princeton: Princeton University Press).
Goh, E. (2007), "Southeast Asian Perspectives on the China Challenge," *Journal of Strategic Studies* 30:4–5, 809–32.
Goh, E. (2008), "Great Powers and Hierarchical Order in Southeast Asia: Analyzing Regional Security Strategies," *International Security* 32:3, 113–57.
Goh, E. (2011), "Institutions and the great power bargain in East Asia: ASEAN's limited 'brokerage' role," *International Relations of the Asia-Pacific* 11:3, 373–401.
Goldstein, E. (1999), "Neville Chamberlain, the British Official Mind and the Munich Crisis," in Lukes, I. and Goldstein, E. (eds) *The Munich Crisis, 1938, Prelude to World War II*, Portland, OR: Frank Cass.
Gordon, M. (2015), "Kerry Urges Beijing to Halt Actions in South China Sea," *New York Times*, August 5.
Governments of the Member States of ASEAN and the Government of the People's Republic of China. (2002), *Declaration on the Conduct of Parties in the South China Sea* (Phnom Penh).
Graham, R. (1996), *The Great Powers and the Decline of the European States System 1914–1945* (New York: Longman).
Great Britain. Foreign Office. (1990), *British Documents on Foreign Affairs: Reports and Papers from the Foreign Office confidential print. Part II, From the First to Second*

World War. Series F, Europe, 1919–1939. Vol. 22–23, 47, and 49. (Frederick: University Publications of America).
Green, M. (2014), "Regional Security Roles and Challenges," in Hachigian, N. (ed.) *Debating China: The US–China Relationship in Ten Conversations* (Oxford: Oxford University Press).
Guinto, J. and Heath, N. (2012), "China Maps Path to New Conflicts in its Passports," *The Age*, 23 November.
Gulick, E. (1955), *Europe's Classical Balance of Power: A Case History of the Theory and Practice of One of the Great Concepts of European Statecraft* (Ithaca: Cornell University Press).
Haas, E. (1953), "The balance of power: prescription, concept, or propaganda?," *World Politics* 5:4, 442–77.
Haas, M. (2014), "Ideological Polarity and Balancing in Great Power Politics", *Security Studies* 23(4): 715–53.
Haight, J. (1960), "France, the United States, and the Munich Crisis," *Journal of Modern History* 32:4, 340–58.
Hammerström, M. and Heldt, B. (2002), "The Diffusion of Military Intervention: Testing a Network Diffusion Approach," *International Interactions* 28:4, 355–77.
Harinder, A. (1983), "Britain and the Sudeten Issue, 1938: The Evolution of Policy," *Journal of Contemporary History* 18:2, 233–59.
Harris, G. (2016), "Vietnam Arms Embargo to Be Fully Lifted, Obama Says in Hanoi", *New York Times*, 23 May.
He, K. (2012), "Undermining Adversaries: Unipolarity, Threat Perception and Negative Balancing Strategies After the Cold War," *Security Studies* 21:2, 154–91.
He, K. and Feng, H. (2012), "Debating China's assertiveness: Taking China's power and interests seriously," *International Politics* 49: 633–44.
Hemmings, J. (2011), "Law not War in the South China Sea," *The Diplomat*, November 23.
Herman, J. (1980), "Soviet Peace Efforts on the Eve of World War Two: A Review of the Soviet Documents," *Journal of Contemporary History* 15:3, 577–602.
Hernandez, J. (2015), "Warily Eyeing China, Philippines May Invite US Back to Subic Bay," *New York Times*, 19 September.
Herz, J. (1950), "Idealist Internationalism and the Security Dilemma," *World Politics* 2:2, 157–80.
Hirschman, A. (1980), *National Power and the Structure of Foreign Trade* (Berkeley: University of California Press).
Hitchins, K. (1994), *Rumania, 1866–1947* (Oxford: Clarendon Press).
Hoisington, W. (1971), "The Struggle for Economic Influence in Southeastern Europe: The French Failure in Romania, 1940," *Journal of Modern History* 43:3, 468–82.
Holden, A. (1976), "Bulgaria's Entry into the First World War: A Diplomatic Study, 1913–1915," Dissertation (University of Illinois).
Holmes, J. (2012), "The Sino-Japanese Naval War of 2012," *Foreign Policy*, 20 August.
Hopf, T. (2010), "The Logic of Habit in International Relations," *European Journal of International Relations* 16:4, 539–61.
Hoptner, J. (1962), *Yugoslavia in Crisis, 1934–1941* (New York: Columbia University Press).
Houweling, H. and Siccama, J. (1988), *Studies of War* (Dordrecht: Nijhoff).
Hughes, J. (1988), "The Origins of World War II in Europe: British Deterrence Failure and German Expansionism," *Journal of Interdisciplinary History* 18:4, 851–91.
Hume, D. (1898), *Essays. Moral, Political and Literary* (New York: Longmans, Green).

Hunt, L. and Jiang, S. (2016), "South China Sea: China may establish air defense zone after losing court ruling", *CNN*, 13 July.

Huth, P., and Russett, B. (1984), "What Makes Deterrence Work? Cases from 1900 to 1980," *World Politics* 36:4, 496–526.

Huth, P., Croco, S., and Appel, B. (2011), "Does International Law Promote the Peaceful Settlement of International Disputes? Evidence from the Study of Territorial Conflicts since 1945," *American Political Science Review* 105(2): 415–36.

Iklé, F. (1964), *How Nations Negotiate* (New York: Harper and Row).

Ives, M. (2016a), "Vietnam Faces Last-Minute Maneuvering for Communist Party Leadership", *New York Times*, 18 January.

Ives, M. (2016b), "Vietnam's Communist Party Gives Old-Guard Leader a New Five Year Term", *New York Times*, 27 January.

Jackson, P. (1998), "Intelligence and the End of Appeasement," in Boyce, R. (ed.) *French Foreign and Defense Policy 1918–1940* (New York: Routledge).

Jervis, R. (1978), "Cooperation Under the Security Dilemma," *World Politics* 30:2, 167–214.

Jervis, R. (1994), "What Do We Want to Deter and How Do We Deter It?," in Ederington, L. and Mazarr, M. (eds) *Turning Point* (Boulder: Westview Press).

Johnston, A. (2011), "How New and Assertive Is China's New Assertiveness?," *International Security* 37:4, 7–48.

Jones, D. (1994), "Balancing and Bandwagoning in Militarized Interstate Disputes", in Wayman, F. and Diehl, P. (eds) *Reconstructing Realpolitik* (Ann Arbor: University of Michigan Press).

Joyce, K., Ghosn, F., and Bayer, R. (2014), "When and Whom to Join: The Expansion of Ongoing Violent Interstate Conflicts," *British Journal of Political Science* 44:1, 205–38.

Jukes, G. (1991), "The Red Army and the Munich Crisis," *Journal of Contemporary History* 26:2, 195–214.

Kang, D. (2009), "Between Balancing and Bandwagoning: South Korea's Response to China," *Journal of East Asian Studies* 9:1, 1–28.

Kaplan, R. (2011), "The South China Sea is the Future of Conflict," *Foreign Policy* September/October, 76–86.

Katona, G. (1939), "Hungary in the German Orbit," *Foreign Affairs* 17(3): 599–610.

Kaufmann, J. (1988), "Unusual Aspects of a Unique Fortification: The Maginot Line," *Military Affairs* 52:2, 69–74.

Kaufman, R. (1992), "'To Balance or to Bandwagon?' Alignment Decisions in 1930s Europe," *Security Studies* 1:3, 417–47.

Kaufman, S., Little, R., and Wohlforth, W. (eds). (2007), *Balance of Power in World History* (London: Palgrave MacMillan).

Kennedy, P. (1989), *The Rise and Fall of the Great Powers: Economic Change and Military Conflict from 1500 to 2000* (New York: Fontana Press).

Keohane, R. (1982), "The Demand for International Regimes," *International Organization* 36:2, 325–55.

Keohane, R. (1986), "Reciprocity in International Relations," *International Organization* 40:1, 1–27.

Keohane, R. and Martin, L. (1995), "The Promise of Institutionalist Theory," *International Security* 20:1, 39–51.

Keohane, R. and Nye, J. (1974), "Transgovernmental Relations and International Organization," *World Politics* 27:1, 39–62.

Keohane, R., Haftendorn, H., and Wallander, C. (1999), "Conclusions", in Haftendorn, H., Keohane, R. and Wallander, C. (eds) *Imperfect Unions: Security Institutions over Time and Space* (Oxford: Oxford University Press).

Koo, M. (2009), *Island Disputes and Maritime Regime Building in East Asia: Between a Rock and a Hard Place* (New York: Springer).

Krebs, R. and Rapport, A. (2012), "International Relations and the Psychology of Time Horizons," *International Studies Quarterly* 56:3, 530–43.

Krizman, B. (1978), *Vanjska Politika Jugoslovenske Drzave 1918–1941* (Zagreb: Sveuciliste Zgb-Ins.za hrv. po.).

Kroenig, M. (2015), "Why Democracies Dominate: America's Edge over China," *National Interest* 138, 38–46.

Kupchan, C. and Kupchan, C. (1995), "The Promise of Collective Security," *International Security* 20:1, 52–61.

Kydd, A. (1997a), "Game Theory and the Spiral Model," *World Politics* 49:3, 371–400.

Kydd, A. (1997b), "Sheep in Sheep's Clothing: Why Security Seekers Do Not Fight Each Other," *Security Studies* 7:1, 114–55.

Lacaze, Y. (1998), "Daladier, Bonnet and the Decision-making Process During the Munich Crisis, 1938," in Boyce, R. (ed.) *French Foreign and Defense Policy 1918–1940* (New York: Routledge).

Lake, D. (2001), "Beyond Anarchy: The Importance of Security Institutions," *International Security* 26:1, 129–60.

Landler, M. and Forsythe, M. (2016), "Chinese Missiles in South China Sea Underscore a Growing Conflict Risk", *New York Times*, 17 February.

Layne, C. (1993), "The Unipolar Illusion: Why New Great Powers Will Rise," *International Security* 17:4, 5–51.

Layne, C. (2006), "The Unipolar Illusion Revisited: The Coming End of the United States' Unipolar Moment," *International Security* 31:2, 7–41.

Layne, C. (2008), "Security Studies and the Use of History: Neville Chamberlain's Grand Strategy Revisited," *Security Studies* 17:3, 397–437.

Leeds, B. (2005), "Alliances and the Expansion and Escalation of Militarized Interstate Disputes," in Mintz, A. and Russett, B. (eds) *New Directions for International Relations: Confronting the Method-of-Analysis Problem* (New York: Lexington Books).

Leitz, C. (1997), "Arms as Levers: 'Matériel' and Raw Materials in Germany's Trade with Romania in the 1930s," *The International History Review* 19:2, 312–32.

Levy, J. (1994), "Learning and Foreign Policy: Sweeping a Conceptual Minefield," *International Organization* 48:2, 279–312.

Levy, J. (2002), "Balances and Balancing: Concepts, Propositions, and Research Design," in Vasquez, J. and Elman, C. (eds).*Realism and the Balancing of Power: A New Debate* (Upper Saddle River, NJ: Prentice Hall).

Levy, J. and Thompson, W. (2005), "Hegemonic Threats and Great Power Balancing in Europe, 1495–1999," *Security Studies* 14:1, 1–33.

Levy, J. and Thompson, W. (2010), "Balancing on Land and at Sea: Do States Ally Against the Leading Global Power?," *International Security* 35:1, 7–43.

Li, M. (2010), "Reconciling Assertiveness and Cooperation? China's Changing Approach to the South China Sea Dispute," *Security Challenges* 6:2, 49–68.

Liddell Hart, B. (1960), *Deterrent or Defence* (London: Stevens and Sons).

Lieber, K. and Alexander, G. (2005), "Waiting for Balancing: Why the World Isn't Pushing Back," *International Security* 24:1, 109–39.

Lim, Y. (2014), *China's Naval Power: An Offensive Realist Approach* (Aldershot: Ashgate).

Lukač, D. (1979), *Dileme Stojadinovićeve Spoljne Politike U Vreme Utemeljivanja Osovine Rim – Berlin* (Belgrade: Srpska akademija nauka i umetnosti, Balkanološki institute).

Lukes, I. (1999), "Stalin and Czechoslovakia in 1938–39: An Autopsy of a Myth," in Lukes, I. and Goldstein, E. (eds) *The Munich Crisis, 1938, Prelude to World War II*, Portland, OR: Frank Cass.

Macartney, C. (1938), "Hungary and the Present Crisis," *International Affairs* 17:6, 749–68.

Marks, F. (1985), "Six Between Roosevelt and Hitler: America's Role in the Appeasement of Nazi Germany," *The Historical Journal* 28:4, 969–82.

Mastaduno, M. (2002), "Incomplete Hegemony and Security Order in the Asia-Pacific," in Ikenberry, G. (ed.) *America Unrivaled: The Future of the Balance of Power* (Ithaca: Cornell University Press).

Mastro, O. (2016), "The Vulnerability of Rising Powers: The Logic Behind China's Low Military Transparency", *Asian Security* 12(2): 63–81.

Mattingly, G. (1988), *Renaissance Diplomacy* (New York: Dover).

McDonald, P. (2015), "Great Powers, Hierarchy, and Endogenous Regimes: Rethinking the Domestic Causes of Peace," *International Organization* 69(3): 557–88.

McKay, D. and Scott, H. (1995), *The Rise of the Great Powers 1648–1815* (New York: Longman).

Mearsheimer, J. (2001), *The Tragedy of Great Power Politics* (New York: W. W. Norton).

Mearsheimer, J. (2010), "The Gathering Storm: China's Challenge to US Power in Asia," *Chinese Journal of International Politics* 3:4, 381–96.

Melin, M. and Koch, M. (2010), "Jumping into the Fray: Alliances, Power, Institutions, and the Timing of Conflict Expansion," *International Interactions* 36:1, 1–27.

Men, J. (2007), "The Construction of the China–ASEAN Free Trade Area: A Study of China's Active Involvement," *Global Society* 21(2): 249–68.

Ministry of Foreign Affairs of the People's Republic of China. (2015), "Foreign Ministry Spokesperson Hua Chunying's Remarks on US Defense Secretary Carter's Speech Relating to the Issue of the South China Sea at the Shangri-La Dialogue," May 30.

Mirkovich, N. (1941), "Jugoslavia's Choice," *Foreign Affairs* 20:1, 131–51.

Mogato, M., Martina, M., and Blanchard, B. (2016), "ASEAN deadlocked on South China Sea, Cambodia blocks statement," *Reuters*, 26 July.

Morgenthau, H. (1973), *Politics Among Nations* (New York: Knopf).

Most, B. and Starr, H. (1980), "Diffusion, Reinforcement, Geo-Politics and the Spread of War," *American Political Science Review* 74:4, 932–46.

Mullany, G. (2014), "Philippines Jails Chinese Sailors in Fish Dispute," *New York Times*, May 10.

Mullany, G. and Barboza, D. (2014), "Vietnam Squares Off with China in Disputed Seas," *New York Times*, 7 May.

Murphy, A. (2010), "Beyond Balancing and Bandwagoning: Thailand's Response to China's Rise," *Asian Security* 6:1, 1–27.

Murray, W. (1984), *The Change in the European Balance of Power, 1938–1939: The Path to Ruin* (Princeton: Princeton University Press).

Newman, M. (1978), "The Origins of Munich: British Policy in Danubian Europe, 1933–1937," *The Historical Journal* 21:2, 371–86.

Nexon, D. (2009), "The Balance of Power in the Balance," *World Politics* 61:2, 330–59.

Nye, J. (2002), "Limits of American Power," *Political Science Quarterly* 117:4, 545–59.

Offner, A. (1977), "Appeasement Revisited: The United States, Great Britain, and Germany: 1933–1940," *Journal of American History* 64:2, 373–93.

Oneal, J. (1990), "The Theory of Collective Action and Burden Sharing in NATO," *International Organization* 44:3, 379–402.

Orange, V. (2006), "The German Air Force is Already 'The Most Powerful in Europe': Two Royal Air Force Officers Report on a Visit to Germany, 6–15 October 1936," *The Journal of Military History* 70:4, 1011–28.

Ostrom, E. (1990), *Governing the Commons: The Evolution of Institutions for Collective Action* (Cambridge: Cambridge University Press).

Ott, M. (2011), "Competing Claims in the South China Sea," *Current History* September, 236–41.

Overy, R. (1999), "Germany and the Munich Crisis: A Mutilated Victory?," in Lukes, I. and Goldstein, E. (eds) *The Munich Crisis, 1938, Prelude to World War II*, Portland, OR: Frank Cass.

Oye, K. (1986), *Cooperation Under Anarchy* (Princeton: Princeton University Press).

Paddock, R. (2016), "Mysterious Blast in Philippines Fuels Rodrigo Duterte's 'Hatred' of US," *New York Times*, 13 May.

Pape, R. (2005), "Soft Balancing Against the United States," *International Security* 30:1, 7–45.

Parent, J. and Rosato, S. (2015), "Balancing in Neorealism," *International Security* 40:2, 51–86.

Parker, R. (1956), "The First Capitulation: France and the Rhineland Crisis of 1936," *World Politics* 8:3, 355–73.

Pastor, P. (2004), "Hungarian-Soviet Diplomatic Relations 1935–1941: A Failed Rapprochement," *Europe-Asia Studies* 56:5, 731–50.

Paul, T. (2004), "Introduction: The Enduring Axioms of Balance," in Paul, T., Wirtz, J. and Fortmann, M. (eds) *Balance of Power: Theory and Practice in the 21st Century* (Palo Alto: Stanford University Press).

Paul, T. (2005), "Soft Balancing in the Age of U.S. Primacy," *International Security* 24:1, 46–71.

Pearson, F., Baumann, R., and Pickering, J. (1994), "Military Intervention and Realpolitik," in Wayman, F. and Diehl, P. (eds) *Reconstructing Realpolitik* (Ann Arbor: University of Michigan Press).

Perlez, J. (2014a), "China and Vietnam Point Fingers After Clash," *New York Times*, 27 May.

Perlez, J. (2014b), "Malaysia Risks Enraging China by Inviting US Spy Flight," *New York Times*, 13 September.

Perlez, J. (2015a), "In Victory for Philippines, Hague Court to Hear Dispute Over South China Sea," *New York Times*, 30 October.

Perlez, J. (2015b), "US Admiral, in Beijing, Defends Patrols in South China Sea", *New York Times*, 3 November.

Perlez, J. (2015c), "Xi Hosts 56 Nations at Founding of Asian Infrastructure Bank," *New York Times*, 29 June.

Perlez, J. (2016a), "Beijing Rejects South China Sea Case Ahead of July 12 Ruling," *New York Times*, 30 June.

Perlez, J. (2016b), "Courting New President, China Slows Island-Building Off Philippine Coast," *New York Times*, 25 September.

Perlez, J. (2016c), "US Carriers Sail in Western Pacific, Hoping China Takes Notice", *New York Times*, 18 June.

Perlez, J. (2016d), "Why Might Vietnam Let US Military Return? China," *New York Times*, 19 May.

Perlez, J. and Bradsher, K. (2014), "In High Seas, China Moves Unilaterally," *New York Times*, 9 May.

Perlez, J. and Buckley, C. (2014), "China's Leader, Seeking to Build Its Muscle, Pushes Overhaul of the Military," *New York Times*, 24 May.

Permanent Court of Arbitration. 2016. "Press Release: The South China Sea Arbitration (The Philippines v. The People's Republic of China)," 12 July (The Hague: Permanent Court of Arbitration).

Powell, R. (1999), *In the Shadow of Power: States and Strategies in International Politics* (Princeton: Princeton University Press).

Powell, R. (2004), "Bargaining and Learning While Fighting," *American Journal of Political Science* 48:2, 344–61.

Powell, R. (2006), "War as a Commitment Problem," *International Organization* 60:1, 169–203.

Powell, R. (2012), "Persistent Fighting and Shifting Power," *American Journal of Political Science* 56:3, 620–37.

Prazmowska, A. (1986), "Poland's Foreign Policy: September 1938–September 1939," *The Historical Journal* 29:4, 853–73.

Press, D. (2005), "The Credibility of Power: Assessing Threats during the 'Appeasement' Crises of the 1930s," *International Security* 29:3, 136–69.

Rafferty, K. (2003), "An Institutionalist's Reinterpretation of Cold War Alliance Systems: Insights for Alliance Theory," *Canadian Journal of Political Science* 36:2, 341–62.

Ragsdale, H. (1998), "The Munich Crisis and the Issue of the Red Army Transit across Romania," *Russian Review* 57:4, 614–7.

Raknerud, A. and Hegre, H. (1997), "The Hazard of War: Reassessing the Evidence for the Democratic Peace," *Journal of Peace Research* 34:4, 385–404.

Rapp-Hooper, M. (2015a), "America's Security Role in the South China Sea," *Statement before the House Committee on Foreign Affairs Subcommittee on Asia and the Pacific*, 23 July.

Rapp-Hooper, M. (2015b), "Six Summertime Steps in the South China Sea," *CSIS Asia Program*, 6 August.

Rauchhaus, R. (2009), "Evaluating the Nuclear Peace Hypothesis: A Quantitative Approach," *Journal of Peace Research* 53:2, 258–77.

Reiter, D. (1995), "Exploding the Powder Keg Myth: Preemptive Wars Almost Never Happen," *International Security* 20:2, 5–34.

Reiter, D. (1999), "Military Strategy and the Outbreak of International Conflict: Quantitative Empirical Tests 1903–1994," *International Studies Quarterly* 43:2, 366–87.

Reiter, D. (2009), *How Wars End* (Princeton: Princeton University Press).

Renzi, W. (1987), *In the Shadows of the Sword: Italy's Neutrality and Entrance Into the Great War, 1914–1915* (New York: Peter Lang).

Richardson, Le. (1960), *Statistics of Deadly Quarrels* (Chicago: Quadrangle).

Richardson, Lo. (1999), "The Concert of Europe and Security Management in the Nineteenth Century," in Haftendorn, H., Keohane, R. and Wallander, C. (eds) *Imperfect Unions: Security Institutions over Time and Space* (Oxford: Oxford University Press).

Ripsman, N. and Levy, J. (2008), "Wishful Thinking or Buying Time? The Logic of British Appeasement in the 1930s," *International Security* 33:2, 148–81.

Rosecrance, R. and Lo, C. (1996), "Balancing, Stability, and War: The Mysterious Case of the Napoleonic International System," *International Studies Quarterly* 40:4, 479–500.

Rothschild, J. (1977), *East Central Europe between the Two World Wars* (Seattle: University of Washington Press).

Rothstein, R. (1968), *Alliances and Small Powers* (New York: Columbia University Press).
Roy, D. (2005), "Southeast Asia and China: Balancing or Bandwagoning?," *Contemporary Southeast Asia* 27:2, 305–22.
Russett, B. and Oneal, J. (2001), *Triangulating Peace: Democracy, Interdependence, and International Organizations* (New York: W. W. Norton).
Sakmyster, T. (1973), "Hungary and the Munich Crisis: The Revisionist Dilemma," *Slavic Review* 32:4, 725–40.
Sakmyster, T. (1980), *Hungary, the Great Powers, and the Danubian Crisis, 1936–1939* (Athens: University of Georgia Press).
Sakwa, G. (1973), "The Franco-Polish Alliance and the Remilitarization of the Rhineland," *The Historical Journal* 16:1, 125–46.
Sanger, D. (2016), "Despite Obama's Moves, Asian Nations Skeptical of US Commitment," *New York Times*, 23 May.
Sanger, D. and Broad, W. (2015), "China Makes Some Missiles More Powerful," *New York Times*, 16 May.
Sanger, D. and Gladstone, R. (2015), "Piling Sand in a Disputed Sea, China Literally Gains Ground," *New York Times*, 8 April.
Sanger, D. and Gladstone, R. (2016), "New Photos Cast Doubt on China's Vow Not to Militarize Disputed Islands," *New York Times*, 8 August.
Sanger, D. and Landler, M. (2014), "Obama's Strategic Shift to Asia is Hobbled by Pressure at Home and Crises Abroad," *New York Times*, 21 April.
Sarkees, M. and Wayman, F. (2010), *Resort to War: 1816–2007* (Washington: CQ Press).
Savic, I. and Shirkey, Z. (2009), "Trust in the Balance: Asymmetric Information, Commitment Problems and Balancing Behavior," *Journal of Theoretical Politics* 21:4, 483–508.
Scanlon, C. (2014), "Is Shinzo Abe Fanning Nationalist Flames?," *BBC News*, April 23.
Schelling, T. (1966), *Arms and Influence* (New Haven: Yale University Press).
Schroeder, P. (1972), *Austria, Great Britain, and the Crimean War: The Destruction of the Concert of Europe* (Ithaca: Cornell University Press).
Schroeder, P. (1994), "Historical Reality vs. Neo-Realist Theory," *International Security* 19:1, 108–48.
Schuker, S. (1986), "France and the Remilitarization of the Rhineland, 1936," *French Historical Studies* 14:3, 299–338.
Schweller, R. (1994), "Bandwagoning for Profit: Bringing the Revisionist State Back In," *International Security* 19:1, 72–107.
Schweller, R. (1997), "New Realist Research on Alliances: Refining, Not Refuting, Waltz's Balancing Proposition," *American Political Science Review* 91:4, 927–30.
Schweller, R. (2006), *Unanswered Threats: Political Constraints on the Balance of Power* (Princeton: Princeton University Press).
Schweller, R. (2011), "The Future is Uncertain and the End is Always Near," *Cambridge Review of International Affairs* 24:2, 175–84.
Science Letter (1938), "In Sudeten, Germany Would Add to Raw Material Needs," 34:14, 213.
Selden, Z. (2013), "Balancing Against or Balancing With? The Spectrum of Alignment and the Endurance of American Hegemony," *Security Studies* 22:2, 330–64.
Shear, M. (2015), "Obama Calls on Beijing to Stop Construction in South China Sea," *New York Times*, 18 November.
Shirer, W. (1984), *The Nightmare Years, 1930–1940* (Boston: Little, Brown).
Shirkey, Z. (2009), *Is This a Private Fight of Can Anybody Join? The Spread of Interstate War* (Aldershot: Ashgate).

Shirkey, Z. (2012), *Joining the Fray: Outside Military Intervention in Civil Wars* (Aldershot: Ashgate).

Siverson, R. and King, J. (1979), "Alliances and the Expansion of War, 1815–1965," in Singer, J. and Wallace, M. (eds) *To Auger Well* (Beverly Hills: Sage).

Siverson, R. and Starr, H. (1991), *The Diffusion of War: A Study of Opportunity and Willingness* (Ann Arbor: University of Michigan Press).

Slantchev, B. (2004), "How Initiators End Their Wars: The Duration of Warfare and the Terms of Peace," *American Journal of Political Science* 48:4, 813–29.

Slantchev, B. and Tarar, A. (2011), "Mutual Optimism as a Rationalist Explanation of War," *American Journal of Political Science* 55:1, 135–48.

Smith, A. (1995), "Alliance Formation and War," *International Studies Quarterly* 39:4, 405–25.

Snyder, G. (1965), "The Balance of Power and the Balance of Terror," in Seaburt, P. (ed.) *The Balance of Power* (Scranton: Chandler).

Spaulding, R. (1990), "German Trade Policy in Eastern Europe, 1890–1990: Preconditions for Applying International Trade Leverage," *International Organization*, 45:3, 343–68.

Spitzer, K. (2013), "Why Japan's Biggest Defense-Spending Hike in Over Two Decades Isn't Going to Buy Much," *Time*, 2 September.

Stanley, E. (2009), *Paths to Peace: Domestic Coalition Shifts, War Termination and the Korean War* (Palo Alto: Stanford University Press).

Starr, H. and Most, B. (1976), "The Substance and Study of Borders in International Relations Research," *International Studies Quarterly* 20:4, 581–620.

Steiner, Z. (2011), *The Triumph of the Dark: European International History 1933–1939* (Oxford: Oxford University Press).

Storey, I. (2011), *Southeast Asia and the Rise of China: The search for security* (London: Routledge).

Strang, G. (1996), "Once More unto the Breach: Britain's Guarantee to Poland, March 1939," *Journal of Contemporary History* 31:4, 721–52.

Strang, G. (1999), "War and Peace: Mussolini's Road to Munich," in Lukes, I. and Goldstein, E., (eds) *The Munich Crisis, 1938, Prelude to World War II*, Portland, OR: Frank Cass.

Taliaferro, J. (2001), "Security Seeking under Anarchy: Defensive Realism Reconsidered," *International Security* 25:3, 128–61.

Tams, C. (1999), "The Functions of a European Security and Defense Identity and its Institutional Forms," in Haftendorn, H., Keohane, R. and Wallander, C. (eds) *Imperfect Unions: Security Institutions over Time and Space* (Oxford: Oxford University Press).

Thomas, M. (1999), "France and the Czechoslovak Crisis," in Lukes, I. and Goldstein, E. (eds) *The Munich Crisis, 1938, Prelude to World War II*, Portland, OR: Frank Cass.

Torrey, G. (1998), *Romania and World War I: A Collection of Studies* (Portland: Center for Romanian Studies).

Tuong L. (2014), "Vietnam's Overdue Alliance with America," *New York Times*, July 11.

Tuschoff, C. (1999), "Alliance Cohesion and Peaceful Change in NATO," in Haftendorn, H., Keohane, R. and Wallander, C., (eds) *Imperfect Unions: Security Institutions over Time and Space* (Oxford: Oxford University Press).

Twomey, C. (2014), "Military Developments," in Hachigian, N. (ed.) *Debating China: The US–China Relationship in Ten Conversations* (Oxford: Oxford University Press).

Vasquez, J. (1997), "The Realist Paradigm and Degeneration versus Progressive Research Programs: An Appraisal of Neotraditional Research on Waltz's Balancing Proposition," *American Political Science Review* 91:4, 899–912.

Vasquez, J. and Elman, C. (eds). (2003), *Realism and the Balancing of Power: A New Debate*. (Upper Saddle River, NJ: Prentice Hall).
Wagner, R. (2004), "Bargaining, War, and Alliances," *Conflict Management and Peace Science* 21:3, 215–31.
Wagner, R. (2007), *War and the State: The Theory of International Politics* (Ann Arbor: University of Michigan Press).
Walker, S. and Watson, G. (1994), "Integrative Complexity and British Decisions during the Munich and Polish Crises," *Journal of Conflict Resolution* 38:1, 3–23.
Wallander, C. and Keohane, R. (1999), "Risk, Threat, and Security Institutions," in Haftendorn, H., Keohane, R., and Wallander, C. (eds) *Imperfect Unions: Security Institutions over Time and Space* (Oxford: Oxford University Press).
Wallensteen, P. and Sollenberg, M. (1998), "Armed Conflict and Regional Conflict Complexes, 1989–97," *Journal of Peace Research* 35:5, 621–34.
Wall Street Journal. (2011), "Asia Pushes Back Against China," 19 November.
Walt, S. (1985), "Alliance Formation and the Balance of World Power," *International Security* 9:4, 3–43.
Walt, S. (1987), *The Origins of Alliances* (Ithaca: Cornell University Press).
Walt, S. (2010), "Balancing act (Asian version)," *Foreign Policy*, 3 May.
Waltz, K. (1979), *Theory of International Politics* (New York: McGraw Hill).
Waltz, K. (2000), "Structural Realism After the Cold War," *International Security* 25:1, 5–41.
Wandycz, P. (1981), "The Little Entente: Sixty Years Later," *The Slavonic and East European Review* 59:4, 548–64.
Wandycz, P. (1988a), *Polish Diplomacy 1914–1945: Aims and Achievements* (London: Orbis Books).
Wandycz, P. (1988b), *The Twilight of French Eastern Alliances, 1926–1936: French–Czechoslovak–Polish Relations from Locarno to the Remilitarization of the Rhineland* (Princeton: Princeton University Press).
Ward, M. and Gleditsch, K. (2002), "Location, Location, Location: An MCMC Approach to Modeling the Spatial Context of War and Peace," *Political Analysis* 10:3, 244–60.
Watson, A. (1992), *The Evolution of International Society*. (London: Routledge).
Weber, K. (1997), "Hierarchy Amidst Anarchy: A Transactions Cost to International Security Cooperation," *International Studies Quarterly* 41:2, 321–40.
Weinberg, G. (1999), "Reflections on Munich After 60 Years," in Lukes, I. and Goldstein, E. (eds) *The Munich Crisis, 1938, Prelude to World War II*, Portland, OR: Frank Cass.
Weinberger, S. (2015), "What Happened at Subi Reef?," *Duck of Minerva*, 9 November.
Weisiger, A. (2013), *Logics of War: Explanations for Limited and Unlimited Conflicts* (Ithaca: Cornell University Press).
Wendt, A. (1999), *Social Theory of International Politics* (Cambridge: Cambridge University Press).
Werner, S. (2000), "Deterring Intervention: The Stakes of War and Third-Party Involvement," *American Journal of Political Science* 44:4, 720–32.
Whaley, F. (2014), "US and Philippines Hold Joint Military Exercises," *New York Times*, 29 September.
Whaley, F. (2016a), "Eye on China, US and Philippines Ramp Up Military Alliance," *New York Times*, 12 April.
Whaley, F. (2016b), "US and Philippines Bolster Air and Sea Patrols in South China Sea," *New York Times*, 14 April.
Whitaker, B. (2010), "Soft Balancing Among Weak States? Evidence from Africa," *International Affairs* 86:5, 1109–27.

Wolfers, A. (1962), *Discord and Collaboration: Essays on International Politics* (Baltimore: John Hopkins Press).

Wolford, S. (2014), "The Survival and Breakdown of Victorious War Coalitions," Working Paper (University of Texas).

Wong, E. (2014), "China's hard Line: 'No Room for Compromise'," *New York Times*, 8 March.

Wong, E. (2015), "China Says it Could Set Up Air Defense Zone in South China Sea," *New York Times*, 31 May.

Wong, E. and Buckley, C. (2015), "China's Military Budget Increasing 10% for 2015, Official Says," *New York Times*, 4 March.

Wong, E. and Perlez, J. (2015), "As Tensions with US Grow, Beijing Says It Will Stop Building Artificial Islands in South China Sea," *New York Times*, 16 June.

Wong, E., Perlez, J., and Buckley, C. (2015), "China Announces Cuts of 300,000 Troops at Military Parade Showing Its Might," *New York Times*, 2 September.

Wright, Q. (1965), *A Study of War*. (Chicago: University of Chicago Press).

Wu X. (2014), "Regional Security Roles and Challenges," in Hachigian, N. (ed.) *Debating China: The US–China Relationship in Ten Conversations* (Oxford: Oxford University Press).

Young, R. (1996), *France and the Origins of the Second World War* (New York: St. Martin's).

Zacher, M. (2001), "The Territorial Integrity Norm: International Boundaries and the Use of Force," *International Organization* 55:2, 215–50.

Index

accommodation *see* appeasement
aggressor *see* challenger
Albania 75, 82, 83, 97
Alexander I, King of Yugoslavia 79
alignment *see* alliances
alliances 3, 6, 9, 11–14, 18–20, 36, 40–2, 45–7, 49, 54–5, 59, 62–3, 65, 71–6, 78–9, 80–1, 86, 90, 92–7, 101, 103–4, 109–11, 113–14, 117, 119–22, 124–6, 136–7, 140–1, 143; defection 47; formation 36, 74, 119, 121, 141, 147–8
Anschluss 53, 56–7, 59, 77, 81, 91, 94, 95
Anti-Comintern Pact 82, 92
Antonescu, Ion 88, 98
appeasement 3, 12, 15, 51, 55, 57, 61, 63–4, 146, 148
Aquino III, Benigno S. 133, 139
armament 3, 6–7, 12, 18, 20, 22, 36, 49–51, 53, 56, 58–9, 62–5, 76, 78, 80, 82, 83, 86–7, 89, 90, 93–5, 97, 101, 148
Asia 65, 117, 118, 120, 123, 128, 136, 142, 143, 146, 149; *see also* Southeast Asia
Asian Infrastructure Investment Bank 129
Association of Southeast Asian Nations (ASEAN) 11, 116, 125–7, 129–30, 137–9, 141
ASEAN Regional Forum (ARF) 127, 138–9, 141
Austria 37, 72–3, 75, 97, 107, 110, 124, 142; and the *Anschluss* 53, 55, 57, 59, 64–5, 81, 91; *see also* Austria-Hungary
Austria-Hungary 100; *see also* Austria
Axis 81–5, 88, 92, 93–4, 97, 146

Balance of Power Theory 17, 19
Balance of Threat Theory 9, 67, 109, 114
balancing 1–14, 16–48, 55, 63–4, 67–75, 79, 86, 89, 92–6, 99–104, 106–7, 109–14, 118–24, 126, 130, 136–7, 140–1, 144–9; asymmetric/soft 2, 14; automatic 18–19, 25, 39; against capabilities/power 18, 21–2; against intentions 1–3, 5–7, 10, 12, 16, 18, 21–2, 24–6, 28–9, 31, 35–7, 39–41, 44–8, 74; against threats 1–2, 6–7, 17–18, 21–2; external *see* alliances; collective *see* alliances; internal *see* armament
balancer(s) 1–3, 5, 7, 9–11, 13, 16, 19–22, 24, 30–5, 37, 39–44, 46, 48, 65, 68, 71–2, 74, 94, 100, 104, 106, 109, 111–13, 118, 120, 123–4, 145–8
Baldwin, Stanley 51, 58
Balkan Entente 79, 82, 86, 94; *see also* Balkan Pact
Balkan Pact 97; *see also* Balkan Entente
Balkans 73, 82–4, 97
bandwagoning 1–2, 8–9, 11–13, 17, 19–20, 47, 64, 67–71, 73–5, 79, 88–9, 91–6, 99–107, 109–13, 118, 120–2, 126–7, 130, 140, 146–9; for protection 9, 79; for spoils 9, 67, 79, 89, 91–2; for territorial vs. non–territorial spoils 103–6, 109–13
bargaining 3, 20, 26, 68, 83, 105, 113, 138, 146; bargaining theories of war 99, 112–13
Beck, Józef 55, 76–8, 96, 97
Belgium 17, 37, 51, 71, 76, 100, 102, 103, 107
beliefs 1, 24, 43–4, 47–8, 52–3, 57–8, 62–3, 93
Beneš, Edvard 55, 57, 80–1
Bessarabia 83, 85, 88–9
Biddle, Drexel 65, 76–7
Blum, Leon 80
Bonnet, Georges 54–6, 61
Britain 7, 10, 12, 17, 24, 37, 47, 63, 64, 65, 71, 73, 75, 93, 94, 100, 102, 107, 114,

123, 142, 146, 147, 148; relations with Hungary 91–2; relations with Poland 77–8; and the Rhineland Crisis 48, 50–3; relations with Romania 86, 87, 97; Sudetenland Crisis 53–4, 56–8, 60–3, 66, 122; relations with Yugoslavia 80, 84, 97
British Dominions 57
Brunei 13, 122, 125, 131, 143
buck-passing 12, 19–20, 64, 118, 137, 145; to other states 2–3, 6, 10, 39, 43, 46–7, 122; to the future *see* delay
Bukovina 83, 88–9, 98
Bulgaria 74, 75, 79, 83, 97, 107, 114, 121; relations with Romania 85, 86, 88, 97, 98, 110, 124, 125
Bullitt, William 55, 60, 62

Cadogan, Alexander 58
Cambodia 107, 108, 125, 139
Carol II, King of Romania 56, 85–8, 96, 97
Carpatho–Ukraine 78, 87, 91–2, 97
challenger(s) 1–3, 5–11, 13–14, 16, 19, 21–46, 67–74, 102, 142, 145–8; nature of 69, 73, 102
Chamberlain, Neville 52–4, 57–8, 60–1, 65, 66, 77, 122
China 1, 4, 10–11, 13, 14, 107, 140–4, 146; and ASEAN 126–7, 137–40; compared to 1930s Europe 120–6; economic ties 127–30; relations with United States 132–7; and the South China Sea 115–20, 130–2
Chłapowski, Alfred 76
Churchill, Winston 58, 65, 83, 97, 98
Ciano, Galeazzo 82
Cincar-Marković, Aleksandar 83
Clinton, Hillary 127
coalition *see* alliances
Cold War 6, 14, 25, 72, 129, 136
collective action problems 19, 43, 118
commitment problems 1–4, 6, 10–11, 13–14, 16, 18–21, 25–6, 31–2, 35–6, 38–40, 64
couverture 49–50
credibility 38, 71
Csáky, István 92
Cvetković, Dragiša 82, 84
Czechoslovakia 36, 66, 75, 95, 96, 97, 107, 122, 124–6, 133; relations with Hungary 89–93; relations with Poland 76–8; and the Rhineland Crisis 49–52; relations with Romania 85–7; and the Sudetenland Crisis 54–7, 59–63; rela-

tions with Yugoslavia 79–82

Daladier, Édouard 54, 60–2, 80, 122
delay 2, 6–7, 10, 12, 35, 39, 41, 44, 46–8, 62–3, 65, 100–1, 105, 114, 122, 142, 145, 147
dependence *see* economic relationships
deterrence 3, 14, 18–20, 33, 45, 61, 66, 135–7, 145, 147–8; dual 135–7
diplomacy 44, 76, 78, 81, 100, 142–3, 146
distribution of power/capabilities/forces *see* balancing of power
Dobruja 85, 88, 98, 110
domestic politics, effect on balancing 8, 14, 46, 64, 96, 125, 144; elections 14, 65
dominant power *see* hegemon
Dowdling, Hugh 58
Duterte, Rodrigo 133

East China Sea 116, 142, 143, 144
economic (inter-)dependence, effect on balancing 9, 11, 72, 94–5, 127–8, 141, 146
Eden, Anthony 51–3, 71, 80, 83
Europe 5, 13, 25, 37, 49, 52, 53, 64, 71, 80, 90, 95, 96, 102, 107, 114, 142; East Central 2, 9, 11, 53, 55, 57, 62, 65, 71, 73, 75–8, 82, 86, 89–94, 118, 119, 120–30, 136, 143, 146–7; Western 19, 25, 36, 48, 79

Fabricius, Wilhelm 87
Felvidék 82
First Vienna Award 91
France 7, 10, 12, 14, 17, 25, 37, 47, 71, 73, 75, 93–4, 97, 100, 107, 110, 114, 122–5, 143, 146–9; relations with Hungary 90, 92; relations with Poland 76–8; and the Rhineland Crisis 48–53; relations with Romania 85–8; and the Sudetenland Crisis 53–65; relations with Yugoslavia 79–83
Franco–Polish Alliance 76
Franco–Yugoslav Accord 80
free riding 6, 136–7
freedom of navigation 124, 127, 134–5, 143

Gafencu, Grigore 87
Gamelin, Maurice 50, 53, 58–60, 63
geography, effect on balancing 57, 67, 71, 74, 94, 121–2, 146; isolation 9, 11, 71, 146; proximity 9, 11, 36, 70–1, 73, 75,

79, 93, 113, 123; small states 63, 68, 71, 73–4, 94, 113, 116, 118, 120, 123, 126–7, 130, 134, 137–8, 146–7
Germany 7, 8, 10–11, 13, 14, 17, 39, 47, 63–4, 65, 66, 69, 71, 73, 75, 93–6, 97, 100, 101, 107, 110, 120–8, 142, 145–9; relations with Hungary 89–92; relations with Poland 76–9; and the Rhineland Crisis 48–53; relations with Romania 85–9; and the Sudetenland Crisis 53–7, 60–2; relations with Yugoslavia 79–81, 83–4
Goebbles, Joseph 90
Gömbös, Gyula 85, 89–90, 96, 98
Göring, Hermann 81–2, 90
Great Depression 49, 95, 128–9
Greece 73, 75, 79, 83, 84, 86, 93, 97, 102, 107, 113, 124
Greenert, Jonathan W. 137

Hailsham, Lord Viscount 52
Halifax, Lord 56–8, 61, 77, 91
Harris, Harry B. 134
hedging 66, 82, 84, 86, 118, 120–1, 124, 130–1, 137, 141–2, 144, 147, 149
hegemon 17–18, 24, 43, 91
Henlein, Konrad 54, 61
Hitler, Adolf 5, 10, 47, 63–4, 69, 75, 94, 96, 133, 142, 146, 148–9; and Hungary 90–2, 94; and Poland 78–9, 93, 94; and the Rhineland Crisis 48–9, 51–2; and Romania 88, 94, 98, 126; and the Sudetenland Crisis 54, 56–7, 59, 61–2, 66; and Yugoslavia 84–5, 94, 97, 126
Horthy, Miklós 89–92, 98
Hungary 12, 36, 55, 56, 75, 77, 78, 89–93, 94, 95, 96, 97, 98; relations with Romania 85–9; relations with Yugoslavia 79, 81–4

Iceland 71
Imrédy, Béla 91–2, 96, 98
India 115, 127, 135
Indonesia 122, 125, 131, 134, 141, 143
information 1, 3–4, 14, 16, 20–31, 33–5, 37, 40, 43–4, 47, 99, 102, 104, 111–14, 149
international institutions 9, 13, 67, 71–4, 94–5, 118, 121, 126–7, 130, 137–41, 143–4, 146
international law 50, 116–17, 134, 137–41, 144
intervention 12–13, 19, 65, 100–1, 103–7, 109–12, 113–14, 123, 149

Iran 4, 7–8, 14, 71, 108
Italy 51, 52, 54, 56, 65, 66, 86, 95, 96, 97, 107, 110, 113, 114, 126; invasion of Greece 83, 93; relations with Yugoslavia 79, 80, 81, 82–3

Jamalul Kiram III 125
Japan 100, 102, 107, 108, 109, 110, 126, 142–3; and 1930s Europe 52, 54, 65; and Southeast Asia 122–3, 124, 127, 135, 137, 142, 143, 144
Jungerth-Arnóthy, Mihály 90

Kánya, Kálmán 90–2, 96
Kerry, John 134
Krofta, Kamil 82

League of Nations 11, 50, 78, 82, 88, 92, 94–5, 126–7
Lee Kuan Kew 138
Lipski, Józef 78
Little Entente 59, 79–82, 85–7, 90–1, 93–4, 97, 126, 127
Litvinov, Maxim 90

MacMillan, Harold 58
Malaysia 13, 115, 117, 122, 125, 130–1, 134, 141, 143
Manila Declaration 133
Mediterranean Sea 52, 80
Michael I, King of Romania 88
Middle East 1, 4, 8, 14, 73, 136, 149
militarization *see* armament
Mischief Reef 115, 142
Molotov-Ribbentrop Pact 87–8, 92, 94
Munich Pact 82
Mussolini, Benito 80, 95, 97, 98

nature of the challenge/challenger's move *see* opportunity type
nature of the challenger *see* challenger
Netherlands 17, 37, 71, 74, 102, 107
nine-dash line 115, 119
Nöel, Léon 77
North Atlantic Treaty Organization (NATO) 19, 72
North Korea 136
Norway 71, 102

Obama, Barak 134–5
opportunity type 8, 10–12, 15, 21, 25–6, 35, 40–1, 45–7, 54, 63, 67, 69, 73, 93, 96, 99, 102, 112, 118, 145–6; intrinsic value/absolute gains 7–8, 10, 16, 22–3,

31, 33–4, 36, 40, 42, 65, 70; relational value/relative gains 10, 31–4, 42, 63, 65

Pacific Ocean 52, 54, 102, 107, 108, 110, 114, 124, 130, 132. 134, 143
Paracel Islands 115, 129, 131, 142
passing the buck *see* buck-passing
Paul, Prince of Yugoslavia 80, 82–4, 96
People's Liberation Army (PLA) 132, 143
People's Liberation Army Navy 119, 140
Permanent Court of Arbitration 11, 139
Peter II, King of Yugoslavia 85
Petrescu-Comnène, Nicolae 66, 98
Philippines 10, 13, 117, 122, 125, 127, 130–2, 139, 143, 147; relations with United States 132–5; and the Vietnam War 70, 105, 107
Piłsudski, Józef 76
Poland 10, 12, 63, 65, 75, 79, 81, 83, 85, 93, 96, 97, 100, 121–2, 124–5, 143, 147; relations with Hungary 90, 92, 10; and the Rhineland Crisis 49, 51, 76–7; relations with Romania 86, 87–8, 97; Sudetenland Crisis 54–5, 56, 77–8
Polish Corridor 76, 78–9, 93–4
Portugal 71, 107
preemption 22, 69, 101
Purić, Bożidar 80–2

rearmament *see* armament
remilitarization *see* armament
resolve 34, 55, 78–9, 86–7, 89–90
respondent *see* balancer
revisionism 68–9, 75–6, 81, 85–6, 88–90
revisionist state/power *see* challenger
rewards *see* spoils
Rhineland 10, 12, 37, 39, 47, 48–55, 61–5, 76, 90, 93–4, 97, 148; and Romania 86, 89; and Yugoslavia 80–1
Rhodes, Ben 135, 137
Romania 12, 54–6, 59, 65, 66, 74, 75, 77, 85–9, 93–6, 97, 98, 99, 107, 110, 114, 121–2, 124–6, 143, 146; relations with Hungary 89–92; relations with Yugoslavia 79, 81–2, 83, 85
Roosevelt, Eleanor 51
Russia 1, 5, 8, 14, 56, 57, 60, 65, 72–3, 78, 83, 100, 107, 108, 131, 136, 149; *see also* Soviet Union

salami-slicing tactics 38, 136
Salonika 83, 84, 85
Sarraut, Albert 50

Scarborough Shoal 131, 133, 139
Schacht, Hjalmar 128
Second Vienna Award 83, 88, 92, 94
security dilemma 7, 74, 136
signal 7, 31, 34, 37, 43–5, 136
Simon, John 52
Simović, Dušan 85
Singapore 13, 116, 133–4, 137–8, 141, 143
Singh, Vikram J. 135
Škoda munition works 54, 57, 81, 87
Slovakia 86, 90–1, 98, 113
South China Sea 1–2, 4, 10–11, 13, 113, 115–20, 130, 132, 140–4, 146; compared to 1930s Europe 121–30; international law and organizations 137–40; and the United States 132–7
Southeast Asia 4, 10–11, 13, 116–18, 140, 142, 147; economic ties 127–30; and international law and organizations 137–8, 140; military aid 121–4; regional organizations 126–7; and the South China Sea 131–2; territorial disputes 124–5; and types of uncertainty 119–21; and the United States 135–6; *see also* Asia
South Johnson Reef 139
South Korea 70, 105, 107, 124
Soviet Union 6, 19, 25, 36, 37, 76, 78, 83, 84, 93, 96, 97, 102, 107, 110, 111, 122, 125, 129, 136, 143; relations with Hungary 90, 92; relations with Romania 85, 86, 88–9; and the Sudetenland Crisis 54, 65, 78–9; *see also* Russia
spoils 1–2, 8–9, 12–13, 20, 35, 46, 67–74, 89, 92, 103–7, 109, 111–14, 118, 148; non-territorial 70, 103, 105–7, 109, 111, 113; territorial 70, 103–4, 106–7, 109
Spratly Islands 115–16, 129, 131
Stalin, Joseph 37, 65, 97, 98
status quo state/power *see* balancer
Stojadinović, Milan 80–2, 86, 96, 97, 98, 126
strategic interaction 16, 19, 33
Subi Reef 115, 134
Sudetenland 10, 12, 39, 47, 48, 53–6, 59, 61–4, 77, 87, 90, 93, 94, 133, 148; and Yugoslavia 81–2
Sweden 71
Switzerland 71, 74

Taiwan 115, 120, 130, 133, 143
Teschen 55, 66; *see also* Těšín

Těšín 66, 77; see also Teschen
Thailand 70, 105, 107, 125, 141
Titulescu, Nicolae 85–6, 97
trade see economic interdependence
transcending 17, 72, 79, 121, 141, 149
Transylvania 83, 85, 88, 92, 98
Treaty of Locarno 53, 76, 86
Treaty of Trianon 89
Tripartite Pact 83–5, 88, 92
Trump, Donald 133
Turkey 65, 71, 73, 79, 86, 97, 107

uncertainty 28, 31, 34, 37, 39–43, 45–8, 63–4, 67, 74, 99, 118–20, 133, 140, 145, 147, 149; balance of power/capabilities 40, 44–6, 52, 63, 74, 119, 145, 149; challenger intentions/type 35, 40, 43–4, 52, 61, 64, 119; external balancing/coalition size 40, 45, 47, 63, 119; opportunity type/challenge 21, 40, 45, 47, 119; timing/value of delay 41, 45–6, 53
United Nations 11, 14, 116, 127, 139
United Nations Convention on the Law of the Sea (UNCLOS) 116–17, 134, 140
United States 14, 19, 24, 35–6, 37, 70, 73, 102, 105, 107, 111, 113; and 1930s Europe 51, 54, 59; and Southeast Asia 117–24, 127, 128, 130–42, 143, 144
United States Navy 119, 132, 134, 140

Vansittart, Robert 51, 66, 77
Versailles, Treaty of 48, 49
Vietnam 10, 13, 70, 105, 108, 115, 117, 119, 122, 125, 127, 128, 130–2, 142, 143, 147; relations with the United States 133–5

Wang Yi 116, 134
White, Hugh 136
World Trade Organization (WTO) 129
World War I 25, 65, 71, 74, 79, 89, 95, 100, 103, 110, 113, 114, 122, 126, 127, 146
World War II 12, 17, 25, 37, 71, 73–4, 85, 96, 99, 102, 105, 107, 110, 111, 114, 132, 133

Xi Jinping (President) 143

Yugoslavia 12, 54, 59, 66, 75, 77, 79–85, 93–6, 97, 98, 99, 102, 121–2, 124–6; relations with Hungary 89–92; relations with Romania 85–6